THE BROKEN TABOO

THE BROKEN TABOO

Sex in the Family

**Blair Justice and
Rita Justice**

HUMAN SCIENCES PRESS
72 Fifth Avenue   3 Henrietta Street
NEW YORK, NY 10011 ● LONDON, WC2E 8LU

Library of Congress Catalog Number 78-23720

ISBN: 0-87705-389-8

Copyright © 1979 by Human Sciences Press
72 Fifth Avenue, New York, New York 10011

Printed in the United States of America
9   9876543

Library of Congress Cataloging in Publication Data

Justice, Blair.
    The broken taboo.

    Bibliography: p.
    Includes index.
    1. Incest.   I. Justice, Rita, joint author.
II. Title.
HQ71.J84   301.41'58   78-23720
ISBN 0-87705-389-8

CONTENTS

ACKNOWLEDGMENTS

This book is a follow-up to our earlier work, *The Abusing Family,* and continues our focus on parents and children. Our deepest thanks go to all the families we have been privileged to work with. Their capacity to change, to reconstitute, and to bring health and happiness into their lives has been heartening. To those friends and clients who spent many hours being interviewed and sharing their family experiences with us, we are immensely grateful.

A number of people and sources were of help to us in writing this book. We particularly appreciate the help of those who assisted in surveying case histories and records at Harris County Child Welfare Unit of incestuous families: Mary Murphy, psychologist and doctoral student at the University of Texas School of Public Health; Jerry Wald, graduate assistant, and our daughter, Cindy. We are grateful to Gene Lege, executive director of Harris County Child Welfare Unit, and his staff for their cooperation in our survey of cases.

We owe special thanks to Doris Krakower for doing much of the typing of the several drafts that went into the manuscript, and to Gay Robertson and her staff for helping type the final manuscript. They are both at the University of Texas School of Public Health.

Blair Justice
Rita Justice

INTRODUCTION

Why a book on incest for the public? Three reasons: growth of the problem, widespread misconceptions about it, and increasing failure of families to assure the sexual welfare of both parent and child.

To underscore these points, we invite parents to consider the following five statements and answer each either "true" or "false":

1. Relatively few people have thoughts about sex with their parents, brothers, sisters, children, or other close relatives.

2. The act of incest is so "unnatural" that only the sick and depraved practice it.

3. If the subject is just ignored, sexual activity between father and daughter or mother and son is not likely to occur.

4. Incest usually involves force, such as a father forcing a daughter into sex.

5.   There is nothing different about today's society or stresses on parents that causes more sex in the family to occur.

Each of these statements is false, as will be demonstrated in the course of our book. One other widespread myth that belongs on the same list is this: The majority of sexual assaults on children is committed by strangers. It is not. Most sexual abuse of children is done by parents, stepparents, uncles, boyfriends of mothers, and relatives who live in the household or come to visit. Case reports collected by police departments and protective service agencies across the country confirm that children are at higher sexual risk in their own homes than on the streets.

People are ignorant of the facts on incest largely because the subject continues to be treated as "so abominable that it must not even be thought about or discussed." It is a taboo, forbidden and prohibited by every culture. But keeping incest as a forbidden subject has not prevented family sex; it simply has prevented recognition of the problem.

What has been forbidden is discussion of the subject, and without discussion little action has been taken toward helping victims and reducing the growth of the problem. The taboo has succeeded in creating such an aura of mystery and dread around the subject that the public likes to believe that incest does not really occur.

To say that people do not think about having sex with their parents, siblings, or children is to deny centuries of evidence. Incest has been an ancient preoccupation of humans. Anthropologists have indicated that the two most common themes reflected in artifacts across cultures are immortality and incest, the desire for perpetual youth and the desire to commit intercourse with forbidden members of the clan, tribe, or family.

Through the ages, cultures have projected thoughts of incest onto their gods, into their myths, music, paintings, and, in more contemporary times, their novels, films, movies. One surveyor of the subject concluded that "it is probably a very rare human being who never has given thought to the possibility of an incestuous contact." The Kinsey interviews on sexual behavior in the United States, based on sizable samples, indicate that males and females alike have such thoughts.

But beyond the thought is the act. No one knows how much incest is practiced in the United States or anywhere else. Authorities agree that the number of cases reported and confirmed represent only a fraction of those that go undisclosed.

A Problem of Growing Magnitude

For many years the number of known cases of incest was cited as one to two per million population in this country; in Europe the range was one to nine per million. The highest for any state was seven cases per million in Washington. If these figures represented anything more than just the smallest tip of the iceberg, we would have little reason to consider the subject. Incest could continue to be treated as a curiosity of social scientists with an interest in exotic behavior.

But evidence is emerging of the magnitude of the problem beneath the surface. As states across the country have passed more effective legislation on the reporting of child abuse, the size of the incest problem is slowly becoming better known. On both a metropolitan area level and state basis, 50 to 500 percent increases in confirmed cases of incest are being reported each year.

For example, in the Houston area, where we work with abusing families, there were 20 cases of sexual abuse per month in 1976 and 40 in 1978, all but a tiny fraction being committed by a family member. In Texas as a whole, the number of confirmed cases that came to the attention of child welfare authorities was 214 in 1974, 630 in 1976, and 1,153 in 1977. And for every reported case, it has been estimated that 20 go undetected.

In Santa Clara County, California, where a pioneer program was launched in the treatment of child sexual abuse, referrals numbered 36 in 1971, 180 in 1974, and 600 in 1977.

The National Center on Child Abuse and Neglect has estimated that at least 100,000 cases of sexual abuse occur each year. Other authorities consider 250,000 to be a conservative estimate.

One researcher states that 4 to 5 percent of the population is involved in incest. Another concluded that "incest implicates at least 5 percent of the population and perhaps up to 15 percent."

As we will see when in Part IV we consider the consequences of incest, a history of sexual abuse is reported among large numbers of prostitutes, drug addicts, runaways, and prison inmates. But to conclude that incest is a problem primarily in the backgrounds of such unseemly types as prostitutes or prison inmates misses the point.

As Dr. Ruth Weeks, of the division of child and adolescent psychiatry at the University of Virginia Medical Center, has noted, many adults involved in incest "are considered 'pillars of the community.' " She added that people who commit incest include "judges, ministers, university professors, doctors, teachers, skilled workers, white collar workers, farmers, and unskilled laborers." We will meet such people in the course of this book.

Persons who have experienced incestuous relations can be found in all walks of life then. Among 412 university freshmen and sophomores, 17 percent reported having experienced some type of physical contact of a sexual nature when they were children. Most of the contacts came from persons related to them by blood or marriage.

A preliminary study by the San Francisco Sexual Trauma Center in both low- and high-income areas of the city found that one out of every four persons had had "negative sexual experiences" before age 15. Many of these experiences were incestuous.

Although the true extent of the incest problem remains unknown, indications are that the incidence of sexual abuse is larger—perhaps many times larger—than that of physical abuse. Yet the attention given to physical abuse of children is much greater than that devoted to sexual abuse. Why does incest remain largely ignored? Among the reasons are:

1. The taboo against talking about it.
2. The refusal by physicians, clergy, relatives, and neighbors who may be aware that incest is going on in a family to report it or become involved.
3. The laws in almost half the states that fail to specify sexual abuse as one of the forms of abuse of children that must be reported.
4. The fiction that only the poor and the pathological engage in incest.
5. The attitude that nothing can be done to prevent it from occurring or to rehabilitate families if it does occur.

Meanwhile, the problem grows. According to one estimate, the incidence of incest has grown from one in a million in 1940 to one in 100 in 1950 to one in 20 in 1970. Whatever the figures are, no one can say for certain that the increase in known cases represents anything other than greater detection, but signs suggest that more incest is actually occurring.

One sign points to what is going on in today's super-stressed and stimulated society. People are living under increased pressures and are finding it harder to meet their needs for closeness, belonging, and nurturing. Some use sex as an attempt to meet these needs, even sex with their children.

MORE SEXUAL PERMISSIVENESS

The sexual climate is more open and more permissive than in times past. Much attention has been given to group sex, swinging sex, kinky sex, mate swapping, transsexual surgery, and to the recognition of homosexuality, bisexuality, sadomasochism, and transvestitism as sexual styles and preferences, rather than sexual problems. Some ask: Why not sex in the family?

Henry Giarretto, director of the Santa Clara program, has noted:

> We teach our girls to be Lolitas and sexual provocateurs from the time they're 2. They get it from television continually, how to flounce their hair, how to shake their butts. Instead of Shirley Temple, we now have Tatum O'Neal and Jodie Foster, who played the young prostitute in *Taxi Driver.*

Kids learn early that being sexy means being wanted. Little girls learn that if they are cute and sexy, they get favors, treats, compliments. Parents are concerned not only about their own sexuality but also about their children not having sexual hang-ups. No one knows how much the more open and healthy acknowledgement of human sexuality is becoming confused with an "anything goes" philosophy toward sex.

The "anything goes" or "do your own thing" philosophy is seen as meaning that what a person does sexually in his or her own home is nobody else's business. In the past, incest laws have been used unjustifiably to punish persons

—consenting adults related by blood or marriage—for their sexual relations, although the relationship was in no way a threat to society or others. Now the issue is not what consenting adults, related or not, do within the confines of their house, but what adults do sexually with children.

Public attitudes on sex are clearly in a state of flux. We will consider some of the ways incest themes have been portrayed in movies, novels, and other depictions of contemporary society that shape public attitudes. We will not be suggesting a reversal of the greater sexual freedom that has been gained, but will emphasize steps for parents to take to assure healthy futures for their children in today's society.

Excessive Change and Stress

An accompaniment to the atmosphere of more sexual freedom today is the relentless stress that rapid social and technological change imposes on American families. For example, almost 50 million Americans change their place of residence each year. This frequent moving from city to city and from one dwelling to another is matched by a constant change in jobs. The time spent on any one job keeps dropping as the number of careers that a person may have while in the labor force keeps rising. Changes are stressful and excessive change equals excessive stress.

No aspect of one's life has escaped the incessant bombardment of change since World War II. Concepts of work, love, time, space, leisure, religion, and sex have all changed. Instant communications have brought alien tongues and competing values and life-styles into the awareness of everyone with a television set or transistor radio. Rapid transportation puts many into face-to-face contact with the new and strange. The number of human contacts an individual has in a day keeps rising, along with

the transience of each contact. Relationships are frag-
mented, modular, fleeting. Fast food replaces regular
meals with conversation. Pill popping has brought altered
states of awareness, and The Pill has freed more people to
practice sex as a solely recreational pursuit with a series of
dispensable and interchangeable partners. People have
become immigrants and strangers in their own land.

The family has historically served as the shock ab-
sorber for the bruised and battered, the stressed and sur-
feited. But many families today are fractured and fragile
and cannot meet the demands placed on them. Families are
stuck in smaller and smaller apartments and houses, with
parents and children having no sense of privacy or space
they can call their own. Instead of a shock-absorber, the
home, for many, has become a pressure-cooker.

Relations between spouses are strained as changing
sex roles and expectations emerge. Boundaries between
parent and child have been overrun: fathers are pals and
mothers playmates; T-shirts and jeans are interchangeable
between generations. Daughters learn to apply eye shadow
long before they reach puberty. Love and affection are
being pursued with a desperation and in the frenzy to find
nurturing in the midst of stress and change, some parents
are turning to their children. One result is incest.

In Part III, where we examine the causes of incest, we
will look with greater detail at the conditions that contribute to sexual misuse and abuse occurring in the home.
These conditions relate directly to the social stresses and
rapid change impacting the family.

If incest is on the increase, as we believe it is, what can
be done to deal with the growing problem? Do laws need
to be changed, public attitudes modified, stress alleviated,
families strengthened, parental boundaries restored, sex
education required, treatment techniques perfected? We

will explore such questions in Part V on "What Can Be Done About Incest."

The purpose of this book is to bring into the open a subject that has been hidden and neglected, and affects many more families than has been imagined. For too long, the subject has been involved in a "conspiracy of silence." We want to let parents know what they can do once they have the facts.

This book grows out of a survey we made of 112 families in which incest occurred. We did intensive group therapy with 20 of the parents involved. Children of these parents were included in the treatment as seemed indicated. Individual therapy was conducted with seven additional young women, all of whom had incestuous experiences as children. Child welfare case records and files were reviewed to help us put together a picture of what incestuous families are like. We also did a comprehensive review of the work of others who have written about incest, and their findings are included in our book.

Part I will discuss what incest is in its various forms, how the taboo against it got started, how incest relates to sexual misuse and abuse, and what problems parents face in drawing the line between affection and sexual stimulation. In Part II, we will examine who commits incest and what the characteristics are of the incestuous family; what the father, mother, and child are like. Part III will explore why incest occurs, the causes, and the roles played by participants and nonparticipants.

In Part IV, we will consider incest cues and consequences, what signs appear when incest occurs, what psychological and emotional marks are left by the experience, and what the factors are that both minimize and exacerbate the damage. In Part V we will discuss what parents can do to keep the problem from occurring in their family, what steps they can take to insure the sexual welfare of their children and themselves, and what can be done if incest does occur.

In each chapter, where we cite the work of others or offer quotations and cases from their material, the sources can be found by page number in the Notes at the back of the book. We have also used the Notes occasionally for elaboration on points made in a given chapter. All names attached to cases in this book are fictitious.

Part I

WHAT INCEST IS

Chapter 1

MORE THAN A MATTER OF SEX

If a father has a habit of taking baths with his 12-year-old daughter and caressing her breasts, what is this kind of intimate physical contact called? If a mother fondles her 8-year-old son as she sleeps with her body pressed against his every night, what is the name for this type of behavior?

Under the prevailing definition of incest used by psychologists, psychiatrists and social workers, both of these activities are incestuous. Incest is any sexual activity—intimate physical contact that is sexually arousing between nonmarried members of a family.

That activity may be oral-genital relations, mutual masturbation, fondling and caressing erogenous areas of the body, or actual intercourse. More recent laws are consistent with this definition of incest.

Historically, incest laws were first concerned with marriage, not sex. The laws prohibited certain persons, related to each other by blood or marriage, from marrying each other. What degree of relationship was considered too close for marriage is something that varied widely from culture to culture, country to country, even state to state.

Where there was any mention of what kind of sexual act is involved in incest, that act was intercourse. But some laws provided penalties for incest regardless of whether intercourse occurred. If two relatives married each other, then they were guilty of incest regardless of what kind of sexual activity, if any, they engaged in with one another.

Even today, laws in a number of states reflect this emphasis on marriage rather than sex between relatives. In some states, incest is defined as either marriage or sexual intercourse between relatives. In New York, for instance, the definition covers both:

> A person is guilty of incest when he marries or engages in sexual intercourse with a person whom he knows to be related to him, either legitimately or illegitimately, as an ancestor, descendant, brother or sister of either the whole or half blood, uncle, aunt, nephew or niece.

The emphasis on prohibiting intramarriage can be understood in terms of one of the original purposes of the incest taboo. When the human race was struggling for its survival, some means was necessary to develop alliances between clans, tribes, and families. By establishing rules requiring marriage and intercourse outside the family, early humans devised a system for expansion and security of the race.

The emphasis in law on defining incest as sexual intercourse between relatives is also believed to date back to early purposes of the incest taboo. One theory holds that the reason incest has almost universally been prohibited since the time of early man is that inbreeding makes survival of a population less likely. It was believed that defective offspring result when intercourse is permitted between father and daughter, mother and son, brother and sister, or other close relatives. This may explain the origin of the incest taboo in some cultures, but it is not likely that primitive man could have been aware of any association between intrafamily matings and inferior offspring. Studies have shown that biological harm just does not occur that often.

But the incest taboo was seen, correctly or not, as a safeguard against defective offspring. As the facts became better known on inbreeding, a new basis for the taboo emerged. A shift occurred from prohibiting incest on the basis of guarding against defective offspring, and the laws reflected this change.

In Texas, the law was rewritten stating that "protection of family solidarity rather than prevention of genetic defects is the rationale. . . ." The law was broadened to prohibit not only sexual intercourse between nonmarried family members but also "deviate sexual intercourse"—any contact between the genitals of one person and the mouth or anus of another with the intent of arousing sexual passions. A number of states now have the "deviate sexual intercourse" clause in their incest laws.

This broader definition of incest is more in line with current scientific thinking on the problem. As we have noted, many authorities now consider incest to include any sexual activity between parent and child or brother and sister. Most also consider sexual activity between stepparent and stepchild and foster parent and foster child as incest. Most authorities also regard incest as a continuing activity and not a single act.

The National Center on Child Abuse and Neglect uses the term "intrafamily sexual abuse" for incest and defines that as abuse "which is perpetrated on a child by a member of that child's family group" and "includes not only sexual intercourse, but also any act designed to stimulate a child sexually, or to use a child for the sexual stimulation, either of the perpetrator or of another person."

Some authorities classify incestuous relationships that include intercourse as "consummated" and sexual activity that stops short of penetration as nonconsummated. The point, though, is that it is all incest and reflects serious problems in a troubled family. The nature of the sexual act does not determine the negative consequences that a child suffers as much as do the disturbed relationships that gave rise to the sex (see Chapter 11).

PURPOSES OF THE TABOO

Any physical contact of a sexual nature that cuts across generational boundaries is likely to be disruptive in a family and, sooner or later, threaten that family's continued existence. One of the primary reasons for the incest taboo, and one of the theories on its origin, is that sexual activity stirs up passions and jealousies that make harmonious family life impossible. In addition, it confuses family members as to what their duties and roles are—a daughter sleeping with her father takes on the role of a wife while the father often takes on the role of a boyfriend or lover and the mother becomes one of the children. Families bog down and stop working under such strains—so do individuals. Children stop growing and fail to get their needs met. Parents turn inward and shut out the world beyond. The most powerful reason for prohibiting incest is to protect a child's development. To develop, a child must receive both nurturing and encouragement to become a separate person. The needs both to belong and to separate must be met. Incest keeps these and other needs of a child from being met.

The incest taboo, then, serves to protect children's dependency needs as well as their opportunity to develop independence and to fulfill roles outside the family. As noted by social theorist Talcott Parsons, the taboo is the basic mechanism for the child to develop autonomy and social roles during puberty and at the end of adolescence. Carl Jung, pioneer psychoanalyst, also considered the incest taboo as serving the important psychological function of promoting separation and individuation.

Intimate physical contact arouses the most intense feelings that can exist between people, and when these physical feelings are aroused between parent and child, the child cannot grow and separate. Son is tied to mother and daughter to father in the most primitive sense, as if an extension of the original umbilical cord binds the child to parent.

Freud made the point that human culture began with the establishment of the incest taboo, that it was necessary in the original primal family for the sons—having eliminated the father—to foreswear sex with their mother and sisters so that energies would be devoted to cooperative pursuits in the world outside. The whole issue of ambition and accomplishment was seen by Freud as dependent on the child's giving up his incestuous wishes and turning his energy outside the family. This occurs in the resolution of the oedipus complex.

Freud saw sex, including incestuous wishes, as the basic determinant in human behavior. But the central issue of incest goes beyond sex. As Eric Fromm has noted, there is a nonsexual "incestuous striving inherent in man's nature" based on deep needs for roots, belonging, warmth, and protection. Frightened and insecure in the world outside, a person turns inside the family to get his or her needs met and closes the door behind. The more stressful a person finds the world, the more likely he or she will turn inside the family. As we will see, the basic issue in incest is not sex but the need for closeness, nurturing, and stimulation.

We find in working with incestuous families that a central feature to the problem does indeed lie with parents turning to children to meet needs of warmth and closeness in a world that seems frightening and stressful. The fusion that develops between parent and child is almost invariably damaging. The child fails to get basic emotional needs met and is prevented from establishing ties with the world outside that are necessary for growth and experience in relating to others. Parents use the child to ward the world off, to keep from meeting their needs on their own, and to avoid facing the failure of their marriage.

A variation of this kind of family fusion has been identified by Dr. William H. Masters and Virginia E. Johnson, codirectors of the Reproductive Biology Research Foundation in St. Louis, as the "favorite daughter" syndrome or "pseudo-incest." The father singles out one daughter or, if there is only one, he isolates her for himself. She becomes Daddy's girl, spoiled, pampered, immature. Such girls are severely handicapped in developing relationships with boys and, later, with men. They are forever seeking another Daddy. They usually grow up "sexually dysfunctional" and are just as psychologically crippled as girls who have been sexually seduced by their fathers in overt incestuous relationships.

Although we use the term "incest" to mean sexual contacts among family members, we emphasize the role that nonsexual needs play—the need for affection, the need to belong, to have roots, to have a haven from a stressful world, the need to be dependent and to be nurtured. It is the attempt to satisfy these needs by turning to a child that sets the stage for incest (see Part III, "Why Incest Occurs").

Once incest begins, it usually continues for an indefinite time. Research on the 112 families in our survey shows that in the vast majority of cases, the sexual activity continued for well over a year. In fact, the very definition of incest implies that it is not an act of sudden passion, a single episode that is never repeated. It is a pattern of behavior with roots outside the sexual sphere.

TERMS FOR INAPPROPRIATE PHYSICAL CONTACT

As we have noted, incest involves intimate physical contact of some kind. Children need to be hugged, kissed, held. Their feelings of self-esteem depend on receiving lots of affection. Where, then, is the line between physical affection needed by the child and physical contact that is incestuous or sexual?

In a later chapter on parent-child sexuality, we will see that hugging, kissing, caressing spill over into sexual activity when the child gets overstimulated and sexually aroused, or when the adult uses physical contact with the child to meet his or her own needs and gets "turned on."

Some authorities use the term "sexual misuse" to describe exposing a child to sexual stimulation inappropriate to the child's age, development, and role in the family. Sometimes the overstimulation is expressed by the child in physical or behavioral problems—eating or sleeping disturbances or unexplained somatic symptoms. We will discuss such symptoms in later chapters.

We believe that what is inappropriate may also be determined by parents asking themselves whether they are giving physical affection to the child out of their own need for sex, stimulation, love, and nurturing. A mother without a partner who is lonely and isolated may try to satisfy her need for love and warmth through intimate contact with a young son: sleeping with him, fondling, caressing him. A husband whose marriage has gone sour may let passion and need enter into his relationship with his daughter, kissing and embracing her as a lover, not as a father.

"Sexual exploitation" is another term used to describe inappropriate intimate physical contact with children. It refers to "the involvement of dependent, developmentally immature children and adolescents in sexual activities that they do not fully comprehend, are unable to give informed consent to, and that violate the social taboos of family roles."

Although all of this is incestuous behavior, the most common term applied to adults having sexual contact with children is "sexual abuse." The term should not imply that there is one person who is the abuser and another who is the abused; a person who "did it" and a victim. The problem is not that simple; rape may be but not incest.

Incest and sexual misuse or abuse within a family involves the whole family and not just the person who initiates the activity. The nonparticipating spouse is involved in terms of directly or indirectly encouraging the activity. The child is involved in terms of often being an active, not passive, participant or welcoming the activity as a form of special attention. The whole environment of the family is involved in terms of contributing to the conditions under which incest or sexual misuse occurs.

Although the definition is loose and varied, sexual abuse is becoming the most widely-used term. In Texas, it is a matter of court interpretation rather than law. The law in the state covers child abuse and neglect, not sexual abuse per se. One form of child abuse is considered to be sexual abuse, which has come to mean any sexual activity between an adult and a child under 17. This is civil law, under the state's family code. Another law, under the Texas penal code, defines incest, which, as we have seen, relates to sexual intercourse and "deviate sexual intercourse" between specified family members.

In Massachusetts, sexual abuse is covered by a law against physical and emotional injury to children. Would the father who takes baths with his young daughter, and caresses her, be committing sexual abuse? What about the man, cited by another author, who installed a one-way mirror in the bathroom so he could observe his daughter taking showers? Is this sexual abuse? And the stranger who tells a dirty joke to a child walking home from school—is he being sexually abusive? In one of the cases in our survey of families, a father insisted on photographing his 8-year-old daughter in the nude. Is this sexual abuse?

In most states, these are matters of interpretation by a court or by child welfare authorities who intervene. A number of cases outside the home are clearly sexual abuse

—young children, for instance, being enticed into performing sex acts with adults for pornographic pictures—but
these are more often covered by criminal laws on sodomy,
rape, indecency toward a child, etc.

What we are concerned with in this book is incestuous
behavior or sexual misuse inside the home and family. It is
the most common problem of all forms of sexual abuse,
although it does not make as many headlines. Being familiar with the term sexual *abuse* is important because much of
the action against reported cases of incest is taken under
laws governing sexual abuse, not incest. Incest is a crime
and comes under criminal law, which requires the child to
testify and witnesses to corroborate the complaint. The
child must tell what happened over and over, to police, to
the district attorney, to investigators, to the judge, to a
grand jury. There may be a trial in open court, and the
psychological trauma for the child is intense (see Chapter
11). The father, or guilty adult, receives a sentence if the
charge is proved, and a jail or prison term is often the
outcome. The child is left with guilt feelings about having
been responsible for sending her father to jail and breaking
up the family.

All of these are reasons why many authorities prefer
that action be brought under civil law, such as that covering
child abuse or sexual abuse. By court order, a child who is
being abused may be removed from the home and not
returned until the parents have been rehabilitated. The
child does not have to become a witness. Protective social
services can be provided for the family. Unfortunately,
treatment programs for the parents are often not available
or are ineffective, and the abuse—either physical or sexual
—may recur. In Part V, "What Can Be Done About Incest,"
we will discuss treatment and prevention.

For now, we are focusing on what incest is in all its
forms and ramifications. We have looked at what some laws
say it is and what various authorities regard as incest. De-

spite almost universal agreement that incest should be prohibited, definitions of incest vary according to time, place, culture, and circumstance. The fact that behavior considered to be incest in one culture or period is nonincestuous in another belies the argument that all humans have a natural, unwavering instinct against the act. If this were true, no taboo of any kind would be necessary, much less one that changes from country to country, culture to culture. By considering the varied forms that incest has taken in times past, we can get a better idea of what purposes the taboo against it has served and what function it has today.

Chapter 2

INCEST IN HISTORY AND RELIGION

At one time, in the days of early Christianity, a person committed incest if she married her 32nd cousin. Church of England law listed some 30 remote relatives a woman was prohibited to marry under "A Table of Kindred and Affinity, wherein Whosoever are Related are Forbidden in Scripture and our Laws to Marry together." At one extreme were a woman's grandfather, grandmother's husband, or her husband's grandfather. At the other were her son's daughter's husband, her daughter's daughter's husband, her husband's son's son, and her husband's daughter's son. A list of equal length existed for men in terms of women they could not marry.

As mentioned earlier, incest laws and prohibitions have historically been concerned with keeping persons related by blood or marriage from marrying each other. Several practical purposes were served by defining incest in terms of who was forbidden to marry whom. One purpose was to provide a means for better defense and security of fledgling societies. By requiring members of one family to reach out and marry members of another, a society added to its own strength by the network of alliances that developed. Kinship ties multiplied by incest rules, and people had an investment in the survival of the whole group or society.

Marriage outside one's family also came to serve another practical purpose. It provided a fundamental way to meet the economic needs of individuals. Skills from one family were pooled with the strengths of another. The family became an economic organization in terms of producing and consuming. In colonial times in America, for instance, the family produced substantially all that it consumed— with the exception of such things as utensils, tools, salt— and was in effect a small factory. Children were regarded as important productive agents, not potential sources of sexual gratification or partners for marriage. Sex between nonmarried members of a family would disrupt the division of labor and cooperative relationships necessary for smooth functioning of the economic unit. Thus the incest taboo served an important function at this point in history.

The taboo, then, can be largely understood down through the ages by how it contributed to the survival of societies, the economic welfare of families and cooperation between people generally. As we have suggested, it would have been difficult if not impossible for human culture and social development to have started and continued without incest taboos. Anthropologist Leslie White has pointed out:

> Unless some way had been found to establish strong and enduring social ties between families, social evolution could have gone no further on the human level than among the anthropoids.

The incest taboo "is linked with the functioning of every society," in the words of Talcott Parsons. The importance of the taboo in promoting social, as well as economic, ties can be seen from the reply a New Guinea tribal member gave to anthropologist Margaret Mead when asked about why marriage within the family was prohibited. The Arapesh answered:

> What, you would like to marry your sister! What is the matter with you anyway? Don't you want a brother-in-law? Don't you realize that if you marry another man's sister and another man marries your sister, you will have at least two brothers-in-law, while if you marry your own sister you will have none? With whom will you hunt, with whom will you garden, whom will you go to visit?

EXEMPTIONS FROM THE TABOO

The varying ways that incest has been defined can be understood by the particular needs of different cultures, and those in power, at different times in history. For instance, at one time it was important to the Roman Catholic Church to assure its growth by keeping wealth from being concentrated within a narrow range of family alliances. This is one theory for why the Church in the Middle Ages defined incest as being marriage within "the fourth degree of kinship." Some similar reason may have been behind the Church of England's "Table of Kindred and Affinity."

At other times, it has served those in power to make certain exemptions regarding the incest taboo. In Egypt, brother-sister marriages were sanctioned for thousands of years among the ruling dynasties. This was particularly true in the XVII and XVIII dynasties of the Ptolemies, as noted by tax records of the time. Cleopatra was probably the most famous of the Pharaohs who married a sibling. She was both her husband's niece and his sister. Similar royal prerogatives were exercised by the ruling families of ancient Hawaii and the Incas of Peru. By inbreeding, a "pure" blood line was presumably insured for the throne.

In some cultures where incest became a traditional practice of rulers, the custom was eventually adopted by commoners. This occurred in both Egypt and Persia, where families preserved wealth and private property by intramarriage. In the Greek-Egyptian city of Arsinoe, it has been estimated that two-thirds of the marriages during the second century A.D. were incestuous, primarily between brother and sister. Incestuous marriages also were permitted in ancient Arabia.

Whenever incest taboos have been openly broken or exemptions sought, some higher purpose has often been invoked. The sons of Adam are said to have married their sisters so that the human race would continue and the earth be populated. Lot's daughters had similar reasons for seeking intercourse with their father. Among the Hindu-Sakta sect in India, incest was regarded as a higher grade of sexual intercourse and an advanced step toward religious perfection. In more recent times, incest was practiced among Mormons in Utah reportedly as a means for assuring that daughters and sisters would not have to marry outside the church. In 1892, the Utah legislature passed a law against incest after Congress had acted on making polygamy and intrafamily intercourse unlawful.

Some examples of incest can also be found among people who are so isolated that marriage outside the family is impossible. To keep from dying out, they mate among family members.

Where incest has been part of a group's culture or religion, the original purposes of the taboo have been overridden by reasons considered more pressing or noble. In general, however, the taboo has remained in force since before recorded history and the only thing that has varied has been the definition of what incest is.

Marriage among cousins has been one constant issue in definitions through the centuries. In the Middle Ages, the definition of incest was extended to include sixth cousins. At other times, incest has been defined in terms of parallel cousins (cross cousins have actually been encouraged to marry). In traditional Chinese society, a man could marry his mother's brother's daughter but not any person with his own surname.

First or second cousins have usually represented the degree of kinship prohibited by incest laws. In most states today, second cousins can marry and not be guilty of incest. Marriage between any closer kin is likely to be defined as incestuous (except, for example, in Rhode Island, where Jews can marry first cousins). French peasants believed marriage of first cousins caused failures of crops and epidemics among flocks. In Madagascar, headmen and kings may marry sisters and cousins but not their mothers.

In some countries, however, what is forbidden is not only a matter of law, but also of sin. For instance, in England intercourse with a daughter is a crime, marriage with a niece is illegal but not criminal, and marriage with a deceased wife's sister is not illegal or a crime but is a sin. The Church of England, then, regards as incestuous several types of marriage that are valid under the law.

Although most ecclesiastical authorities have historically strongly opposed incest and extended the ban on it to even ridiculous extremes, popes and others have not always refrained from practicing it. Herbert Maisch, German incest scholar, notes that Pope John XII, deposed in 963, was accused of incest with his mother and sisters. Pope Balthasar Cossa confessed to incest and adultery in 1414. Rodrigo Borgia, who became Pope Alexander VI in 1492, committed incest with both his daughter and his son, and in a Papal Bull announced he was the father of one of his daughter's children. Pope John XIII also was apparently removed as pontiff for incest.

Superstition as Basis for Taboo

The purpose of some of the varied definitions of incest has not always been clear. Marriage between sixth cousins, for example, is not going to prevent needed alliances from developing or cause the disruption of any given family in terms of jealousy and passion.

The reason for incest taboos in some cultures is superstition, and there is no rational way to explain why certain remote relatives are forbidden to marry (or, as was once decreed by church law, why even unrelated godparents to the same child could not marry). One theory holds that the origin of all incest taboos can be traced to superstition, that anything pleasurable is bad and since incest involves sex and pleasure, it too is bad and must be banned. Incest angers the gods, according to the superstitious view. Other societies have simply regarded incest as unlucky. In ancient times, all sorts of national catastrophies and social misfortunes were blamed on the existence of incestuous relationships: torrential rains, crop failures in Ireland, sterility among both the women and cattle of Thebes.

Although incest prohibitions existed long before scriptures, one theory holds that biblical injunctions account for the existence of the taboo. It is true that the book of Leviticus (18:6–18), for example, contains a ferocious list of sexual unions labeled a disgrace and shameful: intercourse with mother, sister, son's daughter, father's sister, mother's sister, brother's wife, among other close relatives. But the Mormons' interpretation of such injunctions was that they were meant to regulate marriage "of the children of Israel in the wilderness" in that day, not "those who might live in the latter days."

Certainly, precedent existed in the scriptures for incestuous marriage. Moses was born of the union of his nephew and aunt. Abraham was married to his half-sister. Ham, according to some interpreters, committed incestuous assault on his father, Noah, as he lay in a drunken stupor. The two daughters of Lot made their father drink wine and conceived by him to perpetuate the species. The sons of Adam, Cain and Abel, married their twin sisters for the same reason. And even the union of Adam and Eve, by one interpretation, was incestuous since she was made from his rib. In any event, biblical scriptures do not present convincing evidence for either the origin or later existence of incest taboos.

There is little doubt that superstition plays a part in the horror and dread that the subject of incest incites in some people, but the evidence suggests that incest has been prohibited largely because of more mundane reasons. We have seen that taboos were an early means for promoting the security and survival of societies through interlocking networks of families and that incest prohibitions helped preserve the family as an economic unit by preventing the discord and jealousies that would be aroused by sex among members.

That the very issue of survival was involved in forbidding incest can be seen from the extreme penalties that small societies have traditionally levied against offenders. People were put to death in cultures where group survival depended on mutual aid and cooperation.

But what about today? Our survival does not depend on building up alliances between families through intermarriage. The family no longer serves as a producing and consuming economic unit, demanding that its members work together to assure the security of all. Government has largely taken over functions relating to defense, survival, economic security. So why the continued prohibition of incest? Why keep the taboo in force?

Chapter 3

A NEW LOOK AT INCEST

Modern-day penalties against incest acknowledge that society's survival and economic security are no longer at stake. In England, incest is ranked as a misdemeanor. In the United States, penalties range from a $500 fine and/or 12 months in jail in Virginia to a prison term of one to 50 years in California. In Texas, punishment is a possible fine up to $5,000 and/or imprisonment from two to 10 years. As we have indicated, authorities in a number of states take action against incest under family codes and civil law, which provide no penalties at all in terms of fines or imprisonment.

If the original reasons for the incest taboos are no longer valid, and penalties are no longer severe, what then is the purpose of having prohibitions today?

There is no purpose, according to one view, and there should be no incest laws. R. E. L. Masters, author of *Patterns of Incest,* argues that the incest taboo causes condemnation of innocent people, arouses damaging guilt on the part of children, and punishes people whose relationship was no threat to anyone. He contends that when incest occurs outside the home on the part of consenting adults, no objections should be raised. When it occurs inside the home, other laws exist for taking action: rape, sodomy, endangering the welfare of a child. Masters argues that "morality . . . demands of the parent that he be especially protective of his own children and solicitous of their well-being." The prohibition of incest adds nothing helpful to parental obligation.

We agree that many incest laws, as presently written, have outlived their usefulness. The question of who is forbidden to marry whom is no longer relevant; the issue is not survival of the society or security of the family as an economic unit, the issue is the child, not society. The issue is a child's right to healthy development, free of the problems that come from sexual misuse or inappropriate intimacy. As Dr. Veronica Tisza of the department of psychiatry at Harvard Medical School put it:

> Incest is always an infringement on the rights of the child; it is overthrowing the child's right to be protected from harmful interference with its psychological, social, and sometimes physical development.

It is doubtful that laws can be as effective in securing a child's right to his own development as much as public education and attitude can. Laws can prohibit specific sex acts with children, but incest, as we have seen, is broader than this. Incest endangers the welfare of a child. It is a form of child abuse, and is so classified in many states.

By recognizing incest as a form of child abuse, an important step can be taken toward removing the taboo against discussing the subject. By taking incest out of the category of a dreaded curse or unthinkable abomination and placing it in the context of child abuse, more public attention and action on the problem are likely.

In no way do we suggest that legal action should not be brought against parents engaging in incest. It is a question of what kind of action most contributes to the welfare of the child and the child's family. We favor action brought under child abuse laws, civil laws, rather than under incest laws, criminal laws. If parents refuse to cooperate in going to therapy or making changes, the criminal law can be invoked. But the focus should remain on doing something about abuse of the child, not punishing parents for an unmentionable act.

Recognition that the central issue in incest is welfare of the child will challenge traditional concepts of children being the property of parents. As we pointed out in *The Abusing Family,* children historically have been regarded as property that parents could treat as they saw fit. It has been only in recent times that the issue of children's rights have been raised (see Chapter 16).

Sexual abuse, including incest, has been practiced at various periods in history as a privilege of parents. Slave boys were kept for homosexual use in homes of ancient Greece and Rome. Erotic drawings depicted nude children waiting on adults in sexual embrace. The Roman emperor Tiberius "taught children of the most tender years, whom he called his little fishes, to play between his legs while he was in his bath. Those which had not yet been weaned, but were strong and hearty, he set at fellatio." In France, Louis XIII as a child was hauled into bed by his parents and others and included in their sexual acts. Even now, the practice of parents' masturbating their children can be found among the Arabs, Moslems, the Islamics in Central Asia, the Turkomans, Uzbeks, Kurds and among the Hopi Indians in North America and the Siriono in South America.

In most cultures today, there is still an attitude that parents have a right to do what they please with their children. Fathers who get caught in incest cases often complain that what they were doing in their own homes with their own children is nobody else's business.

So the question of what incest is and how it is regarded depends, in part at least, on how children are considered. To view a child as having the right to develop in a healthy way, to be parented and to have his psychological and emotional needs met is a new way to look at incest.

Public Views and What Influences Them

When the subject of incest comes up, most people do not respond in terms of whether parents have the right to do with their children as they see fit or whether children have the right to their own bodies and a healthy emotional development. Most people find the subject of incest either totally repugnant or they make jokes about it.

These two extremes reflect the ambivalence that marks people's attitudes toward the subject. To much of the public, incest is an evil, a horror, a fascination, an attraction. It repels, offends, perplexes, yet it fascinates. Much of the emotional response toward the subject stems from two sources: the extreme condemnation of incest by Judeo-Christian religion and the theme of tragedy that has been used for centuries to dramatize myths, legends, novels, plays, and poems on incest

Both religion and literature decided a long time ago that the act of incest constitutes a curse that dooms all participants, no matter how innocent, no matter how unaware they were of being related to their incestuous partner. The myth has been widely spread from generation to generation that calamities of such enormity befall incestuous unions that even to speak of the subject is enough to strike fear and repulsion in people's hearts.

We have already mentioned the extreme lengths to which the Church extended definitions of incest from time to time. Such action contributed to the notion that incest is such a curse it can reach out and contaminate even 32nd cousins. Incest became identified in people's minds with witches and witchcraft. At conclaves of the most diabolical of witches, incestuous unions were mandatory. Incest became an act inspired by the devil, and people who practiced it were doomed to hell.

The same doomsday theme ran through literature, which also helped shape public attitudes toward incest. The greatest of the Greek dramas, Sophocles' *Oedipus Rex,* unfolded the tragedies that lay in wait for those involved in incest. It was such a gripping tale that its tragic theme has been picked up by writers and storytellers for the last 2,400 years to portray the curse of incest. The plot has numerous variations, but the central theme is the same: Mother and son—or father and daughter, or sister and brother—have long been separated, the child having been taken away when just a baby. Fate brings them back together without their knowing they are related. Love blossoms, they marry or have intercourse, and then—as though directed by the devil—it is revealed to them that they are near kin. Oedipus tore his eyes out when he learned he had married his mother. Jocasta, his mother, committed suicide. Plays, novels, poems ever since have elaborated upon this tragic story line.

The first treatment of incest by a serious writer in the English language was a play called *'Tis Pity She's a Whore,* staged in 1626. The author, John Ford, focused on the love between a brother and sister, who were swept up by fate into an incestuous relationship and were as doomed as Oedipus 20 centuries earlier. From the time of Oedipus Rex, incest has become a vehicle for writers to express a philosophy of life and an attitude toward man. Sophocles' outlook was that life is tragic and man is doomed; incest was the theme he used to express his kind of gloom. Homer wrote a different version of Oedipus Rex and in his, neither the son nor mother suffered tragic fates. Homer had a different philosophy and gave the story a different ending.

And so it has been down through the ages: Nathaniel Hawthorne used the incest theme as a vehicle for tales of the grotesque and macabre. Herman Melville and, later, Somerset Maugham, used it more traditionally to express tragedy. Marquis de Sade used it as a theme for sadism. William Faulkner used it to express social disintegration. And more recently, E. C. A. de Queiroz used it to depict the corruption and ugliness of an era in Portugal (as Edward Lea did in *Castle of Corruption,* set in post-World War II Germany) and Kate Christie used it to tell a horror story in *Child's Play.*

With these kinds of stories to help shape the public mind, it is no wonder that the subject of incest became the "unthinkable abomination." When Richard Loftus was tried for the murder of his mother, Hortense, his lawyers withheld the fact that the two were incestuous lovers. They believed a jury would be more tolerant of murder than incest.

There is no scientific justification for any of the stories of horror and preordained doom that the public has been given to associate with incest. Incest is not a happy subject, it threatens the emotional welfare of children, but it has nothing to do with curses, devils, and witches, or inevitable death and destruction. These are all myths perpetuated through the ages for purposes of drama, fiction, and religion.

The public has been conditioned to consider the subject in such strong emotional terms that a family makes all kinds of efforts to keep incest a secret. As a consequence, there is no reaching out for help, little enactment of laws that favor rehabilitation rather than punishment, there is little discussion and examination of the subject. Incest is such a taboo subject that the child involved often becomes "the victim nobody believes" because no one wants to believe incest can occur.

Even professionals are not exempt from the idea that incest is so unthinkable that it really does not exist. Cases are missed in emergency rooms because physicians are unwilling to consider the physical evidence of incest. Counselors do not bring the subject up even when a child presents all sorts of cues. Therapists are reluctant to ask if incest is in the background of clients.

An anthology entitled *Taboo Topics* considered incest such a taboo that the subject was not even included. "Complete" editions of the works of John Ford deliberately omitted his play on incest. Books with incest in the title are "lost" from public libraries and articles are cut out of journals. As Dr. Marshall Schechter and Dr. Leo Roberge, of the State University of New York Upstate Medical Center, have noted, incest "data collection and scientific study have been markedly impaired by what has been euphemistically referred to as a 'family affair.'" They pointed out that efforts to study the subject "invariably arouse 'gallows humor,' collusive denial or severe retribution."

In the course of writing this book, we observed that most people reacted to the subject either with unfunny wisecracks or deadly silence. Some reacted with less defensiveness and showed serious interest. Previously, when we were gathering material for our book on physical abuse of children, people would react to the subject with anger toward anyone who would beat a child or with sadness that such a depressing thing goes on or with encouragement for the treatment we provide abusing parents.

With incest, a different cord is struck. The jokes come out or uncomfortable silence ensues. In some instances, we concluded, the subject was hitting too close to home—the people we were talking with had either been involved in incest and had lived with the "secret" ever since or they were practicing incest now. If the subject were pursued in their presence, they became increasingly tense and finally hostile. Others would attempt to dismiss the subject with a joke, such as "the family that lays together stays together."

More than a few people, however, asked serious questions about incest and sought information. One even volunteered, in front of others at a social gathering, "I was one of those children."

MORE OPEN ATTITUDES TOWARD SEX

Though still a minority, the number of people willing to discuss incest openly is growing. Dr. Tisza believes that "the conspiracy of silence" around incest has been broken by a willingness to examine all sexual behavior more openly. Sociologist S. Kirson Weinberg, of the University of Chicago, says permissive attitudes toward sex are largely responsible for more frankness about incest.

The majority of people, however, still express a repulsion or dread toward the subject. Many, as we indicated, are uncomfortable with their own sexual thoughts, impulses, or urges and find the subject too threatening to acknowledge. Often, what people find intensely repulsive, fearful, or horrible is what they also desire in the deep recesses of their beings. The repulsion is a way to keep the desire repressed and out of awareness; making light of the matter, joking about it, is another way. The jokes on incest also reflect the fascination that people have with the subject.

In an era of sexual permissiveness, it is easier for sexual jokes, including those on incest, to gain wider distribution. A magazine like *Playboy* is one source of incest humor. In answer to a reader asking if he would run into problems if he married his second cousin, the "Playboy Adviser" gave accurate information on the legality of such marriages and advised checking a doctor on genetic safety. The advisor then commented: "Clearing this hurdle, you have our blessings. And we can't resist closing with the remark of the anonymous roué who said: 'Incest is fine, as long as it's kept in the family.' "

Other incest humor is along similar lines, such as "incest—it's relative," and "incest is the game the whole family can play." Jokes that reflect a cultural acceptance of incest, such as can be found in parts of the Ozarks and mountains of Kentucky, include "a virgin is a 5-year-old girl who can outrun her pappy and brothers." A variation of this comes from Dr. Weeks, of the University of Virginia Medical Center, who said that when she was growing up, "the definition of a virgin was 'a 14-year-old-girl who doesn't have a brother.' "

It should be noted that rustic incest jokes may provide urbanites a way to deflect their own incestuous impulses. Two California clinicians observed:

> We suspect that rustic incest jokes supply a prejudicial scapegoat for urbanites not entirely immune from incestuous conflicts, and that regional variations in incest behavior are minor.

It is difficult to assess whether the growing climate of sexual permissiveness is resulting in more jokes being generated about incest or whether the old jokes that have long been around are just getting disseminated more widely. (See more on the permissive climate in Part III.) There does seem to be a definite increase in the number of cartoons with incestuous overtones, and these are appearing in a variety of magazines.

Films and books with incest as a theme, or as a part of the story, also seem to be on the increase. *The American Film Institute Catalog of Motion Pictures* listed 5,775 feature films released from 1961 to 1970, with 79 on incest. By comparison, there were 6,606 films listed for 1921–1930, and six were on incest. No catalogue has been compiled for periods other than those two decades.

Many of the more recent films on incest depart from the Sophocles' theme of tragedy and have endings that do not find people committing suicide or going to hell. Dr. Gail Berry of Mount Sinai School of Medicine in New York has even found that "as part of the generalized attack on sexual restrictions, incest has been treated in a lighthearted fashion in certain films and books."

Some films and stories still strike notes invoking the devil and doom but most do not. None of those that do not has received much recognition, so it is not likely they will have much effect on influencing public attitudes about incest. Many were made abroad and released in this country; some are pornographic. A few had major Hollywood stars and these resorted to the doomsday or tragic theme. *The Last Sunset,* with Rock Hudson and Kirk Douglas, was a western melodrama that ended in tragedy. *Chinatown,* with Jack Nicholson, ended in bloody death; and *The Savage Is Loose* starred George C. Scott and illustrated the violent oedipal struggles of a boy who gets stranded with his mother and father on a remote jungle island. In a re-enactment of Freud's primal scene, the son attempts to murder the father by burning him to death and wins the opportunity to have sex with his mother.

A number of contemporary novels on incest also carry out the old doom is inevitable myth. Whether this will change as people adopt less magical and diabolical attitudes toward incest remains to be seen. D. W. Cory and R. E. L. Masters, in their study of incest in literature, concluded that although authors recognize the pointlessness of punishment in incest cases, they must "bow to custom" to achieve publication, so they continue to have their characters punished and the stories end with doom and tragedy.

One new twist that contemporary fiction has brought to the incest theme is to play up stepfather-stepdaughter sex, as in Grace Metalious' *Peyton Place* (which added rape to the storyline), and Vladimir Nabokov's *Lolita*. Paperback novels have best reflected the trend toward anything-goes sex by dealing with incest as simply one of many sex styles and preferences practiced by the protagonists. This is true, for instance, of Willi Peters' *Lesbian Twins* and Don Halliday's *Lust Sisters*, which focused on homosexual incest. More recently, there has been *We, Too.*

As for the part that other art forms have had in molding popular concepts about what incest is, the most certain point that can be made is that all—painting, sculpturing, music—have addressed the subject. The First International Exhibition of Erotic Art in Sweden in 1968 gave the public a candid view of what painters and sculptors have done with incest themes. Frederic Pardo's *Oedipal Trip*, an oil on wood, showed two nude figures, a young male child ejaculating as he straddled the thigh of his smiling mother. Tomi Ungerer's "fellatio machine" bore the caption: "When mother is ill or away." George Segal sculptured *The Legend of Lot*, showing one nude woman standing over a sleeping male figure (father) as another female (her sister) watches.

In music, the most enduring explicit story of incest has been in three operas of Richard Wagner. *Die Walküre* tells the love story of a twin brother and sister. The brother is killed but the sister is allowed to bear his child, who becomes a hero. In *Siegfried*, the child rescues his goddess aunt, and they become lovers. *Die Gotterdammerung (The Twilight of the Gods)* tells of Siegfried's forsaking his wife/aunt and his murder, accomplished with her help. So the incest-means-doom myth continued in opera.

Blues, folk, popular, rock, or soul music has been less explicit with incest. With "baby" being a term of general endearment, no true assessment can be made of the meaning behind many of the countless songs that have "baby" as a theme and part of the title. A similar problem exists with the multitude of songs addressed to "daddy." Some interpreters construe the origin of both "baby" and "daddy" as having incestuous roots. The same observers interpret *I Want a Girl Just Like the Girl Who Married Dear Old Dad* as one of the most lasting tributes to incest.

The question of covert, implicit incestuous behavior, wishes and desires is one last issue that must be examined to understand more fully what incest entails.

UNCONSCIOUS INCEST

The most universal aspect of incest that 20th century writers have presented to the public concerns the powerful unconscious drives that Freud identified as motivating human behavior. These drives are the very basis of Freudian psychology, which holds that the struggle against deep incestuous wishes and impulses is at the very root of why people behave as they do. Such unconscious wishes and impulses can be found in plays of Tennessee Williams (such as *Cat on a Hot Tin Roof*), in D. H. Lawrence's *Sons and Lovers,* and in Eugene O'Neill's *Mourning Becomes Electra.*

The unconscious is that vast part of the mind where people store thoughts, feelings, impulses, wishes, desires that they find unacceptable. By keeping what is unacceptable or painful out of their awareness, they are more comfortable. But Freud saw the unconscious as making continuous efforts to become conscious and interpreted dreams, slips of the tongue, and much other behavior on that basis. Incestuous wishes represent the most powerful of unconscious drives, according to Freud, and require enormous energy to divert into acceptable behavior and activity.

Although Freud's preoccupation with the oedipus (incest) wish is subject to question, psychological evidence confirms that incestuous thoughts and feelings—largely out of one's awareness—do play a part in human behavior.

These may not be strictly sexual in the sense of a child's wanting to have sex with the parent, or the parent's wanting sex with the child. They may represent a child's wanting to claim the parent of the opposite sex all for himself or herself, displacing the parent of the same sex. Or the thoughts and feelings may well represent an attempt to satisfy needs for nurturing or closeness or, as Eric Fromm noted, for a desire to return to what is fantasied as an all-loving-and-secure place. For the child, this may be father's arms or mother's apron strings; for the parent, it may be next to the child's body, demanding his or her affection, warmth, and closeness.

When growing up, most people resolve these issues or come to terms with them in such a way that the incestuous drives become defused or deflected (see Chapters 9 and 12). By midchildhood, a boy has usually settled on giving up his exclusive claim to mother and identifying with father, who, in effect, is seen as winning the competition. A girl renounces her wish for father and models after mother. During adolescence, the final form of renunciation occurs when the youngster completes the job of redirecting his or her energy from inside the family to outside. Much of the young person's personality development and socialization in the world depends on going through this process and coming to terms with it.

With some people, something else happens. They either fail to renounce the longing or lusting for the parent or they never find a satisfactory way to divert themselves outside the family. They may set up self-defeating defenses —diversions—against the incestuous impulses. These may take the form of chronic anxiety, disruptive behavior, or psychosomatic complaints; or circumstances may point them toward more disturbing defenses and diversions: sexual aberrations and sadism.

How parents act toward the child is going to determine in considerable part whether the child negotiates the renunciation and redirection process successfully. A parent may have unsettled incestuous feelings of his or her own. This may lead to unconscious incest or seductive behavior —parading in front of the child nude, keeping the bathroom door open, sleeping with the child, taking baths with the child or with the child watching. Not every glimpse that a child may catch of his parent undressed can be interpreted as involving unconscious incest behavior, but when the parent habitually invites attention to his or her nude body there is more to such behavior than simply being open and free of hang-ups around one's child.

More overtly, a parent may make a practice of giving the child deep, sensual kisses and embraces or playing with the child's genitals. Even if such activity stops short of actual intercourse, it still is likely to create conflicts in the child and problems that may well lead him or her later to psychotherapy. We will explore these issues in detail in Chapter 12 on parent-child sexuality.

Physical contact with sexual overtones may be initiated by the child and not rebuffed by the parent. The French writer Stendahl said:

> I was always in love with my mother. I was always kissing my mother and wishing that we had no clothes on . . . I kissed her with such ardour that she felt a certain degree in duty bound to withdraw. I detested my father when he came and interrupted our embraces. I wanted to kiss her breasts always.

Incestuous impulses are seldom so overt. When they are, they can be dealt with more directly, if the parent is willing, than when the wish for sex between parent and child is disguised and expresses itself covertly. In either case, psychological and social problems for the child are likely to develop if the sexual overtures, covert or otherwise, continue.

This is less true in areas where there is a cultural acceptance of incest and sexual arousal of children by parents in a common practice. As we mentioned, in isolated portions of the Appalachian and Ozark Mountains, cultural incest has been the custom for generations. This is not to say that the child suffers no impairment where incest is accepted; it simply means that in restricted and deprived environments the consequences of impairment are less apparent.

In Part III we will explore more fully all the factors that contribute to incestuous behavior, both overt and covert behavior. In the present chapter we have examined the many sides of incest, the historical views of it, the legal definitions, the way it has been treated in literature and other art, the public conceptions of it, and the role it plays in all human behavior. Now we will look at who commits incest—the characteristics of the fathers, mothers, children involved.

Part II

WHO COMMITS INCEST

Chapter 4

FROM TEACHERS TO TYRANTS

Harry Lewis was an introvert. He came from a family where little effort was made to cultivate friends or have people over for a visit. At school he was a loner who made good grades, shunned girls, and avoided extracurricular activities. He was polite and pleasant when spoken to but he never initiated conversations.

After serving in the army, Harry went to college and became a computer programmer. He married the first girl he ever dated. After a year, the girl said they had made a mistake, that Harry just wanted to stay at home and didn't want her to have friends and that she couldn't go on like that, so they divorced. Harry did well on the job, got promoted, and transferred and worked harder than ever. He went out a few times to bars, discovered he liked to drink and began dating. He met a nice-looking young woman, on the plump side, who liked to cook for him and watch television with him. After awhile, they married and had two children, both daughters.

Harry committed incest with the oldest daughter when she reached 11. It began with his fondling her just-budding breasts in a playful manner. Then, when his wife was out of the house, he began going into the bathroom as his daughter came out of the shower and feeling of her. Later, he would lead her to the bed in her room and press his penis against her. Finally, intercourse occurred, and the family was referred to us for therapy.

Harry Lewis was not mentally ill, he was not subnormal in intelligence, he was not a sex maniac, he was not a drunkard, he was not poverty-stricken and lower class. At 39, he was successful in his career, he was financially comfortable, he was college educated and, as viewed by people who knew him at work, he was a father who cared for his children and was interested in their welfare.

Harry Lewis contradicts all the stereotypes of the person who engages in incest. That person has been typically portrayed as mentally ill, sexually perverted, psychopathic, alcoholic, retarded, uneducated, and unskilled. To be sure, these adjectives fit some people who have sex with their children, but such people are in the minority.

Contrary to findings of earlier studies, many incestuous families present on the surface a picture of being stable and cohesive. Like Harry, the father may seem family-centered, and the mother very home-oriented. The family often puts up a strong "togetherness" front and discourages outsiders from getting to know what is going on at home or even visiting. The father frequently carries being a "family man" to the extreme. He looks to his family to satisfy all his emotional needs and as relations with his wife deteriorate, he turns to a daughter as his sole source of satisfaction.

While many families that come to the attention of the police and the courts are lower-income, they do not present a true picture of families at large involved in incest. For example, average income for the 300 families referred to the Child Sexual Abuse Treatment Program in Santa Clara, California, was $13,413 in 1975. Median educational level was 12.5 years. In our survey, which included families referred both by child welfare authorities and those seen in private practice, even higher income and educational levels were noted.

It is not unusual, then, for the incestuous family to present this kind of profile: they are middle-class people;

the parents have some college, if not a degree, in their background; they have been married more than 10 years; the father is in business, a skilled trade or profession and makes frequent job changes; he is in his late thirties; the mother is slightly younger and does not work; there are three children, and the oldest daughter is approaching puberty.

Fathers most often initiate incest in a family. At least this is true based on cases that are detected and brought to anyone's attention. Some authorities believe that brother-sister incest is more common than any other kind but that less of it gets reported or detected since it is considered less serious and may be handled within the family.

On the basis of known cases, mothers commit incest less frequently than any other family member. In our survey of 112 families, only two cases of mother-son incest were found. Similarly, Weinberg found only two in his study of 203 families in 1955. It should be noted, however, that these are *known* cases. In our experience, mothers engage more frequently in sexual activity that does not get reported: fondling, sleeping with a son, caressing in a sexual way, exposing her body to him, and keeping him tied to her emotionally with implied promises of a sexual payoff.

As for brother-sister incest, there were nine cases in our survey, 37 in Weinberg's and zero in Maisch's in Germany. When we speak of the incestuous family, then, we are most often referring to one in which the father and daughter have sex. Although other family members are usually not directly participating, all are involved in the family system that contributes to the start and continuation of the activity. This is particularly true of the mother, who may play a key role in both what her husband and daughter do. We will develop this point more fully in discussing why incest occurs.

In considering who does it, we are interested in what kind of people they are, what their personalities are like, and what their attitudes are. Because fathers and daughters are the most frequent participants (in terms of known cases), we will focus primarily on them. We will also, though, take a look at the mothers in incest, both from the standpoint of what kind of woman it is who indirectly contributes to her husband and daughter having sex and in terms of the mother who directly participates with a son. In addition, we will take note of the brother and sister who engage in incest.

THE FATHERS

Men who practice sex in the family can be classified into four groups. The first group is made up of what we call symbiotic personalities, and it is by far the one in which most incestuous fathers fall. The second is composed of psychopathic personalities, and the third pedophilic personalities. Last, there is a small "other" group in which we put fathers who engage in incest because the practice is part of the culture in which they were brought up or because they are psychotic. Combined, the last three groups make up no more than 15 to 20 percent of all the fathers who commit incest. We will concentrate, then, on the fathers in the first group.

Symbiotic Personalities

When we were working on *The Abusing Family,* on the causes and treatment of physical child abuse, we discovered that a central problem in these families was that the child was expected to take care of the parents rather than vice versa. That is, the child was turned to for the nurturing, love, comfort, succor, that parents normally give to a child rather than receive. The parents would compete with each other over who was going to take care of whom, and the "loser"

—the parent who ended up making most of the decisions for the family, taking on most of the responsibility and feeling deprived of love and care—would then turn to the child in an attempt to get the love and care he or she failed to find elsewhere. The child, of course, could not meet such a heavy demand and would feel the brunt of the parent's pent-up frustration and anger when the parent got under stress. This central problem is called symbiosis.

The father who becomes involved in incest has a similar problem. Because of the way he was brought up and the kind of parents he had as a child, he hungers for a closeness, a sense of belonging and intimacy that he seldom can verbalize and never has experienced. He has strong unmet needs for warmth, for someone to be close to, for someone to touch and hold him. He does not know how to be close and affectionate in a nonsexual sense or how to meet his needs to belong and have a warm relationship in a non-physical way. For reasons we will discuss later, he turns to sex with his own daughter in an attempt to meet these needs. He seldom is aware of what it is he is needing from the daughter. Most men who commit incest are completely out of touch with their needs and have no experience in meeting them in healthy ways.

Incestuous fathers have symbiotic personalities that are of several types. The types vary according to characteristic ways the men try to satisfy the need for closeness through sex. Some are bullying, others are persuasive, some are shy and play on sympathy and misguided loyalty, still others use alcohol to express their dependency needs and then, claiming loss of control, seek satisfaction of the needs through sex. In order, we call these types the tyrant, the rationalizer, the introvert and the alcoholic.

We will first discuss the introvert, because he most graphically portrays the quality of isolation and distance from people that characterizes all incestuous fathers. Not all are shut in like the introvert—some may even seem to be outgoing—but each type shares the inability to reach out to others, to establish closeness, to get attention and affection through daily human contacts.

Many incestuous fathers present a front of being strong and protective toward their families. Their wives may have married them believing they were men who could be leaned on. Many seem to ask little for themselves. In reality, they are starved for affection and hungry for someone who will nurture and comfort them.

THE INTROVERT.   In some families, a fusion develops between husband and wife, parent and child, or all the family members, from the excessive amount of time they spend together. They may remain indoors virtually shut off from contact with other people. The father is often the most introverted and sets the style for the family. He leaves the house only to go to work. Nights and weekends he goes nowhere. One child in the family often adopts the same pattern and remains locked in the house with the father.

Such was the case with Harry Lewis and his oldest daughter, Annie. As we saw at the opening of this chapter, Harry was successful at his job but he had no friends. He reached out to no one, thinking people would not like him and reject him. He had nothing to say. His wife was not this way. When she saw that all Harry wanted to do was stay at home and watch television, she began to make friends on her own and to go out and play cards. Their younger daughter took after the mother, but Annie became seclusive like her father. The family's frequent moves from one city to another, as Harry got transferred and took on more responsible jobs, made it hard for her to develop friendships, so she did not try.

Harry looked upon his home as a haven from the pressures that kept building up with more responsibilities at work. He felt under a constant bombardment and, deprived of any close relationships, he more and more turned to Annie for comforting. He would lie with his head in her lap as they watched television night after night. They did not talk, but having his daughter close to him became very important to Harry.

His relations with his wife, Susan, deteriorated. It bothered him even to have her talk to him. When she complained of his ignoring her, he would withdraw into a pout. He felt that she was always trying to boss him around and run his life. They stopped having sex together except every month or so.

Harry began eating more, constantly raiding the refrigerator, and snacking all evening, as the stress mounted. Then he began drinking each night and on weekends. Finally, when Susan and his younger daughter were out of the house, he started turning to Annie for sex.

The introvert among incestuous fathers feels under attack from the outside world. He sees the family as a shelter that provides him comfort. He turns more and more inward into the family as the pressures outside continue. Much of the outside stress comes from the introvert's cutting himself off from others, asking help from no one, never confiding or blowing off steam. This type father believes he can trust few people, certainly no one outside his family. He sees his family as the place where he should be able to do as he pleases and no one should betray him.

Some fathers of this type adopt an attitude similar to that of a man who considers his daughter to be his exclusive property. The introvert does not go outside the family to have sex with other women—he may even consider that to be "a sin"—but turns to his daughter, whom he regards as belonging to him. Since she belongs to him, she is a "permissible alternative" to his wife. She is there to help him forget the cruel world outside, the pain and problems that come from people who cannot be trusted, from opportunities that vanish and dreams that fade.

Part of the introvert's seclusiveness and withdrawal is explained by depression. Most of the fathers who fit this type are depressed to varying degrees. They take life very seriously, are easily disappointed and affected by setbacks, and look to a daughter to give them solace. Such was the case with the father of Jan, a daughter who entered therapy with us.

Dan was an architect, a successful one. He and his family lived in an attractive house appointed with handsome pieces of furniture. Even the children's rooms had only the best. Everything looked great—on the surface.

Beneath the surface, things were quite different. Dan was severely depressed, and spent much of his time alone in his room. This had been going on for a long time, even before his first wife, Jan's mother, was committed to a mental hospital. After Dan divorced and remarried an attractive South American woman, things looked better for awhile, for about 18 months. Then he began to pull back into his depression and his new wife reacted with rage and fear.

The only person Dan seemed to be able to respond to during these times was Jan, his 11-year-old daughter. Jan was the oldest daughter and had always held a special place in her father's heart. She seemed to be able to comfort him when no one else could.

Dan would let Jan stay up later than the other children, as a reward for her good grades. During these times, they would sit together, and Dan would caress her. The caressing became more sexual and within a year, the father was having intercourse with the daughter.

When their sexual relationship was discovered by Dan's new wife, she first blamed Dan and then Jan. Finally, the attacks from the step-mother and the continued advances from the father became so stressful that Jan left home at 15. Dan sank back into his depression and his second wife left him. He went on to marry three more wives, all not much older than Jan.

Sociologist S. Kirson Weinberg, in his study of incestuous fathers, identified an "endogamic" type, a father with an "intra-family orientation." All symbiotic personalities turn within the family in an attempt to meet their needs, first to the wife and, then, when relations deteriorate and sex is discontinued between them, to a daughter. All use sex in the family in an effort to satisfy needs that they never learned to fulfill through close contact with others. Weinberg's endogamic type is similar to our introvert father, as illustrated by the case of Ho.

> He never went with other women besides his wife. In all the years that he was employed, he remained at home after working hours. He began to develop a sexual interest in his daughter. She was sexually active and when she sat on his lap, she moved her hips to excite him sexually. His wife was told by a missionary that sex was a sin and would condemn the soul to everlasting hell, so she refused to have relations with her husband. . . . He said his daughter loved him better than his wife and consequently he initiated incest with her. . . .

Sometimes it appears that circumstances, rather than personalities, largely account for incest occurring: a father gets injured or sick and must remain home alone with his daughter while the wife works; a father becomes unemployed and cannot find work. As we will see, the personality type for incest must be present for the circumstances to precipitate the problem. One of the fathers in our therapy group retired from the army at 45, could not find work, virtually stopped looking and began staying at home, where he eventually initiated sexual activity with his oldest daughter, a seductive teenager. He had always been inclined toward developing symbiotic relations, first as a child with his mother, then with the army, later with his wife, and finally with his daughter.

THE RATIONALIZER.   The rationalizer uses lofty words and sentiments or plausible-sounding, but specious, reasons for establishing an incestuous affair with his daughter. Some fathers justify sexual activity with their daughters on the basis of showing them what "love" is. Such a reason sounds plausible to a child. It did, for instance, to Barbara, whose case history was reported by Dr. John Woodbury, a California psychologist, and Elroy Schwartz.

The Lover.   One night when Barbara was 3 and her mother was out of the house, her dad gave her a bath, only he washed her "really too good." The same night, before he went to bed, he came in and took the child to the bathroom "and acted like he was washing her again. Only with his hand." The pattern of "massaging" continued for some time, then her father began "the love game."

> One day he kissed me on the stomach and then he kissed me —he kissed me there. From then on, that was basically the whole idea. . . . It was much different. It was warm. I didn't understand why he was doing it. He said, "Because I love you. This is showing you that I love you."

Barbara and her dad played "the love game" many times, "maybe five times a week," she recalled under hypnosis. In the early grades in elementary school, she got into mild sex play with neighborhood boys under a wooden crate, but this she viewed as "nasty" and knew that if her father caught them, he would "break her neck." When her father played with her sexually, she believed this was all right because he loved her. Dad would bring Barbara presents and give her privileges denied to her brother and sister. When Barbara was 7, her dad started having her kiss his penis and put it in her mouth. When she was a few years older, he would kiss her where her breasts were soon beginning to develop.

> I started wearing a bra when I was in the fourth grade, and then he would kiss me on the breasts. This always repulsed me. I couldn't stand it. . . . maybe because I was used to the other. . . . But I hated it because it tickled, and I can't stand to be tickled. That was all I could relate to it. Now I realize it was much more involved, but at the time, that was all I could think of.

What Barbara later realized was involved was sexual stimulation. As a child she could relate what her father was doing only to "an affectionate game." Her father attempted intercourse with her when she was 8, "but I'm very, very small. It hurt so much I never let him." So "the love game" continued in the form of oral-genital relations.

> I guess I sort of hated him, but really a false hate because I couldn't really hate him. I don't think you can really hate anyone that loves you. As soon as I realized what was involved, I wanted it to end. I wanted it to end because I wanted to be a virgin for my husband. But my father didn't agree, so it didn't end.

It didn't end until Barbara was 16 when, after telling her mother and several other persons who took no action, she informed a juvenile officer she felt she could trust. She refused to file charges, however, because she insisted that she loved her dad and he loved her. So her father and mother began having sessions with the juvenile officer, who sent the dad to a psychiatrist. Nothing changed at home, though. Her father kept wanting to "love" her, so Barbara quit high school and left town.

Barbara's father exemplifies how people can compartmentalize their lives: He worked, he had friends, he went to church, he committed incest. Her dad became religious when she was 5 and began teaching Sunday School. Her mother also taught. The children were baptized and taught prayers to say at home. The family always said grace before dinner. Both father and mother would talk to Barbara about morals. What the dad did with the daughter was something completely separate and apart. A supreme rationalizer, he called it "love."

Among fathers who are symbiotic personalities, a number justify their behavior to some degree on the basis of love for their daughter. A few rationalize their actions in terms of physical intimacy being the highest form of love a father can show his daughter. These are deeply entrenched attitudes. Fathers who espouse love as justification for incest have great unfulfilled needs for warmth and closeness that they confuse with sex, just as they confuse sex with love.

There is a similar kind of father who also has physical intimacies with his daughter out of "love," and stops just short of actual intercourse. He bathes her as a baby, keeps giving her baths when she is old enough to wash herself and starts taking showers with her when she is a preteen. To him she remains his "baby girl." Clinging to this view of her, he exempts himself from any guilt over the intimacies he takes with her. He caresses her as he helps her dress in the morning, he kisses her deeply on the lips when she is leaving the house, he fondles her breasts as she begins to mature. He gives her gifts, money, clothes. When she reaches adolescence, they are like lovers. He writes her passionate letters; they go everywhere together; they hold hands, take long walks, ignore the rest of the world. She is still his "baby girl" and he is her "Daddy." They do everything but sleep together. Their relations are just as incestuous as though they did.

The Teacher.   Barbara's father said he was showing her what love was. Another kind of incestuous father is the one who teaches his daughter about sex and rationalizes the incest on the basis of "sex education." Dr. Richard Sarles, a child psychiatrist at the University of Maryland, cites the case of a stepfather who told his stepdaughter that he wanted to initiate her into sexual experiences "so she could learn right and not get hurt." Another group of researchers had a similar case in which the daughter was given the mother's role and the father provided "sex education" of a physical kind. Sarles notes that this type of father is "often surprised at the concern placed on the incestuous relationship, stating that 'it is a father's duty to teach his daughter the facts of life the right way.'"

Unlike Barbara's dad, these fathers may show little affection for their daughters. Psychiatrists Schechter and Roberge described a father, a Ph.D. in mathematics, who showed no interest in the daughter until she began dating. Then he insisted that he have intercourse with her before anyone else did.

Like Barbara's dad, these fathers may give no indication to anyone outside the family that they would even remotely consider committing incest. In fact, they may even be highly respected and leading members of the community. Such was the case with "Citizen William K.," as presented by Dr. Benjamin Karpman through the eyes of William K's daughter:

> Dad is one of the best known and highly respected men in the community. . . . When he was still a young man, he was elected to an important position in the educational field and held the office for some ten years. . . . While attending college, he worked full time at a government job and supported a family of several children. . . .
>
> Dad never refused to do a favor for anybody who asked him. He went out of his way to offer to do favors for others. . . .
>
> An old lady . . . said that she had never seen another man so devoted to his family. Our neighbors probably shared that opinion. To the casual observer, he probably appears to be a very devoted father. . . .
>
> I have never had an inkling that anybody outside his family had an unkind thought about him. He seemed to be a living example of goodness, kindness, helpfulness, and righteousness, as far as the community was concerned.

William K. never showed any sexual interest in his daughter before she was 15 except one time when she was 11 and he was teaching her how to dance. She could feel "his erect penis touching me with every step he took." She kept pulling away but he seemed to take no notice and kept pressing against her. The daughter also recalled her father "parading around" the house in his underwear, "clutching at the front of it as if he were trying to prevent exposure." The summer that William K's daughter was 15, he took his wife and the rest of the family to his mother-in-law's farm. The daughter drove back to the city with her dad because she was attending summer school.

> It was on the return trip that the "honeymoon" started. . . . Dad began almost immediately to ask questions. He wanted to know if I had any improper advances from boys. When I answered in the negative, he told me that I probably would have and drifted immediately into a dissertation on courtship in France. . . . He then told me about the use of condoms and said that people in France use them all the time. . . .
>
> This led to a description of the penis and its role in the sex act. I expressed surprise at his description of the head and foreskin. To him, this was an invitation to bring forth "exhibit A," his penis.

For the rest of the trip home, William K. would remove his penis from his pants, demonstrate movement of the foreskin back and forth and reach for his daughter's hand to place around the organ. The demonstration was provided, he said, as "education" of his daughter, "to prevent me from experimenting with boys to satisfy my curiosity." William K. also pulled his daughter's dress up so he could stroke her vagina.

The "education" continued at home in his bedroom.

> At first, we merely repeated the play we had enjoyed so much during the afternoon trip homeward. Dad then again assumed the "teacher" role. This was to overcome the guilt of further intimacies in which we were to indulge. . . . He wanted to show me the position the man assumes in sex relations. He had me spread my legs far apart until he was to touch the opening to the vagina with his penis. I did as

> I was told, assuming the role of an obedient child. Although
> I had participated actively in mutual masturbation play in
> the car, with pleasure which must have been apparent, I now
> concealed my enjoyment.

The father insisted he would be careful not to break the hymen, which he said must be saved for his daughter's wedding night. He did, however, have a climax and after the ejaculation, he sent his daughter to the bathroom. There, still acting as teacher, he removed the condom he had worn and showed her what semen looked like. During each night that the family was away, William K. slept with his daughter, continuing her "education."

> After Mom's return, there were a few isolated instances of
> stolen "feels" when she was in other parts of the house. One
> time was after she was in bed. Dad came to my room with
> an erection, felt my body, put my hand on his penis, and
> urged me to play with it. I did for a brief moment, after
> which he went into his room. These experiences produced
> so much guilt in me that I had to stop them. After my first
> refusal, Dad never approached me again.

William K. carefully instructed his daughter never to tell anyone of their physical intimacies. The daughter never spoke to her mother or her two younger sisters of the experience. Later, she had reason to believe that her father also gave sex "training" to the two other sisters. There were indications, she said, that they both received "lessons" similar to hers.

Later, we will discuss the consequences of the kind of "education" William K. gave—the effects on his daughter in terms of her relations with men and her sexual life. Whether the teacher fully convinces himself that what he is doing to his daughter is for her own good or whether he manufactures such a rationalization strictly to alleviate guilt is still an open question. In either case, the teacher is like other symbiotic personalities in his feelings of emotional deprivation and need for closeness. William K. spent his life doing for others, taking on new posts and responsibilities in the community, but never letting himself receive love. Somehow, getting sexually close to his daughter was meant to satisfy his terrible need.

The Protector.   Closely akin to the teacher is the person we call the protector because he takes it upon himself to satisfy his daughter's sexual needs so that she will not have to be exposed to the corrupt minds and manners of men in the world outside. Implicit in this father's sexual attitudes is the idea that "she is going to get it somewhere and it's a lot better that she get it from me than from others." A peculiar moralistic attitude is sometimes adopted by the protector. Dr. B. J. Oliver, Jr. cites a case in which a father contended he had to have intercourse with his daughters to prevent them from having sex with boyfriends, which he regarded as improper.

The rationalization of the protector is that the father does his daughter a service and protects her from unseemly influences by giving her sexual release with him. In reality, what he does is in the interest of serving his own needs, not hers.

Although mostly fathers occupy all the types we have identified and are presenting here, some mothers also fit. For instance, one case was brought to our attention in which a mother rationalized sex with her 11-year-old son on the basis that this would protect him against becoming a homosexual. In her mind, he was showing signs of possibly tending toward homosexuality, so having sex with him was her way of protecting against that outcome.

The Elitist.   A variant of the protector-rationalizer is the father who considers his daughter and himself superior to the rest of the world and wants to preserve the purity of the bloodline. Unlike most other incestuous fathers, this one wants sex with his daughter to produce offspring. He is a modern day counterpart to the royal families (see Part I) that required inbreeding so that the royal blood would remain uncorrupted by genes of lesser mortals. Robert, father of Dianne, who came to therapy with us, was an elitist.

Robert was a systems analyst and an inventor of sorts. He invented a device for jet airplane flaps and sold it to the French government. He took Dianne to Paris when he completed the transaction. Dianne was the apple of her father's eye. Everyone knew that he considered her the most intelligent of the kids. He saw himself as some kind of genius and was willing to consider her his equal. He would caress and kiss her, saying he wanted children by her. "You are so intelligent and I am so intelligent that the children would be simply brilliant."

Since he saw himself so superior, Robert had little to do with anyone except Dianne. He had no friends. He stayed aloof from others wherever he worked. He took pride in the excellent grades that Dianne always made in school and gave her special privileges. Among those was allowing her to stay up late. He would call her to his room and have her stroke and kiss his penis. Although he occasionally became enraged and beat his wife and sons, he never struck Dianne or even criticized her. She was special—like he was.

The "elitist" may, in fact, be intelligent and gifted. But he rationalizes that no one else in the world except his daughter warrants his attention and company. Because he has no skill or experience at making friends or establishing warm and close contacts with people, he rationalizes that no one else deserves him. He picks out his brightest daughter and seeks in her all that he misses from others.

Occasionally a brother and sister, usually of a wealthy family, get the idea that they are too good for the rest of the world and develop an elitist incestuous relationship. Thomas Mann, in his short story, "The Blood of the Walsungs," depicted a brother and sister who found most other people fools and unable to match their superiority and elegance. The brother, particularly, was totally inept at establishing any relationship with people and thus used his sister for the closeness he needed.

Exclusive Property.   Some fathers rationalize incest with their daughters in terms of insisting that children are the exclusive property of parents and it is no one else's business what they do with them. This, of course, is a hangover from the days when, in fact, children were indeed considered the property of parents to dispose of as the parents saw fit. Although residual attitudes remain, neither the law nor prevailing opinion any more recognizes children as property or permits parents exclusive power over them.

A father who practices incest with his daughter in the name of having sexual rights to her may tell her that "this is something all fathers do with their daughters." She may even believe the statement until her association with girlfriends and experience in the outside world tell her otherwise. Dr. A. A. Rosenfeld and his research team at Stanford University School of Medicine cite the case of Mr. D., who asked that his daughter, Mary, manually masturbate him daily from the time she was 2 years old. "He felt that it was his prerogative as a father."

After detection, and in the face of possible prosecution, many fathers protest that they are being dealt with unfairly, that what they were doing was not hurting anyone and was no one else's affair. This is a kind of rationalization after the fact. The kind of rationalizer who has the "exclusive property" attitude convinces himself from the beginning that he has the right to do what he wants with his daughter to serve his needs.

Sexually Free.   Last, a new form of rationalizing father is emerging. In the Introduction, we mentioned the possible effect that the current climate of sexual permissiveness may be having on the growing problem of incest. In later chapters we will relate this idea to why some incest occurs and what can be done about incest. For now, it should be noted that the demand for full freedom of sexual expression is extended by some parents to include sex with their own children. The sexually free type sees sex as just another form of recreation and finds no reason to bar his own child from the fun. The old joke that "incest is a game that the whole family can play" becomes a literal reality. It is true that, like William K's daughter, a child may receive enjoyment from sexual activity with her parent, but this does not mean that the child will suffer no ill effects, as we will see.

The parent who already has convinced himself that having sex with friends and neighbors is simply a form of sexual liberation does not find it difficult to extend his freedom of expression to relatives. We do not know yet how clearly the sexually free parent will emerge as an identifiable incestuous type. In any event, the underlying motivations still stem from a need for warmth and closeness, which remains unsatisfied in the superficial and transient relationships of sexual permissiveness.

This completes the list of the various forms of rationalizers within the group of symbiotic fathers. We will now turn to another common type of symbiotic personality involved in incest.

THE TYRANT.   The primary feature of this father is he is authoritarian. He rules over the family with strict discipline and accountability. He brooks no opposition and relies on intimidation. He may use threats of physical force or actual beatings in demanding submission. However, his daughter usually submits without force being used since the father often has genuine feelings of affection and she is starved for any attention he gives her.

Some tyrants play the part of the proud patriarch, who likes to give the impression of having everything under control at home with wife and children gratefully dependent on him. The patriarch type will go to great lengths to hide any problem at home and to preserve an image of competence. He sees his wife and children as being in his debt and his daughter as owing him sex on demand.

In describing family tyrants, Dr. Herbert Maisch, German expert on incest, said:

> They will not suffer any opposition within the family, they are easily excited, flaring up and quick to anger. From time to time they beat both wife and the children. Outside the family sphere, however, these forms of behavior are hardly in evidence at all.

The tyrant may use bullying tactics to engage his daughter in sex, but he also has affection for her, which she recognizes and responds to. He often has little to do with his wife, who has long since retreated from him sexually and emotionally and has tacitly moved the daughter into the role of wife.

Some of the qualities of the tyrant can be found in several types of incestuous fathers, but we reserve the label for those whose typical mode of family behavior is designed to inspire fear and obedience. Approximately 20 percent of symbiotic personalities can be classified as tyrants. Some have a tendency to drink but drinking is not their most characteristic style as is true with the alcoholic type.

Many tyrants disguise their needs for closeness and intimacy through strong macho attitudes toward sex. Sex is the only way they permit themselves to get close to anyone. They believe that one mark of being a "real man" is to be sexually active and powerful, so to them sex is not for closeness but for expressing manly virility. They have no recognition of how they attempt to satisfy deep needs for warmth through sex. Outside the home their bullying tactics seldom work, so they usually confine themselves to sexual activity with the daughter. If there are any sons, the father demands strict obedience from them but seldom takes much interest in them. They have no conception of how to be close to their sons, or for that matter to any other males. One authoritarian type in therapy with us was Kelly.

Kelly was a former dog trainer for the military and believed that he could train his children and wife using methods he had applied to animals. "What they need is a firm hand," he said. His "firm hand" consisted of beatings whenever anyone in the family did not respond to his commands immediately. A huge man, Kelly browbeat his three daughters and wife into obeying his every whim. As his older daughter reached puberty, he become increasingly possessive of her. He had always hugged and held her a lot. Now he began caressing her, fondling her breasts, and forcing her to feel his penis. He would press himself against her thighs when her found her alone. He became possessive to the point of listening in on the phone calls his daughter made to friends. If he saw the mother and daughter looking as if they were enjoying each other's company, he would find a way to start a fight with one of them and break up the closeness. The daughter complained of his jealous possessiveness but not of the physical intimacies, which she saw as special attention.

This case illustrates the jealousy that often develops on the part of fathers, regardless of type, who engage in sexual activity with their daughters. If they are tyrants, they may become enraged at the sight of their daughter speaking to a boy her age or showing signs of closeness to anyone else, even her mother. The tyrant threatens and intimidates his daughter but usually does not have to force her into being physically intimate. She seeks any sign of affection. To the father, the prospect of someone coming between them is terrifying and produces a violent reaction. The jealousy can reach the point of paranoid behavior on the part of the father.

> A 16-year old man worked as a civil servant and was regarded as irreproachable at work. . . . The marriage and family life had suffered from the outset because of the man's personality . . . he would beat his wife on the least pretext. He ruled despotically over all the members of the family and would not tolerate opposition. . . . Even before it came to incest he controlled his daughter's every word and action, tried to isolate her socially, examined her clothes for signs of sperm and became paranoically jealous. (From Maisch's Case 18).

The tyrant, like most incestuous fathers, can be found on all socioeconomic levels. He can act like a brute at home, a model of decorum outside. Nowhere, however, does he drop his basic distrust of people. It is this quality that keeps him distant from others and hungry for the closeness that he attempts to satisfy physically.

Beneath the bark and bite, a tyrant develops deeply tender feelings for his daughter, who may well reciprocate. But his distrust is so basic he can never drop the authoritarian armor and open himself up to a truly loving relationship. He clings to the macho image and to distorted attitudes toward sex, such as "women are made to be laid" or "a man has got to get his sex wherever he can."

THE ALCOHOLIC.   One of the characteristics of a man addicted to alcohol is a strong need to be dependent and to have someone take care of him. Many alcoholics find this longing for dependency to be painful and unacceptable and "not like a man," so they go to great lengths to hide their dependency. They may pretend to be very self-sufficient, to need no one, to be supermasculine and strong. But sooner or later the bottle gives them away. They drink until they reach a condition that requires someone to step in and take care of them. Sometimes it is a wife, a mother, a daughter, a loyal friend, or when these people give up and are no longer around, sometimes it is the law that steps in and takes charge of the alcoholic by putting him in a jail or a hospital.

From 10 to 15 percent of the men who commit incest are alcoholics. In his survey of fathers, Maisch found 24 percent who were "drinkers," which may or may not mean they were alcoholics. In our study we did not find this high a percent who could be classified as addicted to alcohol, physically as well as psychologically. But, more important, drinking to some degree is involved in a large number of incest cases. Some of the fathers drink whether they are having sex with their daughter, working, or engaging in any other activity. Others are not addicted but have been drinking before they approach their daughter.

That drinking is common among incestuous fathers is understandable in view of the symbiotic personalities that the majority have. The alcoholic seeks succor in drink and uses it as a "lubricant" for getting closer to people, either physically, emotionally, or both. An incestuous father who drinks is trying to blot out his dependency needs at the same time he is turning to his daughter to satisfy them. The alcohol serves to loosen restraints on his behavior so that after the sexual activity, the father often blames the drinking and not himself. If any guilt comes later, he downs it with drink and the cycle starts all over again. This is one of the fathers in our therapy group who used alcohol to blot out all memory of what he did:

Gene, 51, does not remember sexually molesting his three daughters, although he did it several times before his wife turned him in to police. He said he was too drunk to remember anything. When accused of sexual activity with the girls, age 9, 11, and 14, Gene was filled with remorse. He took his wife's word that he had done it, but he professed to be as shocked as she was.

Gene's drinking problem had been going on for a long time, even before he met and married Lillian, a woman 20 years younger. But the drinking had got worse since he was laid off his job as a construction foreman. It was during this period, a time when he and Lillian were fighting a lot and had stopped having sex, that he molested his three adopted daughters, Lillian's children from her first marriage. As Gene's stress became greater, he tried to blot out everything, including pain, with alcohol. Rather than reach out and ask for help, he struggled to hold all his emotions inside, to be strong "like a man."

He had been holding painful feelings inside all his life. When we asked him to describe his father, he said "He hated me because my mother died when I was born." From the beginning of his life, Gene was on his own. His father rejected him, and he was shifted from home to home, with relatives or foster parents taking care of him for awhile and then sending him on.

Gene never received the kind of nurturing necessary to grow out of a symbiotic relationship, and he spent much of his energy keeping his unmet dependency needs out of his awareness. He did this by being gruff and tough, by bossing people around, scaring them, and listening to nothing anyone had to say.

Lillian was the first person Gene ever got close to, and for awhile it looked as if he might drive her away. She did not know how to meet his needs for nurturing any more than he did. In fact, she married him to be taken care of, not to take care of him. He was to be a replacement for the "kind, warm-hearted, good-natured" father she left behind. Instead, he was turning out to be like her mother, who was "self-centered, trying to run everyone's life." To Gene, Lillian was to be the all-giving, all-loving mother he had never had. She turned out to have a terrible temper, provoked him to jealous fits, was tense a lot, and did not trust anyone.

Both Gene and Lillian felt disappointed and cheated, familiar feelings in both of their lives. Gene, in his pain, turned to alcohol and his daughters for whatever succor and nurturance he could get, even if it was through sex and at the risk of abusing them.

In Part V, "What Can Be Done About Incest," we will discuss treatment of people like Gene and others we have mentioned thus far. With the alcoholic, we have completed our look at the first, and by far the largest, category of personalities (the symbiotic) involved in incest. We will now consider psychopathic personalities followed by the pedophilic.

Chapter 5

PSYCHOPATHS AND SEX CULTURES

PSYCHOPATHIC PERSONALITIES

Unlike the symbiotic fathers who turn to sex with their daughters as a way to get human closeness and nurturing, psychopathic personalities seek stimulation, novelty, and excitement. These are people who were so deprived and rejected in their own childhoods that they are driven by a kind of "get-even" aggressiveness and hostility and a powerful need for pleasure and stimulation. Sex is simply one channel in which the hostility and excitement get expressed.

The psychopath (or sociopath) may well be involved at the same time in cop-and-robber games, alcoholic escapades, drug abuse, fights, fast cars, flashy clothes. He goes after sex wherever he can find it or grab it. One of the characteristics of the psychopath is that he feels no guilt and has no appreciation or understanding of love—he is

guiltless and loveless. So sex to him means physical stimulation, and he may seek it from men, women, sons, daughters.

Not all psychopaths are incestuous, but those who are
may be classified as either promiscuous or pansexual. The
promiscuous type is heterosexual but does not confine his
sexual activity to family members. He may carry on affairs
with several women at the same time if he can keep them
attracted. He sees his wife as a source of sex but not the
only source. If she loses interest in him, or he in her, he may
turn to his daughter. Or, if he has a reunion with the daughter after a long separation, he may see her as a new and
stimulating sex partner. Such was the case with Phil.

Phil was a handsome man. He dressed nicely, had a good build and was
the kind of man who easily attracts attention, both with his looks and
smooth manners. He was polite, reserved, and calm when speaking to
authorities or those who might have power over him: police, prison
officials, psychologists. Phil was in our therapy group because his 16-
year-old daughter, Janie, had been placed in a foster home after she was
severely beaten by him.

Phil and Andrea, Janie's mother, divorced when the girl was 2 years
old. After that Phil served two prison terms for possession and sale of
narcotics. He remarried, divorced, then had a common-law wife, who
later died. During each marriage, he carried on affairs with other women.
Phil had two children by his second marriage, and from the first he had
two boys in addition to Janie.

Phil became involved in Janie's life again when her brother was
about to be sentenced to prison for burglary. The brother wrote to his
father asking him to come to the hearing to help him. Phil, who had been
out of touch with Andrea and the children for years, went to his son. The
judge sent the young man to prison, but Phil, after a reunion with Janie
and his other son, decided he should rejoin his ex-wife and "be a father
to the children." Andrea agreed to move to the city where Phil lived and
into the house he had bought. There was no agreement that they would
remarry; in fact, Andrea was still getting a divorce from another man,
a man who had made sexual overtures to Janie, an attractive, well-built
teenager.

With Phil, Janie quickly took over where her mother left off a decade
and a half earlier. Janie and her father would eat meals together while

the rest of the family ate separately. They would go on long rides together and hold hands as they watched television with each other. Father and daughter soon became lovers. And while Phil had sex with his daughter, he continued affairs outside the family.

Phil combined kindness, seductiveness, and brutality. When Janie started showing interest in boys at school, he began accusing her of having sex with them. He started beating her "to get the truth." Child welfare authorities intervened and placed Janie in a foster home. Phil persuaded her to run off and return to him. He lied about knowing where she was until authorities found her back at his house.

As we have seen, psychopathic fathers may not hesitate to beat their children as well as engage in incest with them. Larry, who was referred to therapy with us by child welfare authorities, is another example of a psychopathic father who both physically and sexually abused his daughter.

Dora ran away from home at age 13 and told juvenile authorities that her father first molested her sexually when she was 8 or 9. "He came into the room where my sisters and me slept, and made my sisters go to my mother's room. Then he got into bed with me, and started touching me all over." Another time, she said, "he did it to me when we were at my grandmother's house and everyone else was gone." He hit his daughter several times before he performed sex with her. On another occasion, he struck her in the face, then made her go to the garage with him and "penetrated" her.

Like most incestuous fathers, Larry was extremely possessive of his daughter and would become intensely jealous when he imagined she was showing interest in any other male. After Dora was placed in a residential facility, her father beat her up for "being sexy" with the boys at the children's home.

Like many psychopaths, Larry could be persuasive and disarming as well as abusive and brutal. When he made the first sexual advances to his daughter he told her: "This isn't something I like to do. It's something that fathers have to do for their daughters, to help prepare them for becoming a good woman to a man some day." Psychopaths often sound like rationalizers.

Evidence suggests that some psychopaths may have signs of actual brain damage. Those who are extremely impulsive, aggressive, and disregard all laws and the rights of others may fall into this category. Phil was not one of these. He did come from a background where he was on his own from a very early age, and received little attention from either parent. He never invested himself emotionally in the relations he had with any woman, but he was not as overtly hostile as some other psychopaths. He was more manipulative; the same was true of Larry.

No one knows what percent of incestuous fathers are promiscuous psychopaths, but the number is not large. Even smaller is the number who are pansexual. A pansexual is someone "who imbues all events in his or her life with erotic sexual feeling." It makes no difference whether it is "a cat, the telephone pole, the mailman, or his children. He gets turned on by everything and anything." Boys, as well as girls, are sex objects for him.

Occasionally, the man who is constantly preoccupied with sexual thoughts, feelings, and acts has psychotic as well as psychopathic tendencies. Dr. Frank S. Caprio, a Washington psychiatrist, interviewed the oldest daughter of a man he had diagnosed as suffering from both satyriasis (excessive sex craving in a male) and schizophrenia. The daughter told him:

> My father always carried a big pocket knife. I found out that he once pulled a knife on my sister. He was always beating my sister with his fists. . . . I was 12 years old when he raped me. However, the first time he bothered me was when I was 10, and he had come out of the army. When he raped me, I didn't scream. I was too afraid. He said, "If you tell your mother on me, they will put me in jail." He had relations with me about twice a month. Once a month he would put his mouth to my sex parts and wanted me to put my mouth on his organ. He would suck my breasts and bite them. . . . My sister told me everything a week before he was arrested.

She decided to tell the priest, and I felt relieved. I remember, also, that he would have intercourse three or four times in one afternoon, and one time after another. Another time, he wanted our dog to have intercourse with me. He had rectal intercourse with me twice. He also wanted me to relieve him with my hand. He was never drunk when he had sex relations with me. He also said that he would kill me if anyone else would touch me. Then he would cry and promise not to touch me again.

This kind of incestuous father is rare. The typical person who commits incest is not oversexed, is not a psychopath and—as we will see—does not have psychotic tendencies. Sex is not the basic issue in most incest cases. The basic problem is using sex to fill other needs.

Deciding who is a psychopath is not always easy, since psychopathy is not an all-or-none condition. The marks of a psychopath that are present to varying degrees include inability to maintain close relations with anyone, little sign of a conscience, aggressiveness and impulsiveness, and unremitting pleasure and excitement seeking. The incestuous psychopath, unlike symbiotic personalities, does not develop an emotional attachment to the daughter he uses for sex. Tender feelings, certainly love and deep affection, are missing from his make-up, as if he made a decision early in childhood that no one was worth loving or could be trusted with love.

Some of the chaos and disorganization that mark many families in which incest is practiced can be found in extreme where the psychopath is present. Since he abides by few rules and observes few restraints on his behavior, nothing approaching a well-ordered life is experienced by his family. Weinberg's case of Mr. and Mrs. J. serves as an illustration:

Mr. and Mrs. J. were very promiscuous before and during marriage. Compelled to marry her to avoid a bastardy charge, he separated from her and then divorced her after the birth of two children. He then lived with a common-law wife while Mrs. J. cohabited with a married man. Their two children lived with the father. When his common-law wife went to a relative's home to give birth, the daughter who was slightly past 13 was told by her father it was time to "stretch her open." After forcing her into the bedroom he committed incest. When his wife returned home, he resumed relations with her as well as with other women, but he completely neglected the daughter whom he considered a "sexual side-kick." When he did entertain other women, he barred her from the home. Because of his mistreatment and neglect, the daughter and her brother became habitual truants and delinquents. When he banished the daughter from the home, she was picked up by the police and she told them of the father's incest relations with her.

Some pansexuals are responsible for perpetuating incest in one generation after another. Sarah, in group therapy with us, had a grandfather who carried on incestuous relations with her mother before she was born. A son was born of the union between father and daughter. The son molested Sarah when she was 13. When she was 16, the grandfather took over.

He would call me and my sisters into his room one after another. I wouldn't go at first, but we were living at his house and I didn't want to make him mad. Finally I went and he did it to me. He was really a dirty old man. He was always talking vulgar. Everything he said had sex in it.

As we will see when we discuss the characteristics of daughters who participate in incest, force is not involved in most cases. This is often not true, however, where psychopaths are involved. They may not hesitate to rape the daughter or son they want for sex. The tyrant type of incestuous father may also display aggressiveness and hostility, but he is not as likely to use force. As noted, he also usually has deep feelings involved in the relationship.

The psychopath may turn to children outside his own family for sex if no one else is available. If he finds it stimulating, he may carry on relations simultaneously with adult women and girls, both inside and outside the family. He may also sexually abuse boys, wherever he can find them. However, not all fathers who have sex with boys are psychopaths or pansexuals (see case in Chapter 11, p. 196).

The number of cases of father-son incest is more difficult to determine than is the prevalence of father-daughter incest. Some researchers contend that sexual abuse of boys is widespread. In our survey of 112 families, we found five cases of father-son incest. Weinberg's study of 203 cases included no father-son incest. Maisch had four cases of father-son incest in his series of 78 cases. Sexual abuse of boys in families may be underreported to an even greater degree than incest with girls.

PEDOPHILIAC

Many fathers who commit incest first have sex with their daughter when she is entering puberty and her body is beginning to mature. The rounding of her breasts and hips attracts the father and stimulates him. One type of man, however, is attracted, because of his own immaturity and inadequacy, primarily by young girls who are showing no signs of the physical and sexual development marked by onset of puberty. He is the pedophiliac (pronounced pee-doe-fill-e-ack), which literally means lover of child, or one who has an erotic craving for a child.

Again, only a small percent of incest is committed by this type of father. One reason for this is that the pedophiliac may never marry or have children. One kind of pedophiliac is so arrested in his own sexual development that he avoids adult women out of fear that he is too inadequate to interest them. Emotionally and sexually he is like a child who feels comfortable only around other children. He may be small and have a body more like a child than an adult, or he may have a physical deformity which makes him feel inferior. He indulges in the sex play of children, feeling the genitals, showing his penis. He may hang around schools trying to entice kids with money or candy to "play" with him. Some pedophiliacs are old and lonely and seek children for company as well as sex.

Some men with pedophiliac tendencies do marry and have families. They are inclined to feel inferior, to be emotionally immature and lonely. When they get under pressure or rejected by their wife or when they feel they are getting too old to be an adequate sexual partner for adult women, the tendency to seek out children emerges. They want sexual activity with someone who will not belittle them or reject them. Often, the activity is confined to kissing, caressing, fondling the genitals, and other nonintercourse sex. The pedophiliac who has a child of his own may confine his sexual overtones and activity to that child or he may go beyond the family and look for others.

Most pedophiliacs present no physical threat to children. Many are like the occasional Sunday school teacher or scout leader who makes the local headlines by getting caught molesting children. In a few rare instances, however, a person may have both pedophiliac and psychopathic or psychotic tendencies. This person is dangerous. He is the type whose story is splashed across page one after he has raped or murdered a child. One of the fathers in our survey came to a violent end after rapes both inside and outside the family.

This promiscuous, alcoholic father had served a 10-year prison term for raping an 8-year-old girl. For four years he had infrequently raped and molested all his daughters, ages 10, 7, and 18 months. The mother finally filed charges. The family dynamics were considered unusual because all were willing to discuss the incest. The father threatened suicide if charges against him were not dropped. No one believed the threats. While out of jail on bond, he shot and killed himself. The mother, with the help of welfare payments and insurance, acquired self-confidence and kept the family going after the father's death.

OTHER TYPES

The vast majority of incestuous fathers are fully responsible for their actions, that is, they do not have a brain lesion or organic damage that puts their behavior outside their control, nor do they hear voices or have such fixed delusions that they do not know what they are doing. Approximately 3 percent, however, are psychotic: they have hallucinations and delusions. Perhaps an equal number are psychopaths or pedophiliacs with psychotic tendencies. We have already referred to this combination of characteristics. As we noted, it is the psychotic or the psychopath who is most often responsible for using force in incest.

The remaining "other" type of father still to be mentioned is the one whose culture sanctions incest. In the hollows and the ridges of some areas of the Appalachian and Ozark Mountains, isolated families still practice incest. The oldest daughter is expected to assume her mother's role, both in the kitchen and the bed. The youngest daughter is often introduced to sex by her pappy or brothers. It is not known how much culturally-sanctioned incest still goes on in the United States, but it is not believed to account for more than a small fraction of the total.

Every family, regardless of geography, has its own sex culture in the sense of sharing certain attitudes, expectations, and behavior regarding sex. This is different from the "regional" culture that may endorse or not prohibit certain practices, such as incest. But the family culture is important when considering the question of what persons engage in incest. Earlier, we referred to a sexually-free type who is emerging. This person has a family culture where a "do-your-own-thing" atmosphere prevails. There are other families where such sexual freedom is not openly espoused but the culture is still one that contributes to sexual misuse of the child.

In these families, the father—or mother—sleeps with the child, takes baths with the child, holds, hugs, and fondles the child out of his own need for affection and closeness. Later, there are kisses and caresses that become sexual. Although the parent may not be a rationalizer type in the manner of Barbara's father or the father who babies his daughter, the activity with the child is definitely sexual and qualifies as incestuous.

None of the types we have presented here are "pure" in the sense of standing alone and having no overlap with other types. The four groups—symbiotic, psychopathic, pedophilic, and psychotic—are fairly distinct, but even here, as we have seen, fathers in one group may have some characteristics of another group. The important point is that fathers who practice incest are people who use sex either in an effort to experience closeness and nurturing in human contacts, or as a channel for hostility and stimulation.

As we will see, similar dynamics apply to the daughters and mothers who are involved in incest.

Chapter 6

MOTHERS, DAUGHTERS AND SIBLINGS IN INCEST

THE DAUGHTERS

When Barbara, whose father introduced her to the "love game," was a baby, she was very small and "ugly." She could not keep food down, had to be fed intravenously in the hospital and, when at home, she needed to be held night and day. Out of this experience she grew up with the feeling that she was an unworthy person. In school, she was "a piece of wallpaper" and "inconspicuous." She was "such a goody goody. . . . I was never late for school, I never wore my skirts too short, never wore make-up—I was just a big kiss-ass. I couldn't stand myself."

Barbara was hungry for affection, for approval. She tried to win her mother's love but felt she never could. She would try to help do the ironing but her mother would tell her to go away. The mother never seemed to have time for her or interest in her.

With her father, she got the affection and approval in the form of sexual activity. She took over from the mother in terms of supervising the other children. She became the lady of the house, right down to being her father's sexual partner. She saw that he needed her, and she began to use her "sexual favors" to get gifts, privileges, to stay home from school when she wanted, to go see the Beatles, to use the car. She blackmailed him out of a position of power and control.

Barbara combined a number of characteristics found in girls who get involved in incest. A small percent are forced into sex with their father and never submit even passively. In approximately 90 percent of the cases, no force is necessary. This does not mean that the daughters initiate the activity or openly seek it. Many passively accept it; others see that they can get something out of it and offer no resistance; some quietly encourage it.

One or more of these characteristics typify the incestuous daughter:

1.   She has a poor relationship with her mother, or none at all. The mother may be gone, she may be in the hospital, she may be at home but does not like or want the daughter. The mother may be jealous of her and reject her.

2.   The daughter has low self-esteem. She considers herself unattractive, unloved, inadequate. She may try to compensate for her poor self-image by acting prematurely grown up, adult, and self-sufficient.

3.   She is looking for attention and affection. She often isolates herself from peers out of fear she will be rejected. She wants their friendship but is afraid to reach out for it. She appreciates any sign of recognition and tenderness. She easily falls in love with a father who bestows gifts and attention on her. She may engage in incest for the gifts and privileges it gets her.

4.   She may develop a seductive manner, look, or behavior to attract attention. Little girls learn early in the American culture how to gain favors by adopting the cute

or sexy smile and style of a Marilyn Monroe or a Lolita. She may decide that acting seductive is the only way to get anyone to pay attention to her. She may be the one who initiates sexual activity with the father and gives the come-on to other men.

5.   She may be stuck on her father, making her particularly vulnerable to any advances on his part and increasing the possibility that she will act on her own sexual impulses and initiate activity with him. This point relates to the "oedipal (or Electra) complex," to a fixation on the parent of the opposite sex. For instance, a girl does not identify with her mother and wants to possess the father for herself. If she identified with her mother, she would give up her wish for the father and devote her energies to other concerns (see Chapter 12).

6.   She may try to act as a "rescuer" of her father, sensing that he is unhappy or needs somebody to look after him, to care for him. She may try to "rescue" the whole family, believing she is the only one who can hold things together. Becoming the "lady of the house" may be motivated out of this need to "rescue" as well as to meet her own needs for affection and attention. The rescuing may extend to offering sex to the father to calm him down, to keep him from fighting with the mother or other kids in the family. Daughters of the tyrant type of father often adopt this kind of role.

Even in families where the daughter and mother do not get along, the girl will often protect her from the father's verbal attacks by calming him down with sex. She will go to great lengths to hold a family together that is already deeply split. She often has deep fears of desertion and abandonment and will do any and everything to keep father and mother together.

One young woman recalls how, as a child, she saw sex with her father as an opportunity to help him and the family.

> I thought, now is my big chance to hold the family together, to keep my father from having to go out to drink, to keep my father from having to go out to have prostitutes, to keep my father from having to go out with guys and stay up all night and play poker . . .

Julia, who first had sex with her father at age 13 after her stepmother left the home, would rescue him by servicing his needs for sex and giving him "relief."

> She indicated that sexual relations with her father would often reduce his agitation and anger. She stated that her father tried to fight against "those spells" by reading the Bible for hours at a time. Julia continued: "Men are different from women . . . they need it (sex) more than we do and if they don't get it, it can darn near drive them crazy. If I can give him some relief after all he done for me, why shouldn't I? This is my body and I should be able to give it to who I want . . . ."
>
> Julia indicated that she had become resigned to having sex with her father: "I know it's not right, but it helps him." She said that she did not enjoy sexual intercourse with her father, remarking: "I know it will be different when I do it with somebody I am really in love with. . . ." (Case in Weitzel et al.)

Some fathers encourage their daughters, as they did their wives, into believing that they will go "crazy" if they do not get enough sex and that it is a daughter's duty to keep the father satisfied. A "rescuing" daughter is willing to try.

THE MOTHERS

A mother can be involved in incest in one of two ways: indirectly or directly, through collusion or participation. She is directly involved and participating when she initiates sexual activity with a son or accepts his advances. She is colluding and indirectly involved when her husband carries on sexual activity with their daughter while the mother remains a member of the family. In either case, she cannot escape sharing responsibility for the problem.

Nonparticipant Mothers

Because there are more mothers who allow incest to occur in their homes than there are those who initiate the activity, we will first consider the nonparticipants.

From our own survey and work with incestuous families and from the research of others, we know that a nonparticipating mother has one or more of the following characteristics:

1.   She seeks a role reversal with the daughter. The mother wants to become the child and wants the child to become the mother. This basic symbiotic quality is reflected in nearly all the characteristics of the mothers whose husbands and daughters engage in incest. It expresses the mother's struggling attempt to get the care and nurturing that she missed in her own childhood. In inviting the daughter to take over her role, she is suggesting that the daughter also become her mate's sex partner. She may rationalize her "abandonment" of the daughter on the basis of helping her husband. One mother said: "He gave up smoking and needed something to help him through."

2.   She is frigid or wants no sex with her husband. This is another way of bowing out of her role as a wife and giving reason to the husband to look elsewhere for sex. If he has one of the incestuous personalities already discussed, he is likely to look no further than to the daughter. The mother feels relief when the daughter substitutes for her, as was true in this case described by Drs. Atalay Yorukoglu and J. P. Kemph of the University of Michigan.

> The mother was a beautiful woman . . . She had never expe-
> rienced sexual pleasure with her husband or any other man,
> although she behaved in a seductive manner with most men.
> She actually appreciated those times when her husband did
> not insist on having relations with her. Both the mother and
> the daughter agreed that the mother had never understood
> her husband and that the daughter seemed to be able not
> only to understand but to help her father over acute aggres-
> sive outbursts merely by talking with him. The mother had
> unconsciously encouraged the daughter's becoming the sex-
> ual mate to her husband.

Some mothers lose interest in their husbands, sexually and otherwise, because of the men's drinking, curs-
ing, and other excesses. Yet, they stay in the marriage, and
let the daughter take over.

3.   She keeps herself tired and worn out. This is yet
another invitation for the daughter to take over. The
mother may work long hours outside the home and wants
help from her daughter. This is natural. But if she works
herself into a state of chronic fatigue while her husband
stays home or takes only an occasional job, then she is
failing to confront him and giving messages to her daughter, as well as her husband, that she is abandoning her role.

4.   She is weak and submissive. The mother feels both
economically and emotionally dependent on her husband
and is afraid to assert herself to him, even in the service of
stopping him from having sex with their daughter. She may
see her husband as "a good man except when he is drinking." She expresses fear of bodily harm if she does not do
what her husband tells her or if she tries to prevent him
from doing something he wants to do. If a showdown
comes and she must choose between her husband and her
daughter, she will choose her husband. This mother views
her husband as her prime source of security, if not care and
comfort, and she will do most anything not to lose him.

5.   She becomes "Mom" to her husband. In a few
instances, the mother loses out in a struggle with her hus-

band over who is going to take care of whom and becomes the spouse who carries most of the responsibility and seems in charge of the home. The husband no longer considers "Mom" an eligible sex partner and turns to the daughter. He generally assumes the role of an adolescent in such families.

6. She is indifferent, absent, or promiscuous. The mother who tends to be indifferent may be caring toward other children in the family but not toward the daughter who is left vulnerable for incest with the father. The indifference usually extends also to the father, with the mother saying, in effect, that she does not care what the daughter does as long as she substitutes for her as a mate for the father. The same kind of message is given by the mother who arranges to be gone from the house for extended periods, either working excessively long hours or doing things on her own. The promiscuous mother may not be absent so much as she provides a poor model for the daughter and contributes to a sex culture in the family where normal restraints are not observed.

Some, perhaps many, mothers whose husbands and daughters engage in incest are depressed. The depression may have started before the incest and played a part in the mother's withdrawing sexually from her husband and turning responsibilities over to the daughter.

The role reversal, in which daughter becomes mother and mother becomes daughter, can be passed on from generation to generation. Mrs. L., a woman whose case was reported by another group of therapists, illustrates this point.

> .... the pattern of role reversal was established early in her childhood. She was enjoined by her older sister and her mother to take care of the family and function as an adult well beyond her years.... in her relationship with her mother it was clear that she took care of mother more than mother took care of her....

> Toward her own daughter, Ann, Mrs. L. behaved in much the same way as her mother had behaved. . . . By the age of 7 most of the responsibility for nurturance in the family had been transferred by Mrs. L. to Ann.
>
> When her daughter reached the age of 8, Mrs. L. began to voice suspicions that Ann was having an affair with her husband and was competing with her for him. . . . These accusations were delusional since overt incest did not occur until five years later (case in Lustig et al.).

Mrs. L. was "armed always with an unassailable excuse to reject sexual relations" with her husband, so this was another way that she set Ann up to become involved with the father. In times of conflict between the parents, Ann was frequently commissioned by Mrs. L. to "make up with father." Ann learned to use sex with her father to reduce family tension.

Another clear example of role reversal is provided by a mother and daughter who were referred to Dr. Irving Kaufman and his group at the Judge Baker Guidance Center in Boston.

> June had always seemed older than her years to Mrs. Smith. She said that June seemed more like her mother than her daughter. Although she felt that June's ideas were those of an older girl, she couldn't describe what she meant. She added briefly that June menstruated at 11. Mrs. Smith commented that June could be very good when she wanted, taking over much of the care and responsibility of the home and children. . . .
>
> June often told her mother that she wasn't grown-up. June had to take care of the little ones and made her father's lunch. . . .

Barbara's mother also illustrates the kind of qualities characteristic of the mother whose daughter and husband commit incest. She did very little with Barbara; she did not want to bother with her. And gradually, she turned her house and husband over to her.

> While I was never sure what was going on, I did feel there
> was something wrong with Henry spending so much time
> with Barbara. It got so Barbara was the lady of the house. By
> the time she was 7, she was literally running the house,
> telling me what to do, telling me what to fix for dinner, and
> what the whole family was going to do on the weekends.
> Even with the other children—I'd tell them they couldn't go
> to the park, or some place, and then, moments later, I'd find
> them leaving, and they'd tell me Barbara had said it was all
> right for them to go. Ever since she was a little girl, I didn't
> feel Barbara was my daughter. I felt she was my rival.

The mother's own needs were served by Barbara's
taking over. Even when the mother discovered lewd photos
that the father had made of himself and Barbara, she still
took no action to stop the incest. She refused to believe
reality.

Another mother in our survey refused to believe until
she walked in one day on her 12-year-old daughter performing fellatio—oral-genital relations—with her 40-year-
old father. The incest had been going on for five years, and
the daughter had told her mother several times. After
catching the two in the act, she filed charges, saying: "I
didn't believe it until I saw it myself."

If her husband is jailed, a wife may get her daughter
to deny anything happened so charges will be dropped and
he can return to the family. This is most likely to occur with
the submissive mother who is economically dependent on
her husband. In one of our cases, the incest had been going
on for two years before the daughter got the mother to
report it to police. When the father was jailed without
bond, and the mother saw that her economic lifeline had
been cut, she had the daughter change her story, denying
everything, so the father could be released.

Although a number of mothers will deny that they
knew any sex was going on between the daughter and the
father, most are aware on some level that they contributed

to the conditions making incest possible. They simply pre-fer to keep knowledge of the sex out of their awareness since it serves their emotional needs for the daughter to become the wife as well as mother.

In some instances, of course, it is the mother who reports the incest and brings a stop to it. Often this occurs when the wife seeks retaliation against her husband for some other grievance he has caused her, or it may occur when the sexual advance of the father is a one-episode affair and constitutes more of a rape than ongoing incest.

Mother Participants

As for the mother who is directly involved in incest, partic-ipating in sexual activity with her child, her characteristics are similar to those of the fathers we discussed. She may deeply love her son and rationalize incest as the highest expression of such love, she may consider she is providing him with sex education, she may be seclusive, shut off from the world with her son and turn to him for human contact, or she may be promiscuous and shares sex with her son along with a number of other males. Finally, she may simply be psychotic.

Like the fathers, she tries to use sex as the means to establish closeness and warmth with another human being. She longs to be held, stroked, taken care of. Often she either has no husband or he is extremely passive or absent from the home most of the time.

Some mothers "drift" into sexual activity with their son from caressing and body contact that get out of hand. Such a mother may have had a habit of sleeping with the boy since he was very little. As he matures, she continues to touch him, hold him, kiss him, and arouses sexual feel-ings in both the son and herself.

One mother suggested to her son one cold winter night that he sleep in her bed. He was 10 years old at the time. The sleeping arrangement continued into his adolescence when he began being awakened in the middle of the night by his mother touching his genitals. He began touching her breasts and genitals.

Sometimes the mother combines a seductive manner with a high degree of possessiveness to keep the son by her side. As he grows and begins to have outside interests, she holds him to her by a subtle seductiveness and an intense quality of hovering over him. This mother is not likely to have intercourse with her son but does pet and fondle him, caress and kiss him inappropriately. She keeps implying by her manner that some day she will completely give herself to him.

Dr. David R. Walters described a mother who illustrates several of the characteristics we have mentioned.

> Mrs. M. and her 15-year-old son had slept together since the father left home seven years earlier. Under the guise of "teaching (the boy) sex education," Mrs. M. masturbated her son and asked that he in turn do the same for her. She had sex relations with him a number of times, and was reported by an uncle in whom the boy had confided.

Sometimes it is the son who is the aggressor in incest with the mother. In these cases the mother and son may have been separated for years and when reunited, he sees her as an eligible sexual partner. In other cases, there has been no separation but the mother's attitudes toward sex are very permissive—she may, in fact, be promiscuous—and the son gets the idea that there is no reason he should not have relations with her if everyone else does. Such was true in this case:

> Both mother and son were promiscuous. . . . He had seen her nude frequently and, at times, was unable to enter the home because the mother was "entertaining" some men. He

was particularly disturbed when his mother gave birth to an illegitimate child, because he felt that was not "like a mother." She teased him because she never saw him with girls. Irritated, he asked his mother for intercourse. She told him that she might at some other time. The son was very attracted by the mother but she was completely indiffent to him. He felt that if the other men had relations with her, he should also have that right. . . . He claims that he attempted relations with her when he was helping her in the home and she lay down on the couch and was almost asleep. When he assaulted her, he said, "You said it to me before, and now I'm going to make it come true." He demanded that she fulfill her promise. The two struggled, and the mother stormed, "You low-down, dirty bastard." She got up and went to the police. . . . (Weinberg's case of N.)

Occasionally a son has sex with his mother when he is "the man of the house" and she is dependent on him, emotionally and economically.

Mother-son incest is relatively less common. In the chapters on why incest occurs, we will consider some reasons for this.

BROTHERS and SISTERS

Siblings may engage in sex play during childhood without any incestuous intent. If, however, they get the idea that the parents do not care what they do, or if the sex culture of the family is loose and permissive, the sex play may well lead to more serious sexual activity. Brothers who commit incest do so in the absence of strong parent figures, particularly a father. Sisters often respond with willingness. Sibling incest does not represent so much a certain type personality on the part of the brother and sister as it does a certain set of conditions in the family and characteristics of the parents. The conditions are often chaotic and the parents passive, preoccupied, or sexually loose.

Occasionally, however, the personality of the brother or sister does play a leading role. Sometimes a brother, in adolescence, will start being destructive and delinquent and force a younger sister into sexual activity. To her his behavior may seem brutal, as in this case of ours:

Lisa was a good student. She studied hard and was proud of her academic accomplishments. Her parents were proud of her school work, too. They praised her often and were grateful she was not giving them the kind of trouble her brother, Tom, was. No matter what they did, the parents could not control Tom. Her Dad punished, even beat, him often, but nothing seemed to work. Tom was still stubborn, rebellious, and deceitful. Her Mom would try to win him over with love and presents, but those also failed.

When they were little, Tom and Lisa got along fairly well. They played together a lot and fought some. Maybe they spent more time together than some brothers and sisters. Their parents insisted they go home after school and stay there until Mom and Dad closed the store they owned. No other kids were allowed to come over, since there was no one home to supervise. Once or twice Lisa told her mother about how lonely she got, but when the mother seemed to have no solution, she stopped bringing the subject up. Her mother and father looked so worried and distracted anyway. She did not want to worry them more.

This is why she did not tell them about what first happened when she was 11 and Tom was 14. Tom pushed her down on the floor, hitting her, tearing her clothes, and trying to rape her. She prevented penetration, but Tom masturbated while he pressed against her thighs. Even though she could keep him from having intercourse, he continued to feel her up and masturbate against her several times over the next few years. The storm in Tom seemed to pass as he got older and he never mentioned what he had done to Lisa. She did not mention it either, although lasting emotional scars were left.

Another type of brother who may physically intimidate his sister and force her into sexual relations is the one who is much older than the girl. Bobby, for instance, was 18 and recently discharged from the Army. His sister, Debbie, was 6. A friend gave him some LSD one night, and he raped Debbie. This one-episode kind of incest was not common among the families in our study, but when it did occur, it usually involved rape after the offender had been drinking or taking drugs.

In some cases, either the brother or sister is so shy or introverted that he or she has no outside friends, even during adolescence. For instance, the girl may see her brother as the only "boyfriend" she is likely to have. Gradually, she may begin acting flippant, coy, and finally seductive toward him.

In other cases, a brother and sister who are kept together without much outside contact may become closely attached and build up mutual admiration, which at some point gets converted to sexual attraction.

> . . . . the brother and sister were both somewhat shy of companions of the opposite sex. She had a deep affection for the brother since he was the most admired sibling in the family. . . . Though the sister participant was only 15 years old she tried to look her "best" for the brother. The two were constant companions, frequently talked about sex. When they were in the car alone, the sister would kiss the brother and he would "go on from there." (Weinberg's case of Le.)

Some studies have indicated that the very proximity of a brother and sister growing up together militates against their becoming interested in each other as willing sex partners. The day-to-day familiarity with one another does not spark romantic or sexual desires. Other research contradicts such findings. Certainly brother-sister incest does occur and—as we noted in an earlier chapter—has become the subject of a number of incest novels. In these, as sometimes happens in real life, the brother and sister have such a rapturous love for each other that sex seems inevitable.

Part III

WHY INCEST OCCURS

Chapter 7

WHEN SEX STOPS BETWEEN FATHER
AND MOTHER

Incest has the potential to occur in any family. It is a relationship born out of very human conditions. We all cling to images of being held, succored, and stroked, letting ourselves to be dependent and taken care of. When life becomes stressful we want a haven to retreat to, someone who will give affection and attention. That someone may be a daughter, a son, a mother, a father.

Incest is clearly not the means by which most people, longing for care and nurturing, try to satisfy their needs; for some it is. And the line between the two groups—those who do and those who don't—is often represented only by circumstances and degree.

We all have had incestuous thoughts, feelings, longings. What decides, then, whose thoughts, feelings, longings are converted from fantasy to reality and whose are not?

Whether incest occurs depends on a number of factors: how deprived, rejected, buffeted a person feels; how

unable he or she is to establish human contact and closeness outside of sex and the family; how likely a person is,
on some level of awareness, to see sex as an answer to
feeling rejected, without affection or warmth, and how
much opportunity there is for sex in the family.

   To understand why incest occurs, then, we must consider (1) the personalities of the individuals involved; (2)
their situation, setting, and circumstance, and (3) the
changes or crises that have recently occurred in their lives.

   These points can be represented graphically by the
following figure:

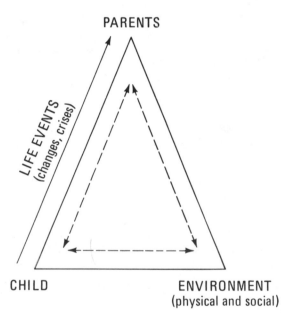

This triangle depicts the major factors involved in the
question of why incest occurs in a family. Looking at the
characteristics of the parents and child as we did in Part II
is not enough. We must also look at their backgrounds and
the roots of their personalities. We must consider their
environment: who sleeps in what room, what privacy there
is, how much stress there is from financial and marital prob-

lems, how much sexual permissiveness or repression there is, how much "innocent" play. We must also know what events have recently occurred: did the mother have to go to the hospital, did she start working at night, is the father now unemployed and staying at home, did father and mother stop having sex with each other? These are the kind of precipitating factors that trigger incest between parent and child.

As can be seen by the dotted lines inside the triangle, there is an interaction between all points. This means that the parents, child, environment, and events constantly affect one another and it is impossible to say what the incest risk is in a family by looking at just one of the factors at a single point in time. All must be considered, and at several points in time.

For instance, a father with little potential for incest in terms of personality may never come close to sex with his daughter provided no predisposing or precipitating factors arise elsewhere on the triangle: no provocative behavior by his daughter, no sexual estrangement from his wife, no undue stress in his environment. If a sexual crisis develops with his wife, and if there is other stress in his life, and he is home alone with a seductive daughter and starts drinking, this father may cross the line to incest. At any given time there must be a balance between points on the triangle between personalities of the parents and the child and the stresses of the environment and life events. Given an excess at any point, incest may occur in any family.

In Part II we considered the types of personalities with the greatest potential for incest, the highest risk. We will return to this subject a little later to learn more about what kind of background such people have, what early sexual experience, and how they are different from other people who are symbiotic or dependent but never commit incest.

For now, we will look at other factors in the triangle— at the changes and crises that precipitate incest and the kind of environment that contributes to its occurring.

CHANGES AND CRISES

One of the characteristics of families in which incest occurs is excessive change. In this respect, incestuous families are very much like families in which physical abuse of children takes place. In our treatment of both physical and sexual abuse cases, we are continually amazed at the amount of stress that families bring into their lives from the constant changes they make. Change—any change, good or bad—requires a person to make an adjustment. In this sense, a change is a demand on a person, a demand to cope with something different, to adjust to something different, to make decisions about the new and unknown. A demand is stress, pressure. Some stress is essential to life and growth. Too much stress means trouble; it wears a person down.

When incestuous families come into therapy, we give them a checklist of some 43 events that may have occurred in their lives, or changes they may have experienced, in the past 12 months. As can be seen from the list in Figure 7-1 on Pages 114–115, these events range from very serious to trivial, from death of spouse and divorce to Christmas and minor violations of the law. The more serious changes require greater readjustment and carry a heavier weight on the scale (the weight is the number at the right of each item). Each person has a life change score for every year he or she lives. That score is computed by adding up the weights or values of each event that has occurred or change he or she has experienced. Research has shown that when the score exceeds 150 for 12 months, the person is at increased risk of getting sick. The higher the score, the greater the risk, and the more serious the illness is likely to be.

What applies to physical illness also applies to emotional disorders and behavioral problems, such as physical or sexual abuse of a child. One person with a high life change score may have a heart attack, another may suffer a severe depression, a third may start beating his child and still a fourth may commit incest. Different people respond in different ways to stress. What they have in common is loss of control—control over either one's physical health, emotional well-being, or behavior.

When we gave the Schedule of Recent Experience or Social Readjustment Rating Scale to 35 abusing parents and compared their scores with those of a matched group of 35 nonabusing parents, the difference was staggering: the abusing parents had an average score of 234, compared with 124 for the nonabusing group.

We have had a similar experience with incestuous families. Scores averaged 240 for a sample to whom we gave the scale. This average represented the amount of change they had made in their lives for the 12 months prior to the time when incest began. What this means is that change was so excessive that it wore them down to the point that they lost the restraints they might normally have over their behavior. When a person bombards himself with change, or when a series of events happens in his life one after another, that person has no time to recoup and regroup. Just as soon as an adjustment to one change is starting to be made another change comes along, and then another, until finally—disaster.

A number of our parents, when first confronted about the excessive change in their lives, protest that they have no control over the changes. However, a careful inspection of the items they check invariably demonstrates that most of the changes were ones they initiated and were well within their control. We are often reminded of the "innocent" series of changes Somerset Maugham wrote that his father made:

> My father ... went to Paris and became solicitor to the British Embassy.... After my mother's death, her maid became my nurse.... I think my father had a romantic mind. He took it into his head to build a house to live in during the summer. He bought a piece of land on the top of a hill at Suresnes.... It was to be like a villa on the Bosphorous and

FIGURE 7–1   Schedule of Recent Experience (SRE)
(Short Form)

1. Under "Number of Occurrences" indicate how many times in the past year each of the events has occurred.
2. Multiply the number under "Scale Value" by the number of occurrences of each event and place the answer under "Your Score."
3. Add the figures under "Your Score" to find your total for the past year.

Life Event	Number of Occurrences	Scale Value	Your Score
Death of spouse	_____	100	_____
Divorce	_____	73	_____
Marital separation from mate	_____	65	_____
Detention in jail or other institution	_____	63	_____
Death of a close family member	_____	63	_____
Major personal injury or illness	_____	53	_____
Marriage	_____	50	_____
Being fired at work	_____	47	_____
Marital reconciliation with mate	_____	45	_____
Retirement from work	_____	45	_____
Major change in the health or behavior of a family member	_____	44	_____
Pregnancy	_____	40	_____
Sexual difficulties	_____	39	_____
Gaining a new family member (e.g., through birth, adoption, oldster moving in, etc.)	_____	39	_____
Major business readjustment (e.g., merger, reorganization, bankruptcy, etc.)	_____	39	_____
Major change in financial state (e.g., a lot worse off or a lot better off than usual)	_____	38	_____
Death of a close friend	_____	37	_____
Changing to a different line of work	_____	36	_____
Major change in the number of arguments with spouse (e.g., either a lot more or a lot less than usual regarding child-rearing, personal habits, etc.)	_____	35	_____
Taking on a mortgage greater than $10,000 (e.g., purchasing a home, business, etc.)	_____	31	_____
Foreclosure on a mortgage or loan	_____	30	_____
Major change in responsibilities at work (e.g., promotion, demotion, lateral transfer)	_____	29	_____
Son or daughter leaving home (e.g., marriage, attending college, etc.)	_____	29	_____

FIGURE 7–1 (continued)

Life Event	Number of Occurrences	Scale Value	Your Score
Total from page 1			____
In-law troubles	____	29	____
Outstanding personal achievement	____	28	____
Wife beginning or ceasing work outside the home	____	26	____
Beginning or ceasing formal schooling	____	26	____
Major change in living conditions (e.g., building a new home, remodeling, deterioration of home or neighborhood)	____	25	____
Revision of personal habits (dress, manners, associations, etc.)	____	24	____
Troubles with the boss	____	23	____
Major change in working hours or conditions	____	20	____
Change in residence	____	20	____
Changing to a new school	____	20	____
Major change in usual type and/or amount of recreation	____	19	____
Major change in church activities (e.g., a lot more or a lot less than usual)	____	19	____
Major change in social activities (e.g., clubs, dancing, movies, visiting, etc.)	____	18	____
Taking on a mortgage or loan less than $10,000 (e.g., purchasing a car, TV, freezer, etc.)	____	17	____
Major change in sleeping habits (a lot more or a lot less sleep, or change in part of day when asleep)	____	16	____
Major change in number of family get-togethers (e.g., a lot more or a lot less than usual)	____	15	____
Major change in eating habits (a lot more or a lot less food intake, or very different meal hours or surroundings)	____	15	____
Vacation	____	13	____
Christmas	____	12	____
Minor violations of the law (e.g., traffic tickets, jay-walking, disturbing the peace, etc.)	____	11	____
This is your total life change score for the past year			____

> on the top floor it was surrounded by loggias. . . . It was a white house and the shutters were painted red. The garden was laid out. The rooms were furnished and then my father died.

Within a relatively short time, Maugham's father had undergone a change in occupation, residence, personal habits, finances, and family. These multiple changes did not kill him, but they contributed to his death.

Similarly, excessive change is not a cause of incest, but it is a contributing condition. For the person with the potential for physical abuse, it contributes to that problem. For the person with the potential for incest, which we will discuss in detail later in Part III, it contributes to sexual abuse. What excessive change does is to bring out tendencies that otherwise may remain under control.

In some families, excessive change may go on for several years before incest occurs, before a father lets go of the control he normally has over his behavior and turns to his daughter as a sexual source of closeness and comfort. This was true in Dianne's family; her father, Robert, kept himself and his family in constant turmoil.

> We moved every six months or a year. I was born in Oregon, then my father took a job in St. Louis, then Chicago, Cleveland, Minneapolis, Detroit. He married and divorced my real mother twice. When he married my stepmother, she had a son the age of my sister and they moved in with us. My father then took on a project in Pittsburgh and we lived in a large stone house there. He would buy a house every time we moved and would take on another mortgage. The year before he began pressuring me to have intercourse with him, he took sleeping pills and would have died if my stepmother hadn't known what to do.

Although some changes are more critical than others in the incestuous family, all mount up in terms of collectively representing a predisposing agent. Harry Lewis, whose story was presented in Part II, is a case in point.

In the 12-month period immediately preceding Harry's turning to his daughter for sex, his life was marked by a change score of 533. Any score of 300 or more places the person into what is considered a major life crisis. Harry was deep in one, and he sought solace from his 12-year-old daughter, Annie. In the preceding year, he had experienced a marital separation, a bout of illness, marital reconciliation, illness of his wife, sex difficulties, change in financial state, trouble with in-laws, wife stopping work, starting a night course, change in living conditions, change in residence, change in recreation, change in social activities, mortgage or loan less than $10,000, change in sleeping habits, Christmas, and a traffic ticket. Of these, the most critical event in Harry's life was that he and his wife stopped having intercourse, or had it only once every month or so. Harry was thus cut off from a major source of strokes (a stroke is a unit of recognition or attention and may be verbal, such as a kind word or greeting, or physical, such as a backrub or sex). As we will see, strokes are necessary for people to maintain themselves and they will go to extremes to get them. Some people get their strokes from friends, others from people they work with.

Harry had no friends and at work he pretty much stayed to himself. So he turned to his daughter. He already spent much of his spare time with her, since she also had few friends and stayed at home a lot as he did. But the two of them mostly just watched television together or Harry would put his head in her lap and she would stroke his hair. After the sexual estrangement from his wife, Harry started drinking and seeking sexual strokes from his daughter.

Another change also occurred about this time. Annie, the daughter, began showing signs of physically maturing, her breasts started developing and her hips rounding. She lost her chubbiness and began growing into a slender young woman. These changes did not escape Harry's notice, just as most fathers become aware of their daughters' developing bodies as they enter puberty. Many incest cases begin during this period and usually culminate in intercourse. Those that occur prior to puberty usually involve sex without intercourse: fondling, oral-genital relations, pressing against the thighs, masturbation.

But regardless of what type of sex occurs, the most common event preceding the onset of incest between father and daughter is sexual estrangement between father and mother. This estrangement most often takes place as a result of increasing tension and hostility between father and mother, but is also may come as a result of the mother's entering a hospital, going to work at night, taking a trip.

In Clare's family, it was a combination of sexual problems between her mother and father plus her mother's going into the hospital.

I was about 12 when it happened. Physically I was well-developed and I had had my menstrual cycle for about three years. My parents were having problems with sex. . . . I know that they had gone to a psychologist to try to sort things out. My mother felt like she was just being used. I know my mother had to go into the hospital. That could have been part of the problem. She evidently wasn't letting my father have anything because he was coming to me. I can't comprehend why he would come to a 12-year-old girl. I would have much rather for him to have gone outside the marriage and to another woman to fill his needs.

In the Smith family, the mother had her own mother living upstairs and went up to sleep with her each night, leaving 11-year-old June with her father. As June interpreted the situation:

All the trouble was her mother's fault. If her mother hadn't quarreled with her father and gone upstairs to sleep with the maternal grandmother, there would not have been any trouble. Her father drank sometimes and it was when he was drinking that he made sexual advances to June.

In each of the cases we have discussed—Harry, Kelly, Dianne, Barbara, William K, Jan, Gene, Phil—sexual intercourse had stopped between father and mother. This is a particularly critical event for symbiotic fathers: they do not have the skill or capacity for cultivating relations elsewhere to make up for the loss of strokes from their wives. At the same time, they may well have the capacity—as we have seen—for rationalizing why they should have sex with their daughter.

Many men, of course, experience sexual difficulties with their wives at some time in marriage and never consider turning to their daughter as a substitute. If they must have immediate sexual strokes, they go outside the family. Others make up the stroke deficiency by increasing contacts with friends or doing something else that is stimulating. They do not have personalities that require others to meet their needs for them or to give them sex because they cannot experience closeness any other way.

In the incestuous family the sexual estrangement between mother and father may well be precipitated by some other event: the father may suffer a depression, as Jan's father did, and alienate his wife; he may lose his job, as Gene did, suffer low self-esteem and have his wife berate him for not "acting like a man."

One event, then, feeds into another, and the potential for incest intensifies if the daughter's reaching puberty happens to coincide. Maisch cites the case of a 41-year-old man who had no satisfactory sexual relationship with his wife.

> He began sexual activities with his daughter a year after her menarche: "She had really always been quite reserved and always dressed and undressed alone. I only ever saw her dressed, all the same I could see that she was already quite well developed."

OPPORTUNITY FOR INCEST

The opportunity for incest may come as part of the sexual separation between mother and father. William K's wife went to her folks' farm, leaving him to "honeymoon" with their oldest daughter for a week. Other mothers get sick and go to the hospital, setting up the final conditions for incest to occur. The predisposing factors, of course, are already present—mother wanting daughter to take over, father wanting warmth and nurturing, daughter wanting attention and affection—but the "last straw" is the mother's actual leaving. This does not mean that it is the mother's "fault" that incest occurs. The father makes the advances but does so when given the opportunity.

Some mothers set up the opportunity by starting to work at night. Others go out to play cards or to visit friends, as was true with Dianne's stepmother.

My stepmother had taken to the habit of going out with women friends of hers. She'd often go to the movies. Daddy would never go. He would have everybody go to bed before me. I made the best grades so I got to stay up the latest. The other kids would have to go to bed. Even if I had already gone to bed, he would call me downstairs to him. He had the room on the lower part of the split level. . . . I felt special.

Still other mothers leave figuratively rather than literally. They do not go out or to the hospital but they become incapacitated at home. They may be far along in pregnancy, or they retire to their rooms with chronic fatigue or ailments, leaving their daughter to become "the lady of the house" and their husband's mate.

One mother actually put her daugher in bed with the father.

> . . . she could not tolerate her husband's snoring and went to sleep in another room. Then out of concern that he would be lonely, she put the daughter in her place in bed with the husband.

With Clare, who was the oldest daughter, her mother was often sick with stomach problems and occasionally went to the hospital. But still, her brothers and sisters were at home, and her father had to be careful as to when he approached Clare.

> He would catch me at times when there was nobody else in the house but us two. He would kiss me, fondle my breasts, and just touch me all over. He even placed his finger up inside of me. This went on for about two or three years, I guess. . . . He wanted to have intercourse but I was too scared to have it.

Sometimes, opportunity for incest comes when the mother is forced to leave the house to take a job because her husband has become unemployed. Maisch found that in 34 percent of the cases in his survey incest occurred while the wife was at work and the husband was at home. Again, nothing will happen unless the predisposing factors we have mentioned are already present. Only then does the mother's absence become a precipitating factor.

Occasionally it is the father who is gone, and all the predisposing factors are present for sex between mother and son. Such was the case with Hortense Loftus and her son, Richard. Hortense was a society woman whose marriage was dull and barren. She had always dreamed of having a son and talked her husband into adopting an 18-month-old boy. The adoption was hidden from Richard Loftus until he was 15. By then, Hortense had made Dickie her entire life. She considered her husband "a necessary evil." Each time he had to be out of town or worked late, the mother would romp and play games with Dickie long after his usual bedtime.

> One of these romps led to the first overt step in the tragedy. Dickie was 11 at the time. He had prepared for bed and was in his pajamas when his mother came into the room in night-dress and kimono. She started to tickle him and he pulled her down on the bed, rolling over and over, pummeling her playfully as he had done many times in the past. He was

laughing and giggling but a new excitement was added to
the game.

Suddenly his mother recognized that he was in a state
of sexual excitation and struggled to free herself but he
would not release her. He pressed closer against her. In
desperation she flung herself from the bed, carrying him
with her to the floor.

The mother freed herself, reprimanded the boy and
left the room. For a long time she no longer visited his
room at night and "carefully avoided any intimacy in touching him." Dickie, who had no friends or outside interests,
fell into sullen silence at home and at school he became a
troublemaker. Nearly a year went by before his father took
another out-of-town trip.

This time there was no party atmosphere. Mother and son
faced each other across the dining room table almost as
strangers. The father was away for nearly a week and each
day the tension grew more and more taut. One evening
Dickie made tentative advances and suddenly his mother's
arms were about him and they were clinging together and
kissing. Then, as Dickie's excitement rose, she thrust him
away from her and ran to her room and locked the door.

Later that same night, Hortense Loftus came to her
son's room and, in the darkness, the forbidden ritual of
incest was made complete.

Mrs. Loftus told Dickie the next day that what had
happened "must never happen again." But changes kept
occurring that seemed to pitch mother and son together
and provide new opportunity for repetition of the sexual
activity. First, the two were in an automobile accident. Mrs.
Loftus escaped serious injury, but Dickie suffered a fractured skull, broken collar bone and a spinal injury. The
mother had to nurse her son back to health. Then, Andrew
Loftus, the father, died. Mrs. Loftus had long talks with
Dickie, now 15, emphasizing that he would be "the man of
the house." Dickie construed this as an invitation to resume

the incestuous relationship, and slipped into his mother's room and made love to her.

From then on, a love-hate relationship developed between the two: love for the sex act and the physical and emotional closeness it brought, hate for self and each other for not having the will or power to stop. After lengthy fights and bitter recrimination, with occasional periods of passionate love in between, the end came when Dickie killed his mother.

Incest does not usually end so dramatically or tragically, but the turbulence that marked Dickie and Hortense Loftus' lives is not uncommon in incestuous families. Although change and crisis alone are not causes of incest, they become potent contributors when parent and child have only each other to turn to in riding out the storm.

In summary, then, the changes that may occur in a family that increase the risk of incest include:

1. Father and mother stop having sex with each other.

2. Parent of the same sex as child becomes incapacitated or is frequently absent from the home.

3. Parent of opposite sex suffers a crisis, such as father becomes unemployed or mother becomes widowed.

4. Daughter is beginning to mature physically.

Now we will consider other conditions that contribute to the risk of incest. We will look at the role played by the physical and social environment of the family—including its sex culture.

Chapter 8

TABOOS IN TWILIGHT

In addition to the personal changes that occur in the life of an individual requiring him to cope with increased stress, changes are also constantly occurring in that person's society and these play a considerable part in shaping the kind of environment in which he and his family live. They affect the size of his home, the opportunity to make friends and know his neighbors, the kind of work he does, the type of movies he sees, the style clothes he wears, the sex values and fantasies he has.

Perhaps the most difficult type of change that American society imposes on people today is transience in human relationships. Families move and relocate at such a rapid rate that, as noted in the Introduction, 50 million Americans change their place of residence each year. Even for people who have the ability to make friends easily, close human contacts are hard to establish because of the transience. Dianne, as we saw, hardly had time to settle in at a school before her father changed to a new job in another city.

No one gets to know anyone else when everything and everyone are in a constant state of flux. Alvin Toffler, in *Future Shock,* quotes one young wife, a veteran of 11 moves in 17 years, as saying:

> When you live in a neighborhood you watch a series of changes take place. One day a new mailman delivers the mail. A few weeks later the girl at the check-out counter at the supermarket disappears and a new one takes her place. Next thing you know, the mechanic at the gas station is replaced. Meanwhile, a neighbor moves out next door and a new family moves in. These changes are taking place all the time, but they are gradual. When you move, you break all these ties at once, and you have to start all over again. You have to find a new pediatrician, a new dentist, a new car mechanic who won't cheat you, and you quit all your organizations and start over again.

As Toffler said, people today have "modular" relationships with one another: they plug into one or two parts of each other's personality to complete a transaction or to get a service, but it is all touch and go. There is no closeness and little warmth. Satisfying strokes are hard to come by these days, and those without the ability to reach out and find closeness are left vulnerable. They may decide sex provides the only closeness, and a daughter is the only one who can be counted on not to reject.

A Harry Lewis feels under attack from all the stress that transience and change bring. Yet he keeps imposing more on himself. He keeps thinking that the next job in the next city will magically give him peace, happiness, a sense of well-being. He keeps chasing elusive dreams, and his frantic pursuit just makes the dream all the more impossible. He is too busy running to see how he has isolated himself and cut himself off from the human contacts that would give him solace. Finally, there is no one to turn to but his daughter.

Transience, then, in American society provides a backdrop for the kind of environment in which families live; the kind of social environment they have; the friends, if any, they have; whom they can call on for help; the neighbors they know; the school chums the kids have.

It is only one element, however, in that backdrop. Many other forces on the societal level exert powerful influences. Television is in everyone's home, shaping values and expectations. The home has become too small for the extended family; aunts, uncles, helping relatives live elsewhere out of reach. Homes have no front porches where people meet and visit, exchanging strokes. People live shut away from each other in air-conditioned boxes, neighborhoods are dead, a sense of community is gone. People work at jobs where they seldom see the consequences of their own efforts. They may produce nothing but paperwork.

In many ways, technological changes have made people's physical and social environment more convenient, easier, more stimulating and exciting. There is more freedom of choice. Supermarket and department store shelves offer a blinding array of diversity. People can put together their own individual styles of diet, dress, transportation, recreation, entertainment.

But close human contact becomes more elusive. Warm strokes are harder to find. The one possible exception is in the area of sex.

CHANGING SEXUAL VALUES

In the midst of the changes that have produced such transience and diversity in contemporary American life, parallel changes have occurred in sexual values and behavior. Emerging on the scene have been the Pill; increased knowledge and use of contraceptives; demand by women for equality and satisfaction in sexual relations; explicit sexual scenes in movies, plays, and novels; sex themes and serials on TV; sex in advertising and pop music; greater tolerance of pornography and public nudity; acceptance of sexual deviancy as individual expressions of sexual style and preference; group sex; recreational sex; wife swapping; sadomasochism in sex; child prostitution.

In November 1967 *Newsweek* magazine featured a special report on "Anything Goes: Taboos in Twilight." Among the points made were:

> (1) . . . the revolution in manners and morals that has produced a climate of candor is very real and unlikely to reverse itself. . . .
>
> (2) "We're going to have to live with a degree of freedom much greater than anything we've known in the past. We're going to have to employ our minds and morals in determining that some things go and other things don't" (quoting Father Walter J. Ong). . . .
>
> (3) "What was once the realm of private knowledge has become public knowledge" (quoting Father John M. Culkin). . . .
>
> (4) The mini-skirt and stay-on cosmetics are symbolic of "girls who don't want to wait" until dark to go to bed with a man (quoting fashion designer Mary Quant). . . .
>
> (5) The shattering of taboos on language, fashion and manners generally is part of a larger disintegration of moral consensus in America. Vast numbers of Americans distrust their government. Catholics in increasing numbers simply ignore the church ban on birth control. The family has changed from a breeding ground of common values into a battleground of generations.

More than a decade later, in February 1978, *Newsweek* published a cover story on "Sex and TV," noting that "the sexual revolution has finally seeped through the looking glass." Prime-time TV has dealt with a lesbian school-teacher and a rape ("All in the Family"), male prostitution ("Baretta"), a white-slave ring specializing in teenagers

("Police Woman"), seduction of a gigolo by a 15-year-old girl ("Aspen"), transsexual surgery, homosexuality, and promiscuity ("Soap"), nymphomania and female frigidity ("What Really Happened to the Class of '65?"), impotency ("MASH"), and "two deflowerings, a teacher exposing himself to his class and a woman achieving her first climatic orgasm—out of wedlock, of course—after ten years of failure" ("Loose Change").

Meanwhile, on the daytime soap operas the sexual activity of main characters far outstrips anything seen at night. As for incestuous topics, appearing either day or night on TV, NBC dealt with an incest fantasy in "Sharon: Portrait of a Mistress," and "Fernwood Forever" had Kathy, a several-times married sexpot, fall for her dad in some hot embraces after he came back with a remade face from falling in a vat of acid at the factory.

It remained, however, to the British-produced, "I, Claudius," shown on public television in the U.S., to depict incest most explicitly. Claudius married his niece, Agrippina, only to be poisoned by her. She engaged in incestuous relations with her son, Nero, who became the Roman emperor and later killed his mother.

Critics of television's permissive treatment of sex contend that "TV tends to glorify sexual activity without impressing on viewers, particularly adolescents, the responsibilities that go along with it." That may be a valid objection. However, the point we are making is that no one's social environment today escapes the effects of the sexual climate of the times. That climate helps shape sexual attitudes and behavior. Its effects are felt in homes throughout the country.

People also cannot escape the effects of transience in American life. As relationships become more impermanent and close human contacts more elusive, sex emerges as an attractive alternative to make up the deficit in strokes.

For people who are already marginal in terms of having little ability to reach out to others, to get the attention and affection they need in daily human interaction, the glories of sex, and the freedom of expression advertised by the sexual revolution seem to provide an easy answer.

Whether the revolution will embrace incest no one knows. We do know that transvestism is promoted through the Cherry Stone Club in Boston, sadomasochism is the purpose of the Eulenspiegel Society in Manhattan, and underground newspapers like the *Fetish Times* in Los Angeles offer features on bondage and carry advertisements for enema clinics and films on nude women wrestling.

Then, too, of course, there is the rise of not just pornography in general but pornography that focuses on incest. In Houston, of 154 cases of pornography investigated by postal authorities, a large percent featured incestuous themes. Ralph Wallace, chairman of the Select Committee on Pornography of the Texas House of Representatives, reported that all the publications were "low-key" in how they began their portrayal of incest. "They start with pictures of the whole family fully clothed and looking like any other normal American family. By the time you get to the last page, everybody is nude and having sex with everybody else."

The 1970 Commission on Obscenity and Pornography came to the conclusion that exposure to erotica induces no antisocial behavior. It is not known whether the Commission included incestuous material in its study, but its findings were highly controversial and rejected outright by then President Richard Nixon.

Whether pornography has any negative effects on people's behavior is an open question, but the fact remains that it is on the increase and reflects changing attitudes and standards toward sex. Where these changes will lead us is the subject of a number of predictions.

Dr. Stanley Lesse, a New York psychiatrist, says that "we are rapidly approaching a concept of 'sex on demand.' Men and women are likely to have sexual relationships whenever they might desire them, perhaps even in public." Dr. Charles Socarides, psychiatrist at Albert Einstein College of Medicine in New York, sees the "clinical fallout" that will come from sexual freedom as including erosion of sexual identity and gender role, "wholesale assault on the nuclear family," downgrading of maternal functioning, and "depreciation and eradication of the two-sex exclusive pair model of sexual relations."

Chuck Ryder, counselor at the American Institute of Family Relations in Hollywood, contends that one consequence of our being in an age where very little is considered taboo is that more women are admitting that they are proud that they had incestuous relations with their fathers and were taught how to make love.

Whatever the outcome of the sexual revolution, the climate of permissiveness is likely to stay. It is a fact of life that must be dealt with in considering the sex culture and climate of any given family. It is an inescapable part of the environment's backdrop.

FAMILY SEX CULTURE

As we noted in Part II, every family has a shared set of attitudes, assumptions and expectations about sex. We have just discussed one possible source of those attitudes and expectations—the sexual climate of the society in which the family lives.

Inside the family, the sex culture is expressed in terms of such things as (1) the amount of overt sex that is observed in the family, (2) the amount of disrobing that goes on, (3) the kind of "play" that a parent engages in with offspring or sanctions between brother and sister, (4) the kind of language used and sexual references made, (5) the degree to which rights of a family member to keep his or her body private are respected.

The sex culture in incestuous families is either lax or repressive. In some families, such as those studied by Weinberg, it is loose: children routinely observe their parents in the sex act; they see their father or mother carrying on sexual relations with lovers; parents and children sleep in the same room, if not the same bed; they bathe together; fathers show the children obscene books and tell dirty jokes; few restraints are observed in behavior or language.

In Sarah's family, it was the grandfather who set the standards, loose as they were. He had sex with his daughter and granddaughters, not caring who watched. He went around the house half naked. He couldn't carry on a conversation without references to "cunts," "screwing and fucking."

Such families are in the minority. More typical was Dianne's family and the kind of sexual tone her father, Robert, set.

My father was bawdy at times and liked to tell dirty jokes he learned in the Army. He encouraged my brothers to read *Playboy* and he would tease me about my developing bosoms when I got to be about 11. The first physical contact I remember with him was when I was about 6. He used to come to my room at night. It was all very playful. There was a lot of romping and caressing. It was not distinctly sexual. I thought it was just play.

The playful romping gradually took on sexual overtones, however.

By the time I was 9, my father would have me take off my pajamas and play with him nude. He was also nude. I would sit on top of his chest and we would talk and play. It was all very pleasant. I don't remember his getting an erection. But then a little later, he began fondling me and caressing and kissing me in a very sexual way.

The activity between father and daughter had es-
calated to another level by the next year.

When I was 10, my father would clear everybody else out of the house
or have them go to bed and then he would call me to the living room,
where he had a favorite chair. He would sit on his chair, open his robe
and have me stroke his penis or suck on it. He would try to French kiss
me. He would stimulate me intensely. He would also show me what
happened when he climaxed. He jacked off to show me.

The sex culture in a number of incestuous families is
such that fathers stimulate daughters starting sometimes at
an early age. The stimulation takes the guise of playful
romping and no one objects. It is only later that the child
recognizes that more than play is involved. By then, the
caressing and touching is being done more furtively and is
overtly sexual.

With Barbara, the early play began with her father
bathing her. Then he began feeling her genitals in her
room and introducing her to the "love game."

In other families, the first contacts are made when
parent and child sleep together. A mother, divorced or
widowed, takes comfort in wrapping her arms around her
little boy. This progresses to fondling, caressing, and sexual byplay. The "little boy" grows up and both mother and
son start to want more serious sex, as in this case:

The mother bathed or helped bathe him until he was 15. As
he matured, he became more sexually discontented. The
mother frequently fondled him like a child. They often em-
braced and he attempted to fondle the mother. She disap-
proved of his actions while she was married, but after her
quarrel with her third husband, she became more encouraging to him. They slept in the same room and each saw the
other nude. The mother, a nervous, high-strung, and emotional person, frequently became excited by the son's body.
Later she asked him to sleep with her (Weinberg's case
of V).

As we emphasized in Part I, parents need to give their children physical affection. It is only when the physical intimacy is carried on to the point of meeting the parent's own need for sex and closeness that it becomes a problem. The crossing of the line to that point is often easier in a family where sexual permissiveness is the standard.

In some incestuous families, the sexual climate is dominated not by permissiveness but repression. Sex is such a taboo topic that a major issue is made out of a child catching a glimpse of his or her parent getting dressed or putting on a robe. Bathroom doors are not only closed but locked when a family member takes a shower. Mother and father have separate beds. The children have separate rooms. Television is prohibited from fear that an objectionable reference to sex or even the human body will be made on a program. No movie stronger than *Bambi* or *The Wizard of Oz* is approved. Shorts are not worn by parents or children. Curse words are condemned. Obscenities are considered a sin.

The complete suppression of sex in a family is sometimes a cover-up and compensation for powerful incestuous wishes. In cases like William K., whom we discussed in Part II, the home may appear very proper and the father have the reputation of a model community leader. A father may display a righteous attitude toward the subject of sex while at the same time committing incest with a daughter.

Children, in turn, constantly have their curiosity aroused and are intrigued when sex is suppressed in the home. They reason that there must be something intensely inviting about the subject for it to be such a taboo. Clandestinely, then, they may experiment with sex among themselves or act seductively toward a parent in an effort to learn more.

Related to the sex culture of a family is another factor that may contribute to the potential for incest. This is the blurring of lines and boundaries between generations.

When a mother pushes a daughter into becoming "the lady of the house," the daughter may also assume the role of wife to the father and demarcation between generations is lost.

When such blurring occurs, the parent starts treating the child as an equal and an eligible sex partner. The thrusting of the child into a position of pseudoequality may come from the mother, from the child himself or herself, or from the father. In Dianne's case, it came from the father.

My father considered me as his equal in intelligence. He saw us both as superior to the rest of the world. He didn't want to love me as a child but as a woman. He wanted to have children by me. I kept saying: "I want you to love me as a Daddy." He kept saying: "I don't want to love you that way. I love you as a woman."

Dianne was 10 years old at the time.

In other cases, the breaching of boundaries comes in the opposite direction: rather than the parent trying to make an adult out of the child, the parent tries to become a playmate of the child. Again there is a pseudoequality; the generations dress alike, talk alike, and play alike. The play may take the form of being "free and spontaneous" in terms of wearing no clothes around the house and tickling and romping. There is nothing wrong, of course, with tickling and romping. It just may get out of hand when both playmates are nude and become sexually aroused.

ISOLATION AND HOSTILITY

Other factors in the family's social environment may serve as predisposing agents in incest. We have already indicated that when a parent or child becomes isolated, sex within the family may be resorted to in an attempt to gain warmth, closeness, or nurturing and attention. Most of the fathers we discussed in Part II are inclined by personality to cut themselves off from others and become isolated in the sense of having few, if any, friends and little close contact with anyone outside the family.

The daughters, also, are characterized by a quality of loneliness. The family environment, then, is often marked by isolation. The isolation is often encouraged by a father who does everything with his daughter and virtually shuts off all contact with others. One father reported:

> Since she was a little child, we always played together. I took her for rides and taught her how to drive when she was old enough. When she was little, she climbed all over me in the bed, asking me to tell her stories. When we went for a ride, she wanted to sit on my lap. I bathed her and watched her grow and become womanlike. The wife was jealous and bawled me out, but we paid little attention to her. She never went with boys and had few friends. We were always together (Weinberg's case of H.).

Besides isolation, which is only intensified by the transience that we discussed, another prevailing condition in the family is hostility between father and mother. They have a disturbed sex life, and they may argue over money, the children, or any number of other things. The hostility between parents may not be overt. From a distance, the husband and wife may seem to get along. But, underneath, there is deep dissatisfaction and disagreement with much pent-up anger.

In Dianne's family, her father and stepmother would go for months without speaking. Hostility hung between them. Robert, her father, would go to his study and ignore his wife. He would send for Dianne to keep him company and give him affection. Robert would occasionally fly into rages and beat his wife. Every few months the two would make up and be civil to each other again. But the fighting would recur and the hostility returned.

One reason behind a father's turning to a daughter for sex may be to express hostility and anger toward his wife. Walters, who has treated a number of cases of sexual abuse, believes "the basic reasons for being involved with one's child is anger toward one's spouse," although in our experience and that of others there is much more involved: For example, the father has little capacity for developing relations outside the family, and the daughter may encourage his advances out of her needs for attention and affection.

Nevertheless, animosity between the spouses is characteristic of the family environment. On top of this, one or both parents may take to drinking, and something may happen to cause the father to be home a lot and the mother absent. Maisch found that in 70 percent of the cases in his study there were such situational factors in the environment that gave rise to "temptation."

PHYSICAL ENVIRONMENT

Early studies of incest were inclined to place great emphasis on lack of space in living conditions as an important factor in why incest occurred. We now know that the condition of parent and child sleeping in the same room, or even the same bed, is not a cause of incest. It may be a predisposing agent, but it must be considered alongside the other conditions in the family environment that contribute to the potential for incest.

In cases where parent and child sleep together and sexual activity ensues, it is almost invariably found that lack of space or other beds was not the reason such a sleeping arrangement occurred. The reason was that the parent wanted to sleep with the child. In one study, 18 percent of the cases involved parent and child sleeping in the same bed "but in only one case was there an urgent situation of need where both were forced to sleep in the same bed, and even in this case other arrangements could conceivably have been made."

A father may manufacture a reason to start occupying the same bed with his daughter when she begins to develop physically. Maisch cites such a case:

> The subject was 43 years old at the start of the incest, which was with his own daughter and which went on for two years. Under various pretexts he came to an agreement with his wife about sleeping which . . . enabled him to share his bed with his daughter. "My daughter, who was then 14, had just previously had her first period and was already quite a young woman. The shape of her body excited me." About six months after the conscious introduction of this sleeping arrangement which provided opportunities for physical contacts between the two incest partners (stroking, manipulation of the genitals) coitus first occurred.

In Weinberg's study of 203 incestuous families, 64 percent lived in housing below the minimum standard of one person per room. However, he found that in only two cases were fathers compelled to sleep with daughters because of congested quarters, "and in one of these cases, another sleeping arrangement was possible." Some families had parents and children sleeping in the same room although there were other rooms available in the house or apartment.

Congestion, then, may be used as an excuse for a parent to sleep with a child, although other arrangements could be made. Overcrowding may contribute to the potential for incest, but usually this is true only because parents are not motivated to make other arrangements.

In our survey of 112 families, congestion was not prevalent. In fact, it was not uncommon for daughters to have their own rooms. In some cases, the father made sure the daughter had her own room so that he could carry on incestuous relations with her in privacy. Dianne, for instance, always had her own room despite the frequent moves the family made and the fact that there were six other children. She was her father's favorite and he rewarded her with her own room. The arrangement also made it easier for him to visit Dianne at night and engage in sexual activity.

In cases where the father cannot afford a separate room even for his favorite daughter, lack of privacy may not restrain him from sexual contacts with her. This was true of Clare's father, who could not always arrange for the two to be home alone, so he would come to her bed at night.

Several times I'd already be in bed and he'd wake me up at night. I slept with my sister in a big king-size bed. What he'd do to keep someone from walking in on us would be to loosen the light bulb in the socket so it wouldn't turn on at the switch near the door. He would fondle and feel me up while my sister was asleep in the same bed. As far as I know, she never knew it.

In summary, the physical environment is seldom so crowded within a family that a parent and child must sleep in the same bed or, in most cases, even in the same room. Crowded conditions may be used as an excuse by a father to sleep with his daughter or a mother to sleep with her son. The deciding factor is not the environment but the motivations, conscious or unconscious, of the parents.

Chapter 9

FANTASIES OF AN ALL-LOVING MOTHER

In Part II we discussed what kind of fathers and mothers commit incest. We called them symbiotic personalities, people who are hungry for nurturing and closeness and turn to a child for it. Some are introverts, some are tyrants, others are alcoholics.

There are an untold number of introverts, tyrants, alcoholics, and other symbiotic types who get bombarded with stress, have few friends, and are in a bad marriage, but only certain ones commit incest.

What decides?

To answer this question, we need to look at the background and childhood of parents who become involved in incest. With an incestuous father, for instance, three things usually stand out in his developmental history:

1. He never got over a fixation with his own mother.
2. He never identified with his father.
3. He was encouraged to be "the little man of the house" or to take care of his parents' emotional needs.

For a person to be fixated with his mother does not necessarily mean he has a close relationship with her. Often the mother is emotionally distant but implies that if he pleases her enough or does enough for her, then she will allow him to become close. He remains hungry, then, for closeness and keeps seeking it in a woman.

He seeks even more. He stays stuck at the developmental level of wanting total possession of his mother and the unlimited love he thinks that will bring. This quest for the impossible dates back to when little boys first fall in love with their mothers at about age 3, which usually marks the start of what is known as the oedipal stage. He sees total possession of mother as possible if father was not present. In families where the father is a distant or absent figure, this hope for unlimited love from mother often remains alive. The boy fails to identify with his father and stays fixated with mother.

In most families, a boy ends the oedipal stage of courting mother by deciding that mother belongs to father and identifying with the father in terms of directing his energy to interests and pursuits outside the home: friends, accomplishments, ambitious plans for the future. He relinquishes his incestuous wishes and settles for other relationships and projects.

If the son has no father and lives alone with his mother, what then? Unresolved oedipal feelings are not inevitable. In most instances, the mother has a brother, father, neighbor, or some other male figure with whom the boy can identify. As long as she does not encourage her son to remain in the oedipal stage as her "little man," the boy will not likely have problems.

In cases, however, where there is no father or he stays aloof and the mother is intent on keeping the son involved with her, the boy may never give up his oedipal strivings or complete that stage of his development. At some level of his awareness, he remains stuck on mother, clinging to the fantasy that she represents boundless love and limitless caring. In reality, she may be indifferent and uncaring or she may be seductive and smothering. But regardless, he stays convinced that in mother—or a woman like her—unlimited love is possible if he can possess her totally.

With fathers who later commit incest, they may first pursue this fantasy with the woman they marry. They try to turn her into the "good mother," the all-loving, all-caring mother who will satisfy their incestuous wishes. But she turns out to have faults and does not want to mother the man she married and be possessed by him. When their marriage deteriorates to the point of her removing herself as even his sexual partner, he then transfers his fantasy and longings to a daughter.

The daughter becomes "the good mother" or reminds the father of what his wife was like when they were first married and she still had promise of being the all-loving figure. The father now turns his wife into the "bad mother," the rejecting mother, and hides his incest with the daughter believing that the wife would punish him if she found out.

Such a theme runs through the background of many incestuous fathers. It is an age-old theme of unsettled oedipal conflicts and dependency on mother. In reality, many of the fathers got very little love and nurturing from their mothers and this is a basic reason that they become symbiotic personalities and want someone to satisfy their needs as adults. But on top of the lack of nurturing, they received little opportunity to identify with their father or some other male figure, and the normal incestuous wishes and fantasies that a boy has from about age 3 to 6 or 7 never were rechanneled into other dreams and activities. Such individuals never gave up the idea of winning mother as a wife and having her bestow love without limits.

Some fathers had mothers who were overtly seductive or overly attentive rather than simply unnurturing. In either case, the child was kept dependent and given only pseudolove and nurturing. In later life when that child has a daughter of his own, he expects her to provide the love and nurturing he always wanted. She also is expected to provide sex when the wife ceases being a partner.

Dianne's father, Robert, had the kind of background we have discussed here.

Robert and his father never had much to do with each other. He always addressed his father very formally. There was no intimacy between them or close sharing of any kind. They had sort of a gentlemen's agreement that they would be courteous but cautious with each other.

Robert's father was in the Navy and was away from home for long periods. During one four-year period, he took all his leave overseas, not even returning home for a week's visit. Robert's mother was hurt, incensed, and humiliated. She made Robert her escort and the man of the house.

She was not a gushing mother or even an overtly seductive one. She was aggressive and ran everyone's life who was around her. Robert's development was arrested in the oedipal stage, and he later sought from a succession of four wives the unlimited love that he fantasied his mother embodied.

Finally, with Dianne, Robert thought he could fulfill his fantasy. But she wanted him to love her like a Daddy. He kept insisting he wanted to love her like a woman. If he loved her as a father, he would have to be on the giving end of love and nurturing. He wanted to be on the receiving end, as he was—or fantasied he could be—with his mother.

Robert remained emotionally tied to his mother. He always took his family to visit her at Christmas, again having very little to do with his father, who finally retired from the Navy. After living all over the country, he moved to the same little town where his mother lived, buying a house only a short distance away.

By staying so preoccupied with his mother, Robert never learned to cultivate close relationships with others. He never learned to reach out, to have friends or warm relations with even his wives and children. The only way Robert knew to be close was through sex.

Robert's mother gave him a "don't-grow-up" message. He was expected always to be dependent on her and consider her as the central figure in his life. He complied completely.

Symbiotic personalities, such as those that become involved in incest with their daughters, can be traced back to a mother's keeping her child so dependent that he never learns what it means to grow up and reach out to others or to a mother's never allowing her child to be dependent and receive love and nurturing. In either case, the outcome is the same: the child is expected to meet the needs of the parent. The parent has a need for the child not to grow up, to remain dependent, or the parent has a need for the child to do all the loving and nurturing. In both instances, the child does not feel loved because the parent's needs come first. The child grows up seeking the love and nurturing he never received. Erroneously, he fantasies that mother embodies all-embracing, unlimited love if only he could possess her and this is the fantasy he pursues with his daughter, whom he believes he can possess.

"F." was another father whose background is typical in terms of the dependent relationship he had with his mother.

> The relationship to the mother was far closer than to the father. She was the stronger, a woman of considerable force, dominant but very warm. F. describes her as gay and high-spirited, with a temper. As he grew up, she permitted him a good deal of liberty, did not object to his love affairs, but he remained very much under her control. He gave her most of his money, but more important, when at age 19 he fell in love with a young girl and wanted to marry, the mother broke off the match. She said he was too young, and she did not like the girl. As a result, he continued to live at home until his mother's death when he was 36, and then he drifted into a marriage with a neighbor's daughter (Cormier, Kennedy, and Sangowicz's case of F.).

As we noted, when the father initiates sexual activity with a daughter, he often sees in her his mother—the "good" mother—or a former wife or his present wife when she was young and he still fantasied her as all-loving.

> F. had four daughters, followed by three sons. His favorite
> child was his oldest daughter, who at a very early age acted
> as a substitute mother for the younger children. He found
> her bright and sharp, resembling his own mother. . . . One
> night, when the wife was away, and he was in a state of
> intoxication, he initiated sexual relations.

It is often a memory of the mother's "beauty" that a
father clings to and transfers to his daughter. In a case
involving "Mr. R." and his daughter Kathleen, he compared her to his own mother, "whom he remembered as a
beautiful, selfish, promiscuous woman who had never
loved him." Mr. R's wife accused him of behaving flirta-
tiously toward Kathleen, saying that

> he kissed her as if he were "making love to a grown woman."
> She complained that Mr. R. preferred going out with Kath-
> leen to staying home with her. . . . Mr. R. expressed mixed
> feelings about Kathleen. He described her beauty and tal-
> ents with enthusiasm, and told of his plans to make her a
> child actress, a ballet dancer or a photographer's model. . . .
> He felt, however, that Kathleen was selfish and cold and that
> she did not appreciate what he was doing for her (Case of
> Mr. R. from Weiss et al.).

Barbara reminded her father, Henry, of his first wife,
Tina, "a beautiful woman with a fascinating personality"
(and a symbol of the all-loving mother). During sex, the
father mistakenly called his daughter "Tina." At other
times, he would tell her: "You're just like Tina. You look
like Tina. You talk and think like Tina. You're Tina."

Barbara complained that her father was "terribly in-
considerate," not just because he called her "Tina" but in
other ways, too. Dianne also remembered that her father
was "ugly" to his wives and to women generally. Incestuous
fathers often are left with hostile feelings from the lack of
nurturing they received from their parents. As children,
they could not trust their parents to meet their needs. They

grow up with distrust toward people, particularly women. Just as they project to a daughter a fantasy of the good and loving mother, they also project to other women their anger toward the bad and rejecting mother.

With some fathers, the anger toward mother is on a more conscious and overt level. Mr. R., for example, attributed his failure in life to his mother's rejection of him. At the same time, however, he clung to images of a beautiful and loving mother and projected these to his daughter. Although anger toward the rejecting mother is often displayed to other women, it may be directed toward the mother herself. Even though it is, the fantasy of a loving mother is kept alive simultaneously.

While the mother is the parent who continues to stir fantasies and feelings in the man who commits incest, it is his father who plays a key role initially in those feelings not getting settled. By the father's being distant or absent, the child not only has no male figure with whom to identify but he also has no male figure to restrain him in his incestuous fantasies toward mother.

If mother and father are constantly at odds and clearly are unhappy with one another, such conflict invites the child to think he can move in and take the mother over. With the majority of the incestuous men we studied, there had been chronic conflict between their parents or the father had been absent or aloof. They had no male figure to tell them that mother was, in effect, off limits. A strong father at home who loves his wife makes it clear to his son that she belongs to him and the boy will have to grow up and find a wife of his own.

Harry Lewis, who illustrated the introverted type of incestuous father, had a father he remembers as a "gruff, stern man who was not at home much." Harry spent very little time with his father and never identified with him. He grew up a lonely and frightened individual who turned to his daughter for what he never got in his own childhood.

Some men who commit incest never had mothers they can remember. Gene, the alcoholic, was one of these men. His mother died when he was born and his father "hated me for it." Gene's father would have little to do with him, and he grew up fantasizing about a mother who would give him everything he had missed. He kept looking for this all-giving figure in one woman and wife after another, and finally turned to his daughters.

The turning to a daughter often occurs not only when she is beginning to take the shape of a woman but also when the father is starting to look back on his life with regrets and wishes he could start over. He remembers at some level of awareness his first love, his falling in love with mother, and nothing since has ever seemed quite as good and promising. What he tries to do is to restore the feelings of the first love, to substitute daughter for mother.

If he had settled those early incestuous feelings through a strong identity with his father and had directed his efforts and energies outside the family, he would be much less vulnerable to fantasies that his daughter is the answer to his loneliness and need for love. He would have discovered other ways to satisfy his needs, he would not see sex as the only way to be close, he would have the social skills for cultivating warm relationships outside the family, and he would have the motivation to reach out to others.

Contributing to the incestuous father's viewing sex as the answer to his needs is often a childhood of sexual stimulation or repression. This may or may not have come from the mother. It may be the distant father who tells dirty jokes, parades nude around the house, refers to all women in a sexual manner or fondles the child. In any event, the child, who is already grappling with oedipal feelings toward the mother, has his attention further fixed on sex. At the other extreme is an atmosphere in which sex is considered dirty or sinful and never to be mentioned. The effect is similar: the mystery and prohibition of the subject feed the child's imagination and fantasies and contribute to keeping them alive long after the oedipal stage is normally completed.

MOTIVATIONS OF COLLUSIVE MOTHERS

Just as incestuous fathers remain emotionally tied to their mothers or to a fantasy of one, similar dynamics are at work in the mother whose daughter becomes involved in incest. In fact, all the family members—father, mother, daughter—appear to be searching for an all-loving mother figure.

The collusive mother often had a father who abandoned her and her mother either literally or figuratively. Her mother was generally stern and unloving but she was all there was to cling to. If she had sons, she pampered them but she was hostile to the daughter and described her as being like her deserting husband. As soon as the daughter could leave the house, she married but invariably picked a husband who would mistreat her and give her reason to desert him sexually.

When her daughter came along, she made her into the image of her own unloving mother. Meanwhile, she continued to try to get her own mother to love her and give her the nurturing she never got as a child. She would either move in with the mother or keep in close contact. The continued pursuit of the mother invariably led to more rebuffs, and only her daughter was left as any hope of offering love and nurturing. But her daughter was left alone much of the time with the father, who was looking for a new sexual partner and someone to take care of him. The daughter assumed both roles.

The mother, then, often plays a key role in whether incest occurs. By "abandoning" her daughter in terms of not offering adequate parenting or protection and expecting that daughter to assume her responsibilities, she invites hostility and revenge from the daughter. By "abandoning" her husband in terms of withdrawing from him sexually, she invites him to turn to the daughter.

BACKGROUND OF INCESTUOUS MOTHERS

As we have noted, mother-son incest is uncommon compared with the other types of incest that occur. Why this is so is not fully understood. We suspect that one reason is that mothers are less likely than men to substitute physical intimacy for other forms of closeness. A woman who has had the experience of carrying a baby inside of her, giving birth, holding and feeding the child has known a kind of closeness that a father misses. She may still hunger for love and nurturing in life but she is less inclined to seek it through physical contact with the child to whom she gave birth.

Even in instances where in her own childhood a mother fails to identify with her own mother and does not end the oedipal attachment to her father, she is not as likely to project her incestuous wishes on to a son. She may smother him with too much attention, she may be overly protective, she may be seductive. But she usually stops short of incest.

In cases where a mother does not stop short, she may be widowed or divorced and, in moving her son into the role of "man of the house," reactivates old, unsettled feelings of incest she had toward her father. Other mothers, like Hortense Loftus, go into marriage believing that if only they have a son, life will be complete. A son comes along and they are totally preoccupied with him; they totally possess him. In the process of possessing him, they slide from "innocent" physical play with the son to physical intimacy and incest.

Mothers who are promiscuous come from backgrounds of excessive early sexual stimulation, loose standards in the family, or beliefs that a male must be serviced with sex for him to feel affection for a woman or even to have any interest in her. The promiscuity, as we have seen, may extend to sex with their son.

Only in cases in which incestuous mothers and fathers come from homes where loose standards prevail is it likely that there is little awareness of the strong taboo against incest and religious sanctions against it. When a mother or father breaks the taboo it is not that they have never learned there was one, it is that the psychological and situational forces that predispose them toward incest are stronger than the taboo.

THE CHILD'S BACKGROUND

The last point on the triangle of why incest occurs is the child. The child's contribution to factors causing the problem is usually weaker than that of the parents or the environment. In some instances, a daughter may be so seductive toward her father that she represents a primary reason as to why incest occurs. But even in these instances, the father must have, to some degree, the kind of background and personality we have discussed in order for him to respond sexually to the daughter and be willing to engage in incest with her.

In most cases, we look to the parent, to the stress and changes he is experiencing, and to the conditions of the family and home to find the principal reasons for incest occurring. However, the child cannot be ignored. As we saw in Part II, children who are involved in incestuous relationships have certain characteristics. These include being starved for affection and attention, having a poor relationship with mother, and acting as a "rescuer" of the father and the family as a whole.

How these characteristics come to be—what their background is—relates primarily to the role reversal that occurs in the family. As we have pointed out, the child is often called on to do the loving and nurturing in the family. The child takes on the role of parent and the parent becomes the child.

What the child misses in this process is receiving the love and nurturing she needs. She may become very responsible and efficient in being "the little parent" in the family, but at the same time she is starved for love and care-taking. She is also angry, perhaps not consciously, at having been pushed into the parent role and missing being a child. The anger is involved in the poor relationship that the daughter invariably has with the mother.

The "rescuing" that is characteristic of some daughters is part of the efforts by the child to bear the responsibility of the parents' happiness and welfare. As we have seen, a daughter may rescue a depressed and unhappy father by giving him sex or rescue her mother from being beaten or verbally assailed by calming the father down with sex.

The hunger for affection, the anger toward mother, the eagerness to rescue, all make the daughter particularly vulnerable to a father who makes sexual overtures or is presented the opportunity. Dianne, Barbara, and most of the other daughters we have discussed had this vulnerability. They were lonely and isolated, they had a poor relationship with their mothers, they welcomed attention from their fathers, and they knew how to please their fathers.

One other factor in making a daughter vulnerable, and in understanding her contribution to incest occurring, is the oedipal love that daughter may have for father and vice versa. This love may be present before incest begins or it may come to the surface afterwards. It involves early feelings that the daughter, as well as the father, never settled.

The daughter is not likely to have identified with her mother or redirected the early incestuous fantasies she had toward her father.

Sexuality is a fact of life for all children (see Chapter 12), whether there is genuine love of a parent or not and whether a child is hungry for affection or not. A child can become sexually aroused and passively cooperate, as was true of Dianne and Barbara, or start initiating sex with a parent, as was true of Dickie. A child with the kind of background and personality that we have discussed is at a higher risk of becoming involved in incest. But, given the right set of circumstances and a parent with the potential, any child may end up becoming involved. In the last analysis, it is the parent, regardless of how seductive or inviting a child behaves, who bears the responsibility for deciding whether to engage in incestuous relations.

SUMMARY

Incest, as we have seen, has no single cause and can be understood only by looking at the interaction of certain conditions that act as predisposing and precipitating agents. For father-daughter incest, these include:

1. The father clings to a fantasy of an all-loving mother and sees in the daughter a chance to pursue it.

2. The father is bombarded by stress, much of it coming from multiple changes he and his family are constantly making, and seeks a source of comfort and nurturing. He often starts drinking more.

3. The father and mother stop having sex and his source of physical intimacy and affectionate strokes dries up.

4. The mother starts work at night, gets sick, or in some other way arranges to leave the father and daughter

alone together. The mother "abandons" both her daughter and husband.

5. The daughter is hungry for attention and affection and is willing to rescue her father from his unhappiness.

6. The sexual climate of the family is lax, loose, or repressive.

Part IV

CUES AND CONSEQUENCES
OF INCEST

Chapter 10

CUES THAT INCEST IS GOING ON

When an incestuous relationship is going on in a family, there are signs or cues that are given off. These cues can be seen in the behavior of the family members: the daughter, father, mother, and even the siblings. We will look first at the cues in the daughter.

CUES IN THE DAUGHTER

One of the most obvious signs that incest is taking place can be seen in the mood and behavior of the daughter. She is frequently depressed. Dianne (see Part III) describes herself during the period she was involved in sex with her father:

I was constantly depressed. That was probably very apparent. I don't remember laughing and having fun at all in high school. I didn't partici- pate in any student activities until my senior year and then only peripherally. I had a way of speaking which was very caustic. I think the way I held myself, it was very stooped. I didn't stand up straight at all and I didn't dress with care. I very much had a low opinion of myself. I carried a great deal of shame about the whole thing. I was *very* shy. I was convinced that anybody who saw me could tell that I was bad and that no man would ever want me because I was so bad.

Cindy, a 10-year-old, had reactions similar to Dianne's:

Cindy had become withdrawn, suspicious of all people but more so of men. The girl was shy and would not play with other children for fear that they were staring at her or talking about her. . . . Cindy had been having trouble in school, and her grades had been slipping steadily. She would cry frequently and often become depressed. (Case from Finch.)

Although depression is a common cue in many daughters involved in incest, the child may welcome the incest as an expression of affection by her father. The child in an incestuous family is often starved for strokes and recognition, but the kind of affection that is involved in incest cannot meet her needs for nurturance and dependence.

With many daughters, as we have indicated, another cue is that they function as a parent to the family. Dianne took on that role for awhile in her family.

After Dad had gone to another state to work, there were a lot of times when he didn't send any money, so we were in severe financial straits. My stepmother felt she couldn't get a job because her accent was so strong, and I had already been working since the age of 15 at one job or another. That winter, many times my paycheck was the only money coming in and everything was turned over to her. That Christmas I bought gifts for the kids and things to fill up the stockings. And she was just nasty to me. I turned over my money to her and she wouldn't give me bus fare. So I had to walk to work which was five miles and cold.

Clare (see Part III), in talking of her relationship with her mother, said:

I was doing a lot of the cooking and cleaning, making sure the kids had clothes to wear to school. During the summer, we were pretty much by ourselves.

One "symptom," then, of incest is a blurring of generational lines, where a child is being treated as an adult, and the parent behaves as a child.

Secretiveness is another cue given off by many daughters involved in incest. It is not surprising that, after being admonished repeatedly by their fathers not to tell about the incest, these girls become secretive about other aspects of their lives, too. Such was the case with Dianne.

I have a great tendency, which I have just recently gotten in touch with, of needing to keep secrets, of needing to keep a part of my life secret. I don't want to tell people what I do, and most of the time I'm not doing anything that would be a problem, but I just don't want to tell. My feelings are secret. I like to go and do as I please, with people not really knowing. Certain people will have certain glimpses of this part of my life or that part.

The secretiveness can take the form of being withdrawn, keeping to oneself. The child may have no friends and spend little time involved with family members, other than the father. Dianne goes on to say,

I never had anybody to talk to. It was almost like there was too much privacy. I felt incredibly burdened with all that was going on and an inability to cope with it or sort it out and had absolutely *nobody* I could have confided in.

There may also be some physical cues of incest in the adolescent and preadolescent. The most common ones are venereal diseases and other types of genital infections, and pregnancy. Unfortunately, all of these physical cues can be hidden for some time. In many cases, there are no physical signs, or at least none that would be apparent without a gynecological examination.

While depression, excessive responsibility, and secretiveness are common cues in adolescents and preadolescents, the signs and symptoms of incest can vary widely depending on the age of the child. With an infant or baby, the cues are likely to be primarily physical, such as reddened or traumatized genitalia. But there may also be behavioral cues, including eating problems or changes in the baby's activity level.

According to Drs. Renee Brant and Veronica Tisza, since toddlers and young children have difficulty expressing their fears in words, the signs of incest in a child this age are likely to be physical and behavioral. The physical cues that can appear in a small child are genital irritation, laceration, abrasion, bleeding, discharge, or infection; stomachache; and painful discharge of urine. Venereal disease is not rare in children. In Maryland, for example, a family-centered approach was used to screen for new cases of gonorrhea. Family members of identified cases were screened, and 16 percent of those family members had gonorrhea. The average age of the male child patients was 7 to 10 years. The average age of the female child patients was 3 to 5 years. Venereal disease in a child, thus, must be considered as a cue that incest may be going on.

The behavioral cues in a small child may include enuresis (bedwetting), soiling, hyperactivity, altered sleeping patterns (sleeping a lot or little at all), fears, phobias, overly compulsive behavior, learning problems, compulsive masturbation, precocious sex play, excessive curiosity about sexual matters, and separation anxiety. The following case, cited by Brant and Tisza, illustrates how these behaviors can be the result of the pressures on a child in an incestuous relationship.

> The mother of a 7-year-old girl, the second of three children, called the emergency psychiatrist after she learned

that the child had been engaging in mutual masturbation with her maternal granduncle. He had lost his wife several months earlier, and the child had been sent to spend weekends with him to relieve his loneliness. During this period the child became enuretic. The mother had noticed increased activity level, sleeping problems, night fears, and a surge of sexual curiosity. The child's pre-existing preoccupation with cleanliness also assumed compulsive proportions. The mother learned about the child's experiences from a young aunt in whom the child had confided.

The case of Tim, who was seen in a child development clinic in Houston, is another illustration of the various cues a child involved in incest will show.

Tim was referred to the clinic because of a delayed speech development. He was 6. Tim's mother felt Tim's "character" was changing. In the last few months he had tried to set the house on fire, drank insecticide, and was vicious to animals. She related that Tim had told her of two occasions of sodomy committed on him by his stepfather. She believed him but did not intend to do anything about it because she loved her husband and he was a good provider. The clinic recommended medical and psychiatric care for Tim, but the family did not follow through. A year and a half later, Tim was hospitalized for recurrent bleeding ulcers. His speech had deteriorated to the point he was almost impossible to understand.

Another behavioral cue that may be seen in both young children and later on in adolescents involved in incest is excessive seductiveness. Barbara (see Parts II and II) was seductive. She later told her therapist that there were many times when she was little that she asked her daddy if they could play the "love game," even though parts of the "game" were repulsive to her. Mary V., 5, also illustrated seductiveness in a child who had been involved in incestuous relations.

She showed an unusual preoccupation with genital play, and tended to expose herself or play with the genitals of other children. She liked to fondle and embrace her brother and definitely was the more active partner in their sex relations. In the presence of a man, she had a truly seductive manner; with nurses and the woman physician, she played the role of a baby, but with the male physician, she smiled, cuddled up to him, and tried to win evidence of affection. (Case of Bender and Blau.)

Whether the symptom is bedwetting or seductiveness or any of the others described, it serves as a tension-releasing mechanism for the child. When a child is involved in incest, he or she becomes overstimulated. A child is not ready for the kind of sexual stimulation adults enjoy. When the child receives this kind of excessive stimulation, it creates in her or him painful tension, anxiety, and fright. Fantasies, acted out in daydreams, nightdreams, play, and physical exercise are some means by which children release their built-up tensions. When these methods are not adequate for discharging the excessive tension resulting from overstimulation, other symptoms, like those described, will appear. The symptoms are cues that a child is trying to deal with more tension than she or he can handle.

Excessive tension in a child can certainly be the result of pressures other than incest. Bedwetting or hyperactivity, of course, are not seen only in children of incestuous families. The point here is that a child in any unhealthy situation will give cues that something is wrong. What may be wrong is that incest is going on.

CUES IN THE FATHER

One of the most apparent cues given off by the father in an incestuous relationship is likely to be behavior that indicates the blurring of generational boundaries. In interactions with his daughter, the father may behave impulsively, irrationally, and immaturely, more like a child than parent. Barbara's description of her dad when she would refuse him sex illustrates the "child" position the father assumed.

> He'd start to cry; he'd break up . . . Or he'd get furious. Just blow up, mad, and he'd go in and slam his door and mumble to himself, and he would grab a book and start reading or he'd turn his television way up and he'd slam things around and bang things and break things.

Another example of the blurring of generational lines is seen when a father acts as if he is a young suitor to his daughter and courts her as a boy her age would. He may write her love letters, buy her romantic gifts, try to talk like the kids his daughter's age, or in other ways demonstrate that he wants to be seen not as a parent but as a peer to his daughter. Phil (see Chapter 5) illustrated this cue with his love letters to his daughter and his taking her for frequent drives and talks. Another sign was his making "little friends" with kids in Janie's class at school who would spy on her and report back to him.

Jealousy on the part of the father is another sign that often is present when incest is going on. The jealousy may take the form of extreme overprotectiveness. Kelly, whom we described in Chapter 4, exemplified this overprotective attitude. With his tyrannical behavior, he controlled every action of his children. His 14-year-old daughter was not allowed to go anywhere in the afternoons during the week. She was not allowed to date. In every argument between the children, Kelly intervened. He even listened to his daughter's telephone calls. In that way, he monitored her relationships with her friends, to the point of driving the friends away. This "protective" posture may also be the excuse a father uses for spending excessive time alone with a daughter. He may explain that he is "helping her to get her studies right" or "straightening her out" on some matter.

CUES IN THE MOTHER

Since the daugher in an incestuous family takes on the role of wife and mother, the real mother becomes both a child and a rival to her daughter. The cues in the mother's behavior are seen in her being dependent on the daughter or seeming to compete with her. Examples of mothers being dependent on the daughter were seen in the families of Clare and Dianne. Barbara's mother, too, allowed her to be "literally running the house" by the time Barbara was 7.

Some mothers in incestuous families are content to take the "child" role and let their daughters be the "parent." Other mothers get into overt competition with their daughters for the father's attentions. Mothers who overtly compete may take pains to look younger or may begin using their daughters' attention-getting tactics of crying, flirtatiousness, and sexual boldness with the father as the occasion demands. The extent to which the competitiveness on the part of the mother can go is seen in this report by Dianne of her struggles with her stepmother.

Earlier, when we had first gone to Cincinnati, he had bought me a gold ring, a baroque swirl with seed pearls in it. When my stepmother came back, the ring disappeared, but I hadn't worried very much about it. It turns out my father had taken it one night and hidden it in the bottom of a lamp. Later, after he and my stepmother were finally separated, he opened the lamp one time and gave me my ring back. He was certain that she would take it.

The cue here, then, is that the mother behaves more like one of the children in her relationship to her daughter. Again, there is a blurrring of generational boundaries.

CUES IN THE SIBLINGS

The daughter who submits to her father may become his favorite child. He spends more time with her, takes her out, gives her special favors, and, by doing all this, sets her up to incur the jealous wrath of her siblings and mother. The relationship was clearly seen in the case of Phil and Janie. The special attention she received extended even to their eating meals by themselves, while the mother and brothers ate separately.

When the relationship between the father and daughter is such that the other children are being excluded, this can be a cue that an incestuous relationship exists. The jealousy on the part of the siblings may not be in the open, so those feelings may not be a visible cue. But the excluding of the other children is apparent in many cases.

CUES IN BROTHER-SISTER INCEST

The cues that a brother-sister incestuous relationship exists may be less visible than in father-daughter incest, but there are indicators. The most obvious sign is when a brother and sister behave as boyfriend and girlfriend, as in this case:

> the siblings were both members of the same play group. The brother and the girl's "boyfriend" quarreled as a result of the sister dividing her attention between them. She was promiscuous and the brother was aware of her promiscuity. He, too, was promiscuous. She deliberately fostered the rivalry between her brother and her friend so both would take her out on different occasions. She reacted to the brother as if he were a nonfamilial person by making up for him and trying to "look pretty." (Weinberg's case of Gol.)

Another cue becomes evident when a daughter seems to be fearful of being left alone with her brother and avoids

him whenever possible. Karen, a client of ours, talks of her
fear of her brother:

I knew it might happen any time my parents left us alone, especially if
Jack was upset about something. I tried to make excuses to not stay
home, but my parents didn't want me going anywhere while they were
at work. So all I could do was stay in my room and lock the door. Oh,
he wasn't after me every day, but I never knew when he would be. I really
was afraid of him and hated him. I don't know why my parents couldn't
see that.

Another sign may be that the brother and sister look
embarrassed if they are discovered alone, no matter what
they are doing. Katie and Bob reacted this way.

He and I would get embarrassed if someone came in the room and found
us alone. Usually we weren't even doing anything, but we acted and felt
like we'd been caught anyway.

Finally, a sister caught up in an incestuous relationship
with her brother may express her anger by constantly bait-
ing and antagonizing her brother, knowing that he is unlikely to retaliate for fear she will tell someone about the
incest. Katie said:

One thing anyone could have noticed if they had watched was how I
antagonized my older brother and he never retaliated. I never called him
by his name. I always called him "Stupid." It was my way of getting back
at him and he couldn't do anything because he was afraid I would tell
what he was doing to me.

Since brother-sister incest does not cross generational
boundaries, the switching of roles that takes place in parent-child incest is not present. Even so, there are certain
role expectations that are common to the brother-sister
relationship and violations of these roles, in terms of court-
ship or fearful avoidance, serve as signs that incest may be
going on.

Summary

None of the "signs and symptoms" we have discussed can be construed as conclusive evidence that incest is occurring in a family. All can result from other problems and pressures. But each "cue" deserves attention, and when several are occurring as a pattern or in combination with one another, incest must be considered as a distinct possibility. The cues can be summarized as follows:

Cues in Father-Daughter Incest
Blurring of generational lines
> Father takes "child" position
> Mother takes "child" position
> Daughter takes role of "mother" and "wife" in family
> Father acts as suitor to daughter
> Mother acts as rival to daughter

Father jealous of daughter's being with peers and dating
Father over-possessive of daughter
Father often alone with daughter
Favoritism by father toward daughter over other siblings
Siblings jealous of daughter chosen by father

Daughter depressed
Daughter has poor self-image
Daughter withdrawn
Daughter uninvolved in school activities; grades may fall
Daughter secretive
Daughter excessively seductive

Physical cues
  Pregnancy
  Venereal diseases
  Genital infection, lacerations, abrasions,
    bleeding, discharge
  Stomachache
  Painful discharge of urine

Cues in younger children
  Bedwetting
  Hyperactivity
  Altered sleep patterns
  Fears or phobias
  Overly compulsive behavior
  Learning problems
  Compulsive masturbation
  Precocious sex play
  Excessive curiosity about sex
  Separation anxiety
  Seductiveness

Cues in Brother-Sister Incest
Brother and sister like boyfriend and girlfriend
Sister fearful of being alone with brother
Brother and sister embarrassed when found alone
  together
Sister antagonizing to brother; brother does not
  retaliate

Chapter 11

CONSEQUENCES OF INCEST

What are the consequences of incest? Is incest always harmful? Researchers differ widely in their conclusions about such questions. At one end of the spectrum are those who state that there are no long-lasting negative consequences, that incest is "what you make of it." There are even groups, such as the René Guyon Society, that recommend incest and believe parents should masturbate their child because a "lack of premarital sex leads to divorce, drug abuse, crime and suicide." The same group is also in favor of intercourse between adult and child since an "older person passes on tender, loving mannerisms." At the other end of the spectrum are findings that indicate that incest always has negative consequences for the child, parents, family, and society. So, who is right?

The preponderance of evidence is that an incestuous relationship is damaging. To what degree and how incest is damaging depends on many factors: how the incestuous relationship began, the child's age, the emotional context, how the family reacts, how the incest comes to light, how society reacts, and many other elements. The consequences may be short-term, with the incest causing stresses that can be handled and resolved within a relatively short time, or the incestuous relationship may leave scars that last a lifetime.

The consequences of incest may occur at three different points and times: (1) while the incest is going on; (2) when the incestuous relationship breaks up and is discovered, and (3) when participants have later difficulty in functioning and suffer long-term consequences to themselves or their offspring. We will consider first what happens to the family while a parent and child are incestuously involved.

EFFECTS ON THE FAMILY WHILE INCEST IS GOING ON

When a daughter has sex with her father, she often gains a special power over him, and she can wield that power like a club. Families, like other kinds of organizations, function well only when there are clear lines of authority and clear role expectations. In incestuous families, there is neither; there is a blurring of generational lines.

The child in the incestuous family assumes power over the parents, and sometimes, over the entire family. At the same time, the child is still a child. Role confusion exists for everyone. In father-daughter incest, the daughter does not know at any given time if her father is going to act as a parent or as a lover, and she, therefore, does not know if she should respond as a child or equal to her father. Her power over her father makes her an equal, while chronologically she knows she is a child. The mother in an incestuous family becomes both a parent and a rival to her daughter. Siblings are confused about who is in charge. They see their sister with powers and privileges appropriate to a parent, and yet they know she is their sibling.

When there is this much role confusion, the family ceases to do the jobs required of a family. Children do not get limits set for them, or when limits are set, they may be arbitrary since they are being set by a child, the sibling in power. The "unchosen" siblings feel jealousy and resentment in seeing the "chosen" one receive special privileges from the father.

Dianne describes how the sibling rivalry affected her family.

My father has always done a curious thing with me and my brothers. He's always made what I thought was much too much of the fact of my good grades. It was always an issue in our family. It's not uncommon for girls to be better students in high school, and yet it was such an issue that I was such a good student. It created a lot of resentment, not so much with the little kids because they weren't in direct competition. They could simply admire, but my brothers, I think, had a big problem with it. I didn't realize this at the time, but in talking later with my brother John, I think they were also jealous of the attention I got from Dad. John is extremely bitter about Dad's lack of any feeling towards him. His life is such a mess right now. He traces it all to his relationship with Dad being totally devoid of any acknowledgement of feeling.

So, the children in an incestuous family see a poor model of how to parent. What they see are parents who do not not limits fairly, who excessively favor one child over the other, and who turn to their children for nurturing instead of allowing their children to turn to them. One final effect on the family while the incest is going on is that the father's dependence on his daughter leads, as we noted, to his being jealous and overpossessive. His behavior interferes with her making normal social contacts, and the whole family becomes increasingly isolated.

We will explore now how the father's jealousy and overpossessiveness contribute to the break-up of the incestuous relationship and look at other factors that are also involved.

The Break-up of the Incestuous Relationship

What causes an incestuous relationship to end? What are the factors that break up a relationship that, in most cases, has gone on for months or years? What stops a father from turning to his daughter for sex and stops her from giving in to his wants?

One answer to these questions lies in the nature of human growth and development. It is normal for a child, as he or she grows older, to move away from the family and to turn to peers for support, companionship, and love. In an incestuous family, pressure is put on the child *not* to grow, not to move away. A tension is created between the child's needs for autonomy and independence and the parent's possessiveness. As the child matures into a teenager, the tension becomes even greater. Even so, a child may be ambivalent about getting out of the relationship.

A girl caught up in an incestuous family may welcome the attentions of the parent. Even if she feels there is something wrong with what they are doing, the sexual activity may be the only source of love and attention available to her. So she may be reluctant to turn her father away. She also may feel the strong sense of responsibility we discussed earlier, responsibility to take care of her father and mother by taking over her mother's role in the family.

The child in an incestuous family settles for whatever attentions he or she can get from the parent. After all, to the child an incestuous relationship with a parent seems preferable to no relationship at all. But as the child matures, she feels a greater need to be with peers, to be autonomous, to break away from the hold her parents have on her.

As she becomes more aware of her rights as a person, she becomes less willing to put her needs aside. Teenagers very much want to be like other teenagers, and the girl who is her father's lover *knows* she is not like other girls. In an effort to be more like them, to be "normal," she will struggle to break away. Sometimes she takes direct action to make the break. For instance, she may run away or tell someone about the incest.

More often, she takes a passive course of resistance: avoiding the father, staying away from the home, ignoring the father's rules about how long she can be out. Dianne's resistance took the form of her refusing to go with the family when her father took a new job in another city. She simply announced she was not going.

One night I got up the nerve and said I wasn't going to go. They said, "Fine." So it was all arranged that I would stay. I had a job, and I would support myself.... I didn't hear from them for a long time. My father came to my high school graduation, and I only know because I saw him in the audience from the stage. He didn't speak to me, and when they asked all the parents of the graduates to stand up, he didn't stand up.

Several years later, Dianne again said "no" to her father's overtures for further involvement.

When I was in college, my father came through town twice. When I was a freshman, he asked me to go to California with him, but he didn't make any sexual advances at that time. Oh, I was pretty sure that if I went, I knew what it was going to be.

Dianne did not go to California with her father, and the incestuous relationship was over, largely because she never again put herself in a situation where it could happen. There are many women like Dianne who end the incest by getting out of the home—but at a high cost that we will discuss later.

Clare resisted her father's sexual attentions by telling him she wanted him to stay away from her and by avoiding him.

I just told him to leave me alone. I think evidently he and my mother were beginning to get straightened out. He was mad when I said it and said, "Well, I'm not going to bother you." And I would still be a little leery of him. He was taking us to school one morning, my brother and me, just us three in the truck. I wanted him to drop me off first, and I kept insisting that he drop me off first, because I didn't want to be alone with him in the truck. He just looked at me and said, "Well, I'm not going to bother you, but I'll drop you off first anyway." And that was the last of it, the last I remember. There were times when I wanted to threaten him, to say, "Well, I'm going to tell her what you did," but I never did tell.

A number of girls, either because they can never muster the courage or never have the opportunity to flee, cannot break up the relationship simply by getting away from their father or insisting that he stop. These daughters must have the help of outside intervention, and the intervention comes only after the daughter reports the incest to someone willing to help. Many mothers, as we have seen, are not willing to intervene.

The daughter may report the incest after a particularly painful quarrel with her father, or the quarrel may be over something seemingly trivial. One girl reported her father's sexual involvement with her after he refused to give her a portable radio.

The quarrel is likely to occur if, as the daughter tries to break out of the relationship, the father presses even harder to keep her under his control. He may start spying on her and accusing her of having sex with boyfriends, even if his suspicions are groundless. As we saw, Phil did this with his daughter, Janie. He had kids in her school, his "little friends," spying on Janie and reporting back to him.

Based on their reports and his own suspicions, he accused Janie of having sex during the lunch break at school. He attacked her both verbally and physically, until the family was reported to child welfare authorities and Janie was removed from the home.

Phil's behavior toward Janie while she was in foster care was so much more like that of lover than a father that the authorities became suspicious, and the incest came to light. In Phil's family, as in most incestuous families, the fact that someone outside the home found out about the incest stopped it from continuing.

In a small number of cases, the incest is discovered when the daughter becomes pregnant and names her father as the father of her unborn child. In Weinberg's research, he found that 24 percent of the daughters in his 203 cases became pregnant by their fathers and 9 percent gave birth. We did not find such a relatively high percent in our research. When pregnancy does occur, the girl may be forced to drop out of school or even be forced from the home. Since her condition is kept secret as long as possible, she usually receives no prenatal care, and the incest may not be disclosed to someone outside the family until she actually goes to medical facilities to deliver.

In a few cases the daughter will report the incest after realizing that her father is also molesting her younger sisters and that nothing will stop him but to bring the incest to light. Says one young woman interviewed in the film *Incest: The Victim Nobody Believes*, "One of our sacred pacts for not speaking about what was going on was that he promised he wouldn't touch them (her three younger sisters) as an exchange for silence on my part." She was furious when she discovered he had been molesting them all along.

Sometimes the incest comes to light when the mother, who knows of the relationship, becomes angry and upset with the father about some other matter and takes the child to an emergency room or calls the police. In these instances, the mother is angry with the father rather than really concerned about the child, and when the crisis has passed, the mother may change her story or have the child refuse to testify.

As for brother-sister incestuous relationships, they usually end when one or both of the participants either leaves home or turns his or her attention to peers. If the incest is discovered by one of the parents, pressure from the parent is likely to stop or deter the behavior in most cases.

We have examined the factors involved in the break-up of the incestuous relationship. Now, what are the effects on the family when the incest is discovered?

EFFECTS OF THE DISCOVERY OF INCEST

However the incest is uncovered, the public response to disclosure can have serious effects on the entire family. There are researchers and writers who take the position that the most serious consequences of incest are caused by public response to its discovery. For example, Maisch says:

> It is today a well-tried and proven discovery of psychological and psychiatric research that the harmful effects on the family brought about by the official discovery of the offence and punishment of it are more serious than those which might arise during the course of incest.

Although, in our experience, the most lasting consequences usually come from the disturbed family relationships that gave rise to the incest, we agree that the discovery can produce a traumatic effect. We will consider first the impact on the child.

Effects of the Discovery on the Daughter

STRESSFUL LEGAL INVOLVEMENT.   If criminal charges are filed against the father, the entire family is often caught up in a stressful, confusing, time-consuming, and costly judicial process. Law enforcement personnel keenly feel public pressure to punish "degenerates" who sexually abuse children. In their zeal to prosecute, the needs of the children may become secondary.

The child is questioned in detail to get evidence and is put in the embarrassing position of having to discuss her sexual activity and knowledge with strangers, something that would be difficult for most adults to do. The child's embarrassment is added to if the interrogators show shock, amusement, repulsion, or contempt at her narration.

If the father is arrested, the child faces testifying at an arraignment or preliminary hearing, before a grand jury if there are felony charges, and then again at the actual trial. In many states, the trial is in an adult criminal court, in open court, before a jury. Many families come away from the judicial experience feeling the child has been harmed, rather than helped, by the process.

In a study the American Humane Association conducted of 250 families in which a child had been sexually abused, almost half the families reported having negative experiences about the court process and said that the court experience was bad for the child. This was true for Cindy, the 10-year-old we described in Chapter 10. Cindy's father molested her and was sent to prison.

> The court trial had been traumatic for Cindy. She was interrogated first by the police, then had to tell her story again to the prosecuting attorney, and finally was subjected to cross examination by the defense attorney. She wound up feeling guilty, confused, and overwhelmed by the ordeal.

Not surprisingly, with so many pressures on the child, combined with ambivalence on the part of the mother, criminal charges may be withdrawn soon after they have been filed.

BLAME AND DISBELIEF.   Whether there is legal involvement or not, the daughter who reports incest with her father may simply not be believed, or if she is believed, the blame is placed on her instead of on her father. Dianne suffered on both counts.

My grandmother treated the whole issue of incest as a political type thing, as if it were a story made up to cause damage. She addressed all of her concern at trying to find out why I made up the story. Her theory on it was that my stepmother forced me to do it in order to discredit my father. Even my father will deny to me that he ever touched me. He can look me straight in the eye and not even flinch when he says it was not true.

Her stepmother's reaction, on the other hand, was one of belief but blame. Dianne recalls:

I had to fix their meals and serve them, and then I had to eat in the kitchen by myself because I was too shameful to eat with the rest of the family. That was my stepmother's idea. She treated me as if I were dirt. She took the position that it happened but that it was all my fault, that I had seduced my father, that my seductive airs were such that no red-blooded American male could have refused. It was really treated as completely my fault. The other children were not even corrected if they made fun of me. One time my little brother spit on me in front of her, and she just waved it off. She would just do things like that, unnecessarily mean. It was as if she were really venting her viciousness on me. Christmas passed, and my father came back right around New Year's, and then that's when I was not allowed to eat with the family because my father was there. He said nothing. He raised no objection.

In cases of brother-sister incest, the reaction may also be one of disbelief or blame. When Louise told her mother

that she had seen her older brother and sister having intercourse, her mother would not believe her. "She beat me so
bad until I had cuts and bruises all over my body." Louise
tells what happened when she herself was sexually involved
with a stepbrother.

I first had sexual experience when I was 13. It was with the son of a man
my mother had married. He kept coming around. He was about 19 or
20. My brother kept egging him on. He would get me down on the bed
and wrestle until I was exhausted and my brother would be standing in
the door laughing. I'll never forget that evil laugh. It hurt. This went on
and on for a long time. You keep doing this to someone who's never
experienced sex, and the next thing you know they'll be wanting to
experience sex. That's what happened to me. I was mocked. I was
shamed. I was called, "You whore, you!" I was two weeks late for my
period, and I told my mother. She beat me up. The next thing I know
she was taking me to the doctor. The doctor gave me some kind of pills
to dissolve it. I lived with this shame all my life. My brother and sister
shamed me, called me a whore. I don't know. It got the best of me, until
one day I picked up a foot tub and hit my sister with it. It split her head
open. I took it, took it until I exploded.

Katie was also blamed for her involvement with her
brother.

When I was about 15 or 16 I finally told my mother about it. Her first
reaction was to call Bob a rapist and beat him about the head some. Her
final reaction was to blame the whole situation, including when I was 4,
on me. According to her, I was a whore and had seduced him, even at
4. This was evidently the same reaction her own mother had had about
her and her father when she was 11.

SEXUAL ADVANCES.   Once the daughter is seen as seductive and tainted, she may be approached sexually by men
who view her as now being "fair game." Dr. Roland Summit
and JoAnn Kryso of Harbor General Hospital in Torrance,
California, found this to be true in some of the families they
have worked with.

> A bizarre spinoff of the labeling process is the fascination the girl presents to others. She may be regarded by relatives as dangerously attractive. . . . Publicly deflowered as she is, she is regarded as no longer deserving of respect or protection. We know of at least four cases where male relatives have attempted seduction after a girl admitted incest with her father.

REMOVAL FROM HOME.   Another immediate consequence to the daughter is that she may be removed from the home. Some children are placed in foster homes, others in residential care facilities. Even when given factual explanations, these children often think they are being punished for committing the incest or for telling or for both. Sometimes the fear of being taken from the home is sufficient to keep a child from telling for many years. Says one young woman:

> I can remember not wanting to tell anyone about the incest because I knew it meant I would have to leave the home, that my dad would get so mad at me that he would kick me out and my mother wouldn't believe me and she'd have a nervous breakdown.

Effects on the Father

What happens to the father after the incestuous relationship is discovered? If the affair is brought to the attention of the law, the father may face criminal charges and possible imprisonment. He may be arrested and detained in jail prior to imprisonment. This means he may be fired from his job, putting the family in a state of economic hardship if he was the sole or major breadwinner.

What happens to the father also depends on how the mother reacts. Because there was already serious strain on the marriage prior to the discovery of the incest, there is a high risk of a break-up. Susan, the wife of Harry Lewis, the introverted father, expresses the ambivalence many wives feel when they learn of the incest.

It's shock and horror. "How could you? You just did something that's been taboo for so long." One minute I feel loving and supportive of him and say, "Well, you know, I know you have a problem. I'm going to help you work with it to resolve this." Then the next minute I turn around and I say, "Oh, my God!"

In the face of censure from wives and from society, many fathers experience intense guilt when discovered. Some even become suicidal, as Harry was.

I just started taking every pain pill that I could find in the house, every kind of nerve pill, anything that I thought might do any good at all. But it seems like every time I try taking nerve pills or something, I get too sleepy to keep on, you know, unless I just took a whole bottle at one time and for some reason I can't ever make myself do that. And I don't ever have guts enough to try to commit suicide any other ways.

Other fathers, particularly the rationalizers, have apparently no internal consequences. They see nothing wrong in what they did or they simply deny that the incest ever took place. Dianne's father, as we saw earlier, reacted with denial. But whether the father acknowledges or denies the incestuous relationship, one immediate consequence for him is that he loses companionship of his daughter, and often his family as well.

Effects on the Mother

The effects on the mother in an incestuous family may be as devastating as the effects on the father and daughter. The initial reaction of most mothers in this situation is one of guilt. Susan puts it vividly in describing her feelings and thoughts a few days after discovering Harry's involvement with his daughter, Annie.

I feel anxiety, fear, guilt. I feel that if I had stayed at home.... This happened once a week when I went to play cards right next door in the clubroom of the apartments, and I wasn't but 20 feet away, and I felt like, well, if I had stayed at home and not gone, that maybe this wouldn't have happened. And so I feel guilty on that point and then just a whole myriad of, of feelings, that I need to get rid of and to get a better, healthier outlook on because this is not doing my health, or the health of the baby I'm carrying, any good at all.

Other mothers react decisively to remove the father, often at a cost of economic hardship to themselves, as this mother did.

Upon discovering the incest event, the mother went immediately to the social settlement. They directed her to the police.... They came and arrested the father ... he tried to persuade the mother to compel the daughter to change her plea but the mother turned a deaf ear.... He then told her of the economic difficulties she would have, but she disregarded this argument.... She claims he had always been brutal to her.... He was a chronic alcoholic and so brutal and abusive to the children that his absence had actually relieved the family of the tension and fear which they had from his unpredictable and violent moods. (Weinberg's case of Al.)

The mother in an incestuous family may experience rejection by her friends and even her own family when she takes punitive action against the father. One mother describes her response after her husband's rape of her daughter was discovered.

Two or three neighbors knew it. So when the trial was over, I moved away. I don't go to see them and they're nice people. I'm ashamed. I don't know what they think of me.

When mothers are pressured by their families not to file charges, they experience a loss of family support when they do. Often they have to sever family ties to protect their children. So an immediate impact on the mother when the incest is detected is that she may be, or feels she is, abandoned by her husband, her neighbors, and her family. The mother and daughter may pull closer together in this time of stress and crisis, but many mothers, like Dianne's stepmother, turn their fear and rage against their daughters.

LONG-TERM CONSEQUENCES OF INCEST

Incest does not affect every child to the same extent. Since people are unique, so are their responses to stressful and traumatic events. One factor, apart from individual differences, that affects the consequences is the length of time incest continues. It appears that when the relationship continues for a long time, for several years, the emotional damage to the child is greater. Another factor that influences the long-term consequences of incest is the age of the child at the time of the incestuous relationship.

Incest appears to be least damaging psychologically to the younger child, provided she or he is not physically assaulted and traumatized. As the child approaches adolescence, the psychological risks become greater. The younger child usually does not realize the significance of the sexual behavior and so does not suffer as much guilt. The very young child may not feel as deeply the effects of the family dynamics we previously described: the role-reversal, rivalry, and social isolation. This is not to say that incest has no effect on a small child. Rather, if the child can feel secure, loved, protected, and receive appropriate parenting after the incestuous relationship, the effects are not likely to be as long-lasting.

Unfortunately, many incestuous relationships do result in long-term consequences, as we will see.

Consequences to the Daughter

LOW SELF-ESTEEM, GUILT, AND DEPRESSION.   Perhaps the most pervasive long-term consequences of incest are the effects it may have on the daughter's self-image. These effects stem from years of being weighted down with feelings of both anger and guilt. As a small child, the daughter may not have known the incestuous behavior was wrong and, therefore, she did not put up resistance. Once she realizes society condemns it, she starts blaming herself for having participated.

At the same time, the daughter is often angry at her parents for having exploited instead of protected her and angry at herself for having been unable to do anything to stop the incestuous behavior. She may still believe that she was somehow to blame for what happened and feel burdened by guilt. On top of the anger and guilt, a sense of aloneness and impotence also frequently persists. Because she has no one nurturing her, the daughter comes to believe that no one likes her enough to be willing to take care of her. With no one giving her warmth and protection, she begins to feel hopeless. She may also feel tainted by the experience. In short, the woman often sees herself as worthless and may become seriously depressed. Dianne felt this sense of worthlessness.

The hardest problem I had was that in the period after I left home I was convinced that anybody who saw me could tell that I was bad and that no man would ever want me because I was so bad. That was one of the hardest things to get over. At times the old conviction that I'm a bad woman comes up. To this day, the issue of whether I'm a good or bad woman is alive for me.

Because a daughter involved in incest is caught up in a role reversal, she may feel that she is responsible for the incest happening. For years, or even the rest of her life, she also may feel a sense of responsibility for anything that happens as a result of the incest.

Peggy, a young woman from a prominent family in the West, understands well that the incest was not her fault, and yet she continues to feel responsible for her father's suffering.

My father suffered so much from guilt after what he did to me. He never did anything in his life like that to be guilty about. He tried to commit suicide three times, and spent a summer in a psychiatric unit. Six weeks before my marriage, he shot himself on my bed. I feel like I could have saved him a lot of suffering if I could just have told someone. But there was no way I could say the words.

Peggy's feelings illustrate the extent to which a child in an incestuous family assumes responsibility for the parent, even to the point of feeling guilty about whatever goes wrong in the life of her father years after the incest is over and the child has left home. Some daughters even feel responsible for their father's being the way they are, as this young woman did:

I felt that something was wrong with me and that if I would get okay he would be the father that I never had.

FEELING UNIQUELY DIFFERENT.   The low self-image of daughters from incestuous families is compounded by their sense of being uniquely different from everyone else. Because they never heard anyone talk about incest or even mention that such a thing exists, they believe they are the only ones who have ever had sex with a parent. A young woman in *Incest: The Victim Nobody Believes* felt this.

I realized very soon after the ball got rolling that it was something highly unique or else I would have heard something to that effect beforehand. I would go to school feeling, "Shit, nobody else in the world has gone through what I've

gone through. Nobody else knows anything about this sort
of thing. Nobody imagines, or else they would be able to talk
on this kind of level." And nobody could. I was beyond all
the petty talk of girl friends at school and I just hated most
people in general because they were so petty and they
couldn't imagine the depth of the hell I was going through,
the emotional hell.

Another woman shared those same feelings of being
unique and different from other girls her age.

> I didn't get along with other girls. I felt older than them. For
> one thing, I'd been into sex since 8 years old, and when I
> knew that, I felt different, so I hung around guys a lot.

Peggy describes what the time of incest and the years
following were like for her.

> It wasn't until I was 22 that I even knew anyone else had thought such
> a thing could happen. It wasn't until I read *Peyton Place* that I realized
> someone else knew about it. Even then, I was so naïve that I thought that
> the author just had it in her mind that this could happen, not that it had
> actually ever happened to anyone. My parents would never let me read
> *Peyton Place* as a teenager. It would have saved me six years of suffering
> if they had let me read it. I really believed I was the only one this had
> ever happened to. It would have helped so much just to see *one* poster
> on a bus!

PROBLEMS WITH SEX AND MEN.   Because of her guilt and
anger and her hesitancy to make friends, the daughter from
an incestuous family often develops sexual problems and
has difficulty in relating to men in a satisfying way. She
approaches men with an expectation that they will exploit
her, and when she does approach them, she is often confused about whether she is seeking sex or affection.

This confusion between affection and sex may show up
in sexual dysfunction or promiscuity. Dianne, now 26, had
problems with both.

I think some of the sexual difficulties I have to this day are attributable to my relationship with my father. The first inclination of problems in that area is that once I did start dating, I was very aggressive sexually, and usually more aggressive than the guy. Like the fella who asked me out on my first date was unwilling to go to bed with me. He finally did go to bed with me the night before he left for college and it was a disaster. I had certain promiscuous experiences even through college that left me with uncomfortable feelings, that I didn't like what I was doing. My father never had intercourse with me, but I was excessively stimulated.

The sexual dysfunction that came from it was that for so many years I had made myself so rigid and unresponsive that it's very difficult for me to respond, to relax in a sexual situation because the most familiar feeling is still being oriented to please but to be completely rigid and closed within myself. To this day, if I'm not feeling really OK, I will simply perform sex as a service. What happens with penetration is that if I'm not relaxed, it's painful for me. What happens in those situations is that the pain is experienced as my just desserts. It's masochistic.

I still have a difficulty sorting out situations when men want me. It's very easy for me to snap back to the old way and to not keep myself in the present, because the past was a denial of myself, of my wants or needs or desires.

The confusion between sex and affection or nurturing occurs when sex is the only kind of affection shown the daughter by her father. Also, the sexual acts are often accompanied by nurturing gestures. As a result, the daughter grows up not knowing how to separate the two or even knowing that sex and nurturing *are* different. For these women, sex and affection are seen as the same thing. As one woman explains:

He was very gentle and nurturing with me while he was talking me into doing things for him. I think that's the way I am with men now. I want very badly for a man to like me.

Because of this confusion, these women may not understand a man who is affectionate in nonsexual ways. Since they only know how to relate to men who share their confusion about sex and affection, they tend to pick mates who relate only sexually. If a man does relate to them in a gentle nurturing way, they tend to believe he wants sex, whether he does or not.

A woman with this confusion will tend to make sexual overtures when what she actually wants is affection, nurturing, or approval. She gets sex instead and ends up feeling dissatisfied and used. Her mate becomes confused, hurt, or angry that she is dissatisfied or rejecting. So the confusion between sex and affection affects the marriage.

The marriage may be affected in another way, too. This woman describes how the sexual aspect of her marriage was impaired.

> I remember my first year of marriage. I couldn't understand why I didn't like to make love. Then one day it dawned on me when my husband was touching me on the shoulder, and I said, "That feels just like what my father did to me, and I can't stand it." It was repelling to me. I couldn't stand the feeling of my father's skin against my skin. And I would just get creepy, crawly feelings when he would touch me.

The daughter of William K, the "teacher" described in Chapter 4, saw her sexual relations with her father as forcing her into an unhappy early marriage.

> Guilt overtook me and forced me to press for an early wedding date. Fear of pregnancy and guilt over fornication caused me to get married at age seventeen. The experience with Dad caused me to indulge in fornication. Therefore, he caused me to get married. There was the additional fear of a repetition of the experience with Dad which drove me to fornication. By duplicating the experience with someone else, I reduced the danger of repeating it with Dad.

DISTRUST.   The marital problems for daughters from incestuous families are intensified by the fact that the women have not learned to trust. Time after time, they would turn to their fathers for approval or affection only to end up being used sexually. Such was this woman's experience:

> I remember a time when I'd gotten a good report card and I wanted my Dad to be proud of it. I was pretty bad in school. I rushed in and said, "look what I got!" He told me to sit on his lap. I thought, "Good, he's going to give me attention." I was really trusting, really expecting him to be affectionate with me and approving of my report card. What he did was throw the report card on the ground and start getting sexual with me.

After experiences like this, some young women decide that men cannot be trusted. They hold back their feelings, even from their husbands, and inside they are hiding feelings of hurt, anger, and confusion. Dianne tells of her distrust:

> My initial reaction to advances by a male is usually that they are just out for what they can get. On the other hand, I will often get involved in sexual liaisons where I *know* that that's what's going on. I'll do it, and I'll know that I'll feel bad when it's over, and I still do it. I consider men as selfish creatures who only want me for what they want.

Sometimes, outside of their awareness, daughters from incestuous families will pick husbands who are indeed untrustworthy, immature, and unreliable. It is as if these are the only kind of men to whom they know how to relate. In a sense, the daughters end up creating a self-fulfilling prophecy. They expect to find men untrustworthy and they marry men who are just that. We will say more shortly about how this self-fulfilling prophecy perpetuates incest.

SELF-DESTRUCTIVE BEHAVIOR.   In an effort to blot out their pain and loneliness, many daughters will turn to self-destructive behavior. The self-destructiveness may take the form of drug abuse, prostitution, or even suicide. One

woman talked of her attempts to escape her emotional pain
and at the same time protect her father:

> I spent two years dealing with my craziness, my depression.
> I would just wish I could die when the pain would come up.
> A lot of what I was doing was killing myself for him. Die with
> the secret. I wasn't literally saying, "I'm going to kill my-
> self," but I got high, got loaded. I went through a heavy drug
> addiction. I got hepatitis. I weighed 107 pounds. I was dy-
> ing, and I knew why. I didn't want to face a lot of that stuff.
> I would rather get loaded than face some of the pain I had.
> I had a lot of pain and I had no other outlet to deal with it.

Sometimes these women and girls turn to prostitution
to support their drug habits. Also, being a prostitute is
consistent with how these women see themselves: tainted,
bad, good only for delivering sex. It is not infrequent that
the self-destructive outlet of prostitution is chosen. A survey of 200 prostitutes in Seattle found that 22 percent of
them had been incestuously assaulted as children. The
Chicago Vice Commission came up with similar statistics.
They found that 51 out of 103 women questioned reported
having their first sexual experience with their own fathers.

SEARCH FOR NURTURING AND BELONGING.   All of the consequences we have discussed—low self-esteem, depression,
feeling uniquely different, problems with sex and men, distrust, and self-destructive behavior—grow out of the kind
of parenting the child in the incestuous family receives.
Because many take a position of being responsible for their
parents instead of their parents being responsible for them,
these children never receive the kind of love and nurturing
necessary for healthy growth and development. They feel
abandoned and experience a lack of being part of a "real"
family. They struggle, sometimes all their lives, to get that
nurturing and a feeling of belonging and being cared for.

Louise expresses this struggle in a sad, touching description of herself and her relationship with her mother.

I've been running scared all my life, not knowing where I could put my roots in the ground, not knowing who'll care about me. Like a fool I kept going back to my mother and got treated the same way. When I was separated from my husband, I'd drive to see my mama and wake her up about two or three in the morning. She'd start cussing me the minute I'd walk in, instead of saying, "What in the world are you doing up this time of the night, young'un? Get your fannie in here and go to bed." That's what I wanted, but I got the opposite.

Louise, like other daughters in incestuous families, feels, and rightly so, that the mother has failed to take care of her. Louise's frantic, repetitive efforts are aimed at getting her mother to do the caretaking that she never did and probably never will do.

Many young women suffer from a sense of abandonment, feeling that they were never loved or even a part of a family. Dianne says, in speaking of her family and her father:

I still have a lot of personal pain over not having a family. I have these brothers that never bother to call me. I look them up whenever I go to Atlanta, and they seem to enjoy me, but I never hear from them. The lack of a family is part of a bigger picture of which the incest, I think, is just a small part. My father was not in any way genuine with me, and I never felt that his love was love towards me. I can't say that I believe my father has loved anybody, unless you could call his relationship with his mother love. He claimed he loved me, but it was not a love that I wanted.

Many daughters speak of wishing they had had a "real dad," one who would love them as a father instead of as a lover, one who would parent them, nurture them, and set limits.

Long-Term Consequences to the Father and Mother

As we have already noted, when the incest is discovered, the father in an incestuous family may be attacked, downgraded, and humiliated. Some of these fathers will feel a

sense of guilt that they will carry with them all their lives.
If the father goes to prison, his career and position in the
community may be ruined. Some fathers, although a minority, will be divorced by their wives, thereby losing their
families. A few fathers will try to establish an incestuous
relationship with another daughter or attempt to reestab-
lish a relationship with their wives. As we have seen, a final
group of fathers will go on denying to others, and even to
themselves, that incest ever took place or that there was
anything wrong in their actions. So the long-term consequences of incest for the father can range from serious to
practically none.

Long-term consequences to the mother are probably
the least visible. She often continues to feel the guilt she
felt when she first discovered the relationship, but she usually reconciles with her husband. One pair of psychiatrists
found that in only one of their 20 cases did the wife stay
separated from her husband after three years.

Some mothers will continue to disbelieve their daughters, even in the face of convincing evidence. Here is how
one mother maintained her position of disbelief during an
interview conducted by Dr. Frank Pittman, a psychiatrist at
Colorado Psychopathic Hospital:

Mother:	(shakily) I just can't believe it, I just can't—
Daughter:	Mom—
Mother:	(with a trembling voice) Just can't see how anything like this could possibly happen, and how you could treat me this way.
Daughter:	Because . . .
Mother:	(shouting and weeping) After all I've done for you! I've tried to be a mother to you, I've tried to be a respectable mother and you accuse your father of something that's so horrible, that's—
Daughter:	(shouting) Mother, it's true! You've got to believe it!
Doctor:	(calmly) Mrs. Carlson, Mary—
Mother:	(shouting) She's my daughter and I love her but I cannot believe this!

Doctor:	(loud and calm) Mary, shut up and sit down and be quiet. Mrs. Carlson, have you heard this before?
Daughter and Mother:	(both moan)
Mother:	Yes, I've heard it, but I didn't believe it.
Doctor:	How often . . . how often have you heard it?
Mother:	(sobbing) I've heard it once, once in my life, once.
Daughter:	(shouting) Three times! Three times I've talked to you and you never believed me.
Mother:	You never . . . (tape distorted at this point. Mother moans while Mary describes the times she has told this to her. Mothers holds her hands to her ears.)
Daughter:	(still shouting) . . . The first time was when I was 16 and he wanted me to go to bed with him and I wouldn't. And I told you and everybody said I was crazy and you put me in the hospital. And I told you this spring—And then I told you the other night when you took me to grandmother's house, and I'm telling you now! And it's been the same thing, except you don't, you can't visualize it! (sobs) And you don't understand! (sobbing) You don't understand because *you're* right, and *I'm* right, and *Dad's* right; in our minds we're right, our own feelings *say* we are.

A mother, like Mary's, has a lot of reasons *not* to believe her daughter. If she acknowledges that the incest took place, she may be blamed, her marriage may break up, she may have to move, and she may become the sole support of her family. These are heavy burdens for anyone to bear, and it is understandable, but not acceptable, that a mother would elect the choice with fewer negative consequences for her, that is, the choice of disbelieving her daughter.

It is likely that when a mother does choose to believe her daughter, she assumes she has more to gain by getting rid of her husband than by staying with him. This was the case in the example cited earlier of the woman who turned her husband in to the authorities and divorced him without giving any consideration to reconciliation. The husband was alcoholic and abusive, and she had little to gain by sticking with him. Since most incestuous fathers are not physically abusive, the choice is not an easy one for many mothers. How much they suffer emotionally as a result of disbelieving their daughters and not protecting them, no one can say for sure.

LONG-TERM CONSEQUENCES OF OTHER TYPES OF INCEST

Brother-Sister Incest

Although brother-sister incest is probably the most common type, many researchers believe its long-term consequences are the least damaging because of reasons we discussed earlier, that is, it does not cross generational boundaries and is often an extension of sex play. However, the consequences are serious when there is exploitation, and in all the cases of brother-sister incest we have worked with, there has been exploitation.

This was true in Katie's case. She was seduced into a "game" with her brother when she was 4.

> My brother was 10 or 11 during the first time. It always occurred when my mother was gone to the clinic with Jim (another brother), that is, when Bob knew for sure that they would be gone a long time. Bob had these fantasies about queens and warriors. He made up games for us to play, similar to the old "doctor" routine. But they usually involved some sort of trick that required me to submit to being played with or undressed. . . . One day when no one else was home Bob (who was 14 then) took it into his head to "play" with me some more. . . . This one time I was excited but I did not know what it was about. I just felt it was wrong.

If the mother blames the daughter for being sexually involved with her brother, as was true for both Katie and Louise, the girl feels a sense of estrangement from her family. She also suffers from guilt, knowing she has done something wrong, and she believes what others tell her, that she was at fault and the cause.

Even if the incest is never detected, as is the case for many young women, they may carry with them for the rest of their lives a sense of shame, anger, and fear. The women we have worked with also feel betrayed by their parents. Says one young woman:

I told my mother that my brother was bothering me and she just told me there wasn't anything she could do about it. He bothered me and my two sisters, and she didn't do anything. She should have stopped him or made someone stop him. All she did was tell him to leave us alone.

These same feelings—anger, shame, a feeling of being betrayed—were also present in the few cases we have seen of younger brothers sexually abused by their older male siblings.

Mother-Son Incest

Mother-son incest is less common, and it is fortunate that such is the case for the consequences to the participants may be devastating. The extreme to which the consequences can go were seen in the Loftus case, in which Dickie Loftus eventually murdered his mother. Other cases have far less dramatic but no less tragic endings.

The incestuous relationship between mother and son may stop short of intercourse and still be damaging. Just as the father incestuously involved with a daughter becomes overly possessive and attempts to limit her social activities and interests, so does the mother incestuously involved with her son. She uses seductiveness and a high degree of possessiveness to discourage him from having outside interests, from growing socially and from becoming independent of her. The same role-reversal exists that is characteristic of father-daughter incest in the sense that the son is serving the mother's needs rather than she his.

Dr. William Masters and Virginia Johnson believe the most traumatic incestuous relationship is that between mother and son.

> A mother destroys her son socially when she brings him to her bed, for inevitably she is overprotective and overdemanding. While isolating him as much as possible from peer-group influence, she renders him insecure and extremely self-conscious; usually he becomes a loner. The harder he tries to withdraw from her influence, the tighter she holds the reins.

They go on to say that the boy caught up in an incestuous relationship with his mother is filled with guilt when other boys talk about their sexual interest in girls their own age. If he does approach girls, it is without confidence and he is generally unsuccessful in establishing any kind of relationship with a woman of his own age. If the incest goes on for years, the son may be able to have sex *only* with his mother.

As we have noted, most of the incest that goes on between mother and son seems to be a kind where there is excessive physical contact, which becomes sexually stimulating. Although the consequences of this kind of sexual activity are not likely to be as severe, there are still repercussions. Generally, the mother is giving the son a "don't grow up" or "don't leave me" message as she prolongs physical contact with him, sleeping with him, bathing him, dressing him.

The consequences of excessive involvement by the mother with a son can start showing up fairly early. Dr. Stuart M. Finch, professor of psychiatry at the University of Michigan Medical School, describes the effects seen in a 12-year-old boy:

He was effeminate in demeanor, unathletic and openly stated his preference for being a girl. He lived with his over-protective mother and two maiden aunts. The mother continued to bathe her son, frequently slept in the same bed with him, and referred to him as "my little man of the house." He lacked any adult male with whom to identify. He adopted a feminine role, first because that is what he was surrounded by, and second because he felt totally unfit for taking on the role of being "man" of the house.

Many sons in such relationships never grow up or leave mother. They may grow up physically or even leave physically, but not emotionally. They remain unduly attached to mother with all sorts of consequences in terms of poor relations with both men and women. Some never leave home and simply remain "married" to mother, although no overt sex or intercourse ever occurs.

The son who is turned to sexually by his mother learns not to trust, just as the daughter turned to by her father. This distrust was illustrated in a case studied by Weinberg. The son refused to associate with girls because he feared that he would get diseased or be "fooled" by them.

Since the father is excluded in the families where mother-son incest takes place, the son suffers sexual-identity problems from never having a male role model. Socially he becomes retarded and remains overly involved with his mother. Like the daughters who are involved in incest with their fathers, the sons are forced into taking care of their mothers—at least emotionally—instead of being taken care of themselves. The son suffers the same consequences from this role reversal as does the daughter in father-daughter incest: distrust, low self-image, guilt, and poor social skills. Like the incestuous fathers, some incestuous mothers will experience intense guilt and others will simply deny any wrong-doing or fault. Regardless of the mother's reaction, the son is likely to be affected for life.

Father-Son Incest

As we noted in Part II, father-son incest is rarely reported, perhaps because it violates two moral codes: the one against incest and the one that has previously existed against homosexuality. Nevertheless, when incest does occur between father and son, the consequences can be very serious.

A boy who is sexually abused by his father has to cope both with the stress of the role reversal and a threat to his masculinity. A sexual attack by an adult male often arouses acute anxiety in an adolescent boy, whether the adult is his father or some other male. The boy may feel damaged, dirty, and worthless. If the sexual act is the result of a long-term seductive and possessive relationship, the son is inhibited from growing socially in the same way children involved in other forms of parent-child incest are inhibited. Although homosexuality is more accepted now, the combination of it and incest may still be so stressful to a boy that he retreats into his own world and loses contact with reality. He also may suffer serious physical problems. Tim, the little 6-year-old boy we described under "Cues," both lost contact with reality and suffered physical problems.

Other boys may turn to drugs, as did Dave. Dave, who was 20 and in his sophomore year of college, was brought to a psychiatric hospital after taking LSD. He reported that he had had homosexual experiences with his father beginning at age 12. The hospital staff did not believe him until his father voluntarily confirmed that what Dave said was true. After Dave was hospitalized, his father developed a serious depression and was unable to work for a year. When Dave was able to return to college, his father stopped being depressed.

Dr. J. B. Raybin of the Yale University School of Medicine reported a case of father-son incest that involved three generations. The father, "Mr. A," was a professor and theatre director. Mr. A had been sexually involved with his own father and brother for many years during his youth, but he did not show any signs of emotional consequences as a result of the incest. However, Mr. A's son was hospitalized with a psychotic break, a loss of contact with reality. Mr. A was anxious, depressed, and guilty until his son was out of the hospital. Although Mr. A did not show any overt signs of emotional problems as a result of incest with his own father, he did show behavioral problems, as witnessed by the fact that he turned to his son for sexual satisfaction, just as his father had turned to him. We can conclude that Mr. A, like his son, suffered from the role reversal characteristic of incestuous families. He did not receive the kind of parenting necessary for him to establish a healthy sexual relationship with an adult woman, and he turned instead to his son.

"Boy prostitution" is another form of consequences that father-son incest may take. In large cities across the country, boys can be found on the streets soliciting "tricks" or waiting to be picked up. In the background of many of them is a history of incest or sexual abuse outside the family. They received little or no nurturing at home and are seeking both love and money on the streets. Many are looking for someone who will care for them, and also pay them.

In Houston, an estimated 200 youths are involved in boy prostitution at peak periods. It has become a business in the big cities, where telephone orders can be placed in New York or Los Angeles for a boy to be delivered locally in another part of the country, and where sex can be bought with a credit card. Just as many of the boys come from backgrounds of abuse, so do a number of the men who purchase sex from them.

Consequences to the Next Generation

In Part I, we discussed the idea that the incest taboo was seen, correctly or not, as a safeguard against defective offspring. Although not all offspring from incestuous unions will be biologically defective, and, in fact, some may even be superior, there is evidence that the offspring are more vulnerable to disease and defect than children of nonrelative matings.

One study by Dr. C. O. Carter of the Institute of Child Health in London looked at 13 children who were products of father-daughter and brother-sister matings. He concluded that the risks of death or subnormality or serious illness in these offspring is four times greater than they would be between offspring of first cousins.

Drs. Morton Adams and James Neel at the University of Michigan also studied offspring of incestuous matings. They found that seven out of 18 of the infants were normal at the six-month examination period. The remaining 11 either died or suffered from some degree of illness or defect. Only one in a matched group of infants from nonincestuous unions had any defect of consequence. They concluded that children of incest are a high-risk group. Another study found that children of incestuous matings were more frequently mentally retarded and had more malformations. Thus, there is evidence that children born from incestuous unions may be handicapped.

Is sexual abuse continued from generation to generation? There is strong evidence that it is. Summit and Kryso see it being passed on this way:

> Just as abused children are at risk of becoming abusing parents, sexually abused girls are at risk of selecting an abusive partner and failing to protect their children from intrusion.

Why would a woman who had been sexually abused as a child select a mate who would abuse her children? Several factors play a part in this selection. All of us, to some extent, use the parenting we received as children as a model for how we parent our children. If that model was abusive, we are more likely to be abusive. In addition, we are likely to choose as a partner someone who has a similar view of parenting and how husbands and wives relate. Most of us pick someone for a partner who sees the world pretty much the same as we do. We can relate because we see the world from a similar standpoint.

So a woman who has a parenting model and view of the world that includes a father turning to his child for sex may well marry a man with a similar picture. She may not like such behavior by a man or approve of it, but that is the kind of person to whom she knows how to relate. Her motivation in picking the spouse she does is usually outside her awareness.

As one woman who had been sexually abused said:

> I believe my mother was sexually abused to have married my father who abused me. I also believe that if I didn't deal with where I was with men and my anger toward men that I would have picked a man who would have abused my children because those were the only kinds of men that I knew how to relate to.

Another factor that plays a part in incest being continued through the generations is the struggle to be cared for, the emotional competition, that we have already described. The daughter who is used sexually by her father loses out, so to speak, to her parents in the competition for nurturing. The parents may get their needs met, but she does not. She grows up thinking, "I'll marry someone who will love me and take care of me." Unfortunately, she picks someone who is also looking to be cared for and who shares her confusion about sex and love. When the mates fail to meet each other's expectations, they both turn to the child for nurturing, and the cycle repeats itself.

There is much evidence from our own 112 cases and from cases reported in the literature that incest is passed from one generation to the next. For example, Louise was sexually abused by both her stepbrother and her father, and Louise's mother had had a child by her own father. Katie's mother had been abused by her father, and her grandmother had had a child by her great-grandfather.

There is also another way in which the future generations can be affected by incest. Parents who were sexually abused as children are more likely to be physically and emotionally abusive to their children. Evidence of this problem is seen in research done at Cedar House, a model therapeutic shelter for physically abusing families in Long Beach, California. Ninety percent of the mothers seeking help there for physical child abuse had been sexually abused as children. Some of the young children of these mothers were currently involved in sexual relationships with the man in the house or with adult neighbors or friends. In our experience in working with physically abusive families, we have also found sexual abuse in their backgrounds, but not in as great a percentage as was found at Cedar House.

In summary, the victims of incest are not only those involved in the actual act but their children and their children's children as well.

No Negative Consequences?

Is it possible that there are people who experience no negative consequences from incest? There are such people, but how many no one knows.

Research shows that although most children will suffer consequences from incestuous relations, some will escape with little or no apparent effect. For example, one study of 26 girls who were involved in incest with their fathers found that 23 percent showed no apparent ill effects. The remaining 77 percent were either promiscuous, frigid, or neurotic.

A few studies have suggested that the majority of girls who were involved in incest or were sexually assaulted experienced no lingering consequences. Dr. Richard Sarles, at the University of Maryland School of Medicine, gave a series of psychological tests to girls who had been involved in incest. The results showed that, with the exception of evidence of feelings of frustration, the girls' responses on the tests were not too different from those normally expected from adolescent girls.

In 1937, Drs. Laura Bender and Abraham Blau studied 54 cases of sexual assault on girls. Of those 54, 46 seemed to be none the worse for the experience; many had married. Of those who had suffered consequences, one became psychotic, one hysterical, one "nervous," and three became prostitutes. The important point to note here is that many of these girls were not the victims of sexual abuse by a family member. With the few girls who had experienced incest, the consequences were far from benign.

Research has shown that the length of time required for a child to get over the emotional shock of having sexual experience with an adult is significantly related to whether or not the child knew the adult. If the offender was known to the child, as he certainly would be in the case of incest, the shock was greater. In one study, of those girls who said the shock was more or less permanent in its effect, more than two-thirds knew the adult.

TYPE OF INCEST AND CONSEQUENCE

As we said earlier, the age at which a child becomes involved in incest affects the severity of the impact, just as does the fact of whether the sex occurs with a stranger or with a relative.

Does the type of incest affect the severity of the consequences? There is some evidence to suggest that incest

involving intercourse has the most lingering impact. However, in our studies, we found that nonintercourse incest
seemed to have just as serious an outcome. Again, it is
important to note that it is not the sexual activity itself that
is the problem but the kind of disturbed and troubled relationships in the family that lead to the incest.

This is not to say that child rape and what Summit and
Kryso call "perverse incest," forcing the child into all kinds
of kinky sex, are not going to be more damaging than
incidental sexual contacts that may be carried too far. Any
incest that consistently involves force or takes on the character of orgies, with parents and outsiders alike participating, is destined to be destructive to the child. But these are
not the common types of incest. The most common types,
as we have noted, involve no force and may or may not
include intercourse.

SUMMARY

It is impossible to know precisely the extent of harm that
results from incest, regardless of kind. One reason is that
large numbers of children of incestuous families have not
been systematically followed to see what problems they
have in adulthood. Also, there have been no studies that
match children from incestuous families with children from
similar socioeconomic and family backgrounds but where
no incest has occurred. Finally, emotional abuse is something that can never be fully measured, and we believe that
virtually every child who experienced sex with a parent is
emotionally abused.

There undoubtedly are people who have been through
incestuous relationships and have become successful, functioning adults, just as there are physically abused children
who have done so. Nevertheless, this fact does not recom-

mend sexual and physical abuse as the way to parent children.

Some people, and even organizations, have taken the position that since we do not know for sure what harm results from incest, it is best not to do anything about it. We stand with Summit and Kryso when they state:

> As clinicians involved in the daily tragedies of sexual abuse, we are appalled at such a nihilistic interpretation.

There is no doubt that some children will make it through the incestuous experience with fewer scars than others, just as some soldiers make it through the war with fewer wounds. Nevertheless, few people live through the experience of incest or war without some scars.

Part V

WHAT CAN BE DONE
ABOUT INCEST

On the basis of a national survey, psychologist John Wood-bury concluded that "the probability is that if incest in not taking place in your home—it is taking place on your street."

We do not know, or believe anyone else does, how much sexual abuse is occurring in homes across the country. We do know that reports are sharply increasing, as noted in the Introduction to this book, and that Dr. Wood-bury's estimate that "at least 5 percent of the population and perhaps up to 15 percent" is involved in the problem is as good as any other.

If there were 11 to 33 million cases of anything else in the country, the public outcry would be loud and long. But because the subject is sex and what goes on in the privacy of the home between parent and child there is only silence. Is the silence and inaction due to no one knowing what to do or to people believing that nothing can be done? To some extent, we believe it is. But something can be done.

In Part V, we will discuss three avenues of action: prevention, treatment, and public policy. We will discuss steps that can be taken by both the individual and the public to do something about the problem.

What individual parents can do falls into three categories: (1) what they can do for themselves to meet their own needs, (2) what they should do for the child, and (3) what they should do about parent-child sexuality.

Although no prevention of incest can occur without parents learning how to meet their own needs and the needs of the child, we will look first at parent-child sexuality since it is the area where we find the greatest ignorance and confusion.

Chapter 12

PARENT-CHILD SEXUALITY

Parent-child sexuality is not the same as parent-child sex. It pertains to the relationship that a parent has with a child given the fact that both are sexual creatures subject to stimulation, arousal, and erotic interests. It is something to be acknowledged, accepted, and dealt with.

Sexuality begins in infancy. A little boy, usually while taking a bath, discovers his penis around the age of 1. He will touch it, smile, and conclude that this is a part of the body he can return to for pleasure. A little girl discovers her vulva sometime later, either by randomly exploring her body or being guided by sensations from that region. She too will return to it for pleasure.

The capacity for female orgasm develops early. (Kinsey recorded the case of a 3-year-old girl who masturbated to orgasm regularly.) Boys cannot ejaculate until later, but there is evidence to indicate that they too are capable of climax quite young.

Babies and young children can be powerful sources of sexual stimulation to adults. Some mothers report an erotic or orgasmic response from breast feeding their babies. Others like to touch their baby boy's penis while bathing him and are fascinated by the infantile erection. Fathers are sometimes curious to see their daughters' genitals and to touch them.

Many parents enjoy snuggling under the covers with their children on a cold winter morning. In most cases, incidental sexual contacts are just that, incidental. In some cases, they grow into something more.

Few parents who get involved in incestuous relationships ever intended to have sex with their children. In the beginning, there is seldom any premeditation. For some, the physical contact between parent and child starts innocently, then begins to exceed normal limits of affection and sexual arousal takes over for both. A father, in the habit of helping his daughter with a bath, washes her genitals to the point of orgasm one day. Manual manipulation then becomes part of the routine. Next he asks the daughter to touch his genitals, manually, then orally. Finally, after weeks or months, intercourse occurs. A divorced or widowed mother takes showers with her little boy. Then she has him sleep with her. Next she is feeling his penis and having him touch her genitals. As he grows older he starts to explore her breasts as she pretends to sleep, and to press his thighs against hers.

OEDIPAL PERIOD

Two periods in a child's development are particularly critical in terms of both the child and parent being vulnerable to physical or affectionate contacts going too far. The first is the period from about age 3 to approximately 6, the so-called oedipal stage (for girls, some refer to it as the electra period). It is the time of the "family romance" or "family triangle." This is the period when little girls try to monopolize their fathers and little boys possess their mothers. They are quite seductive about it, either openly or subtly. In *Three Babies,* Deborah was showing such behavior before she was 2:

> she needs to see more of Daddy, so suddenly has decided to call for him to "Open door" at 7 A.M., wastes no time with diaper change, but proceeds to dog his heels, prompting him and imitating shaving and toothbrushing, helping him dress (holds pant legs, gets shoes, helps with shoe horn, etc.). And now eats breakfast in his lap, with smug satisfaction, begrudging him every single bite, and flirting with him. . . . In the evening, greetings are nonchalant until he is settled, and then she monopolizes him in all sorts of activity, after telling Mommy to "Go way."

Ruth, at age 23 months, actively competed with her mother for Daddy's attention. Her mother reported:

> My husband, Ruth and I were having dinner in the dining room, and I went into the kitchen for something. I returned and Ruth said resentfully, "Mommy go in the kitchen. Ruthie and her husband are eating. Mommy don't sit with us."

Some children act out in play what they would like to do in real life with the parent of the opposite sex.

> Pat, who is 5, is staging a scene of his own making in his older sister's doll house. He puts the father and mother to sleep side by side in their room. He puts the boy doll to bed in the room next door. . . . he makes the boy tiptoe into the parents' room, takes the mother out of the father's bed and transfers her into his own. At this point, Pat's tune changes to "Here Comes the Bride." Then, he has the father doll get up from his bed and leave the house. And with this he hums in merry triumph, "Jingle Bells."

A number of children in this stage will climb into bed with their parents to hug and snuggle. They respond to loving contact with their whole bodies, and a father may find himself getting an erection as his little girl hugs him.

Children trust their parents to set the limits on their sexual behavior during this period. For parents to do this, they must be aware of their own potential for arousal and be prepared to deal with both themselves and their child when there is overstimulation.

Parents need to recognize that when children get sexually stimulated, they will seek outlets to express their arousal. Summit and Kryso tell of a mother in a parent-education class who expressed concern for her 5-year-old son attempting intercourse with his female playmate.

> the boy and his friend were stimulated by their habitual perusal of *Penthouse* magazine, which the parents felt should not be hidden away. The boy's sexual interests were further piqued by the mother's pleasure in sharing afternoon showers with him. The mother's obvious pregnancy also aggravated potential oedipal conflicts, as indicated by the child's question, "Mommy, when daddy did it to you before I was born, did he do it in bed or was it here in the shower?"

What separates showing a child plenty of physical affection from overstimulating the child sexually? As we have suggested, there are two criteria by which a parent can judge whether affection has spilled over into sex: (1) If the parent keeps getting an erection, turned on, or sexually aroused by what he or she is doing with the child, the line has been crossed; or (2) if the child starts having unexplained problems of sleeping, eating, and physical complaints or, like the boy in the case above, becomes preoccupied with sex, there has been too much stimulation for the child to handle.

Some parents are so intent on avoiding sexual "hang-ups" in their children that they overstimulate them with sights and scenes of sex. Summit and Kryso also describe a sex counselor who views sexual inhibitions as our greatest social problem.

His solution to the problem was to set up a laboratory of sex education at home. He invited his young son and daughter to watch him and his wife in various sexual activities, and then gave them permission to play with each other in the privacy of their own room. The man expressed pride that his family was so free of sexual hang-ups.

Although sexual activity is not something for a child to watch his parents engage in, it is important for the child to see his mother and father do other things together and to share a happy relationship. If there is open strife or the child senses a rift, the boy or girl may well attempt to widen the breach so he or she can have the parent of the opposite sex for himself or herself. A husband may be unhappy with his spouse but he does not have to encourage his daughter to take her place. A parent needs to make it plain that a mother or father is not an eligible partner for a child.

During the oedipal period, the child may actively court the parent of the opposite sex and see the parent as an eligible partner. This is not the time for a parent to respond to the child's seductiveness or to turn to the child to make up for lack of attention from one's spouse.

APPROACHING ADOLESCENCE

The second critical period comes when a daughter is approaching adolescence and is testing her feminine wiles and ways on her father. She is trying to prepare herself to relate sexually and socially to males outside the home. She needs the support of her parents as she struggles with her new emerging womanhood and sexuality. She is vulnerable to sexual responses from the father.

The father, as we have seen, is vulnerable during this period because of the stresses and strains of approaching midlife and his yearning to recapture the vitality and romance of his youth. He may interpret the flirtatiousness of the budding young woman who is his daughter as an invitation to regain his lost dreams.

We agree with Summit and Kryso on what fathers need to do during this period.

> A father should be harmless to flirt with. He should be approving, admiring, and responsive to her growing sexual attraction, and he should provide a controlled, self-limited prototype of the sensual experience she will develop with other men as an adult.

The mother needs to provide the daughter with a model of a feminine behavior and to share in defining the limits for the "prototype romance" that the daughter carries on with the father. The daughter trusts the parents to set the limits and stand by them.

> Incestuous activity begins when the father needs to bend those limits and the mother chooses to ignore them.

As we have seen, the limits are bent and ignored when the daughter is invited to take over the mother's role and the father starts to treat her as a wife.

> The daughter may have assumed many of the more ingratiating aspects of the wife's role: she greets him fondly after a miserable day at work, puts his food on the table, and entertains him at dinner. After she tucks the younger children into bed, she may pour him a drink and nestle beside him watching television. . . .
>
> Just as the man is flattered and stimulated by his daughter's attentions, the girl is at first gratified by his more open affection. It is not her place to refuse her father, and she lacks the experience or the information to recognize all the implications of his increasing arousal.

During this period of his daughter's development, the father is faced with continuing to give her affection, to touch and hold her, without responding to subtle invitations to exceed the limits of physical contact. French kissing and feeling her breasts and legs are the kinds of contact that exceed the limits and lead to more serious sexual activity.

Sometimes the inappropriate contact comes not from the father but from a grandfather or other relative. One woman, featured in the film *Incest: The Victim Nobody Believes*, recalls that her grandfather would French kiss her and feel her up while her father and mother stood by smiling. She felt confused over what was being done. She did not like it, it did not seem right, but here were her parents smiling approvingly. What was being done and what was not right was that she was being taken advantage of with her parents' sanction.

Other behavior that distresses daughters and may lead to more serious sexual involvement is "household voyeurism." This consists of a father using mirrors or standing outside his daughter's bedroom watching her undress. A few fathers parade nude in front of their daughter, offering a clear invitation to have sex.

Some fathers deal with their daughter's emerging adult sexuality by withdrawing and rejecting. They are so threatened by her attraction that they stop touching and giving her hugs. She is deprived of an important source of affection and emotional support at a time when she needs both.

In every stage of the child's psychosexual development, she needs to learn that having sexual feelings, including sexual feelings toward her father, is part of being human. Feelings are not right or wrong, they are just there, to be accepted and understood. Acting on feelings is a separate matter. Learning the difference between feelings and actions is one of the child's chief tasks and requires persistent guidance from parents.

Do's and Dont's for Parents

For a child to have maximum opportunity to grow and develop, free from sexual entanglements and confusion of roles with the parent, certain guidelines are advisable in the area of parent-child sexuality. As we have seen, this is an area concerned with the sexual stimulation and arousal that naturally occur between a child and parent living together.

Many parents, following the good models of their own childhood, "automatically" provide the kind of parenting necessary for the healthy growth of their children. But even these parents sometimes lose their way and become confused. For parents who have no good models to follow or get confused over the issue of sexuality, a set of guidelines as presented here seems particularly useful for heading off problems before they occur.

1.   Be aware that a child has sexual feelings toward his or her parent and the parent has sexual feelings toward the child. These may express themselves at any age in a variety of ways, but they can be visibly seen during the time of the family romance when the child is approximately 3 to 6 years old and again when the child approaches adolescence.

2.   Don't sleep with the child. We are not talking about a child climbing into bed between his parents on a Sunday morning. We are referring to a regular routine of a parent being in the same bed with a child night after night and the child developing a sensual dependency—a dependency to touch and feel the parent's body. Such a sleeping arrangement also is likely to give rise to a sexual stimulation on the part of both parent and child. In times of stress, when the parent or child particularly needs warmth and support, sex becomes a means for attempting to meet these needs.

3.   Don't overstimulate the child by walking around the house nude, by continuing to take showers or baths

with the child, by performing sex in front of the child, or by French kissing the child.

The parents of a 9-year-old boy took him to a psychologist, concerned that, among other things, he was preoccupied with sex. The psychologist reported:

> I inquired about the sexual atmosphere in the family and found that the mother, who prided herself on having out-grown mid-Victorian taboos about sex, often went around the house in bra and panties. The mother was surprised when I suggested she discontinue this because her boy was finding it too stimulating. "Surely he doesn't notice any-thing special about that, does he?" she asked. Her more realistic husband answered: "Honey, it turns me on, and I'll bet it turns him on, too." He was right.

The time for parents to let the child see them in the nude and to become aware of the adult anatomy is early, when the child is a toddler. This is also the time to start answering the child's questions about babies and sex. When children reach preschool age, many have started to develop a sense of privacy about their bodies and they are uncomfortable with nudity, either on the parent's part or their own part. Other children develop this sense of privacy a little later. Their sense of privacy should not be violated.

4.   Be aware of the sexual aspects of body-contact games played by parent and child. Just as sexual tensions can be released through romping and wrestling, the same games can heighten sexual arousal when they go on too long and lead to overstimulation.

5.   Don't go to the child with complaints and criti-cisms about one's spouse or encourage the child's fantasies of capturing mother or father for himself or herself. The corollary to this is not to use the child as a substitute for one's spouse. The son should not become mother's "little man" or "man of the house" and the daughter should not become her father's "woman" or "best girlfriend." Such

role confusion and pseudomaturity on the part of the child are characteristic of incestuous families, as we have discussed in Part III.

6.   If two parents have drifted apart in terms of having sex with each other, or one has cut the other off, the answer is not to turn to a child to make up the deficit. Go to a marriage counselor or a family therapist. Masturbate more or find someone else (adult), if necessary, but don't take on a child as a sex partner.

7.   Encourage the child to have whatever feelings he or she wants and to express them to the parents. Teach the child the difference between feelings and actions, between feeling angry and hitting, between feeling sexually stimulated and acting on that feeling.

8.   Don't betray the child's trust. A child places trust in the parent to provide protection, approval, and affection. If a parent offers sex as the means of giving the child attention, the child will feel confused and betrayed.

If a schoolgirl runs to her father to show him her good report card and he invites her to sit in his lap, she does not expect him to throw the card on the floor and become sexual with her. If a father does this (see Chapter 11), he is only teaching his daughter a distrust that she is likely to carry with her for years to come.

A daughter being used to satisfy a father's needs soon starts feeling exploited. As we saw in the chapter on consequences of incest, such a feeling can play havoc in a daughter's later relationships with men.

9.   Give the child plenty of physical affection but be aware of the line between "loving sensuality" and "abusive sexuality." As we have noted, if the parent keeps getting sexually aroused from the physical affection or the child starts having unexplained physical problems, the line has been crossed.

When the parent is loving the child for being himself or herself, and expressing that love with kisses, hugs, and touching, that is being physically affectionate. When the parent is being physically intimate with the child to meet his or her own needs for closeness, warmth, stimulation, nurturing, love, or sex, that is being sexually abusive and exploiting the child.

Some fathers, as we have noted, have no intention of getting sexual with their daughters but are turned on by her acting flirty and seductive, just as her body is beginning to take the shape of a woman. Instead of recognizing the flirtatiousness as the daughter's way to test her emerging identity on the closest and safest male around, he flirts back and responds to it as an invitation for sex. In a healthy relationship, the father doesn't flirt back and doesn't use the child to meet his own needs.

Chapter 13

WHAT PARENTS SHOULD DO
ABOUT THEIR OWN NEEDS

The father or mother who lets parent-child sexuality spill over into parent-child sex is likely to be the mother or father who has not learned how to meet his or her needs. What are these needs? Sex is one of them, but only one. The biological need for sex is one of the easiest to fulfill. Prostitutes and pickups, for men and women, can be quickly found in any city. Masturbation, though it may not completely satisfy the need, is even easier.

So what is the problem? Why bring one's own child into the act if the problem is satisfying the need for sex? The reason, as we have pointed out earlier, is that incest has very little to do with satisfying the biological need for sex. What it does have to do with is an attempt to fulfill the needs for closeness, warmth, stimulation, nurturing and love.

People who commit incest never learned how to make friends, to get close to other people, to bring stimulating persons and activities into their lives, to ask for what they need in terms of nurturing. In short, they never learned how to get positive strokes, those units of recognition and acknowledgment that we all must have to maintain any sense of well-being. They are stroke-deprived.

When stress (see Part III) comes into the life of a stroke-deprived person, he becomes desperate for attention and some source of caring and warmth. Even if he knew how to meet these needs in a nonsexual way, which he does not, by now he requires intense strokes, and sex is the only thing he knows how to get. A daughter becomes the most accessible candidate and the person most likely not to reject him. It makes sense, then, for a parent who wants to have a healthy sex life for himself and his daughter to take care of his own needs first so that he will not have to turn to her to satisfy them.

How can he do this? The first step toward getting needs met is to learn to ask for what is needed. When people go to a restaurant, they do not expect the waiter to read their minds and automatically bring what they want. They tell him what they want.

In marriage, though, many people expect their spouses to read their minds and provide them with what they need. We often find that a wife needs to be told that her husband loves her, but she won't ask him to say it. She believes that if he really did love her, she would not have to ask. A stroke is a stroke regardless of whether it is solicited or comes spontaneously. We teach people to ask for strokes when they need them. If they get turned down, then they can find someone else who will give them what they ask for.

Different people have different interpretations of what love is and what kind of acts or behavior by their spouse mean they are loved. A marriage counselor told one couple:

220 THE BROKEN TABOO

The only way you will ever learn what each of you thinks of as a loving act is by expressing it. Marian, you have to *tell* Ray that flowers, or champagne, or something you would not get for yourself is what makes you feel loved. And, Ray, what kind of gift would mean love to you?

Ray's answer was, "You know those dead trees in the back yard, Marian? How about a chain saw?"

A willingness, then, to speak up and share is an essential step toward getting needs met and toward building close relations. Emotional closeness is something that does not just come naturally but requires two people to reach out to each other and share. People who use sex as the only way to get close are usually people who do not know how to get close in any other way. They are alienated emotionally.

Closeness, or intimacy, comes in a variety of forms and, as Marcia Lasswell and Norman Lobsenz point out in *No-Fault Marriage,* it develops from the willingness of two people to do such things as:

1. Confide in each other—tell innermost thoughts and feelings.
2. Share trivialities—tell the small, routine, little things.
3. Be intimate in small ways—read aloud, give a small but unexpected present, do a chore for the other person.
4. Be verbal—put feelings into words.
5. Be physically affectionate—touch, stroke, comfort.

If a husband needs some nurturing after a hard day at the office, he needs to say so and ask for what he wants. We suggest that people ask for a backrub when they need some nurturing and caretaking. Backrubs are "tissue" strokes that help meet nurturing needs.

People have stroke banks that they need to keep well-filled. If they let the banks get depleted, they are not meeting their needs. If they make sure they get nurturing, stimulating, or closeness strokes deposited in their banks every day, they will keep their needs met. They won't have to turn to a child for sex in an attempt to make up a deficit.

What else can people do to meet their needs? They can make a contract with themselves to meet their neighbors, to make a new friend, to ask people over, to give a party, to take a trip, to take up a hobby, to start jogging, or to join a health club. There is now a club or organization for every conceivable interest from hiking and biking to wine collecting. Each provides an opportunity to get around people, to make friends, to do something stimulating, to cultivate closeness. None of these things will magically meet everyone's needs. Needs are not met in one fell swoop, once and for all. Meeting needs is a matter of keeping the stroke bank full and this requires getting strokes every day. To get strokes requires some giving.

For people who are shy, inhibited, introverted or just plain don't know how to ask for what they need, we teach assertiveness training. There are a number of good books now on how to be assertive and some on how to overcome shyness. Reading these is a step toward learning how to reach out.

Some people seem to get plenty of strokes, but still they end up doing something that is sure-fire evidence that they are not getting their needs met. They may be community leaders, in the limelight with lots of attention and recognition. William K., in Chapter 4, was like this. A number of fathers who engage in incest have responsible jobs that bring them a lot of strokes.

But something is missing; they are close to no one. They keep people at arm's length and experience no closeness strokes. There is no real warmth in their lives. They may be at the top in their careers, but they use their jobs to keep distant from other people. Sex is the only way they know to experience closeness and that is simply a physical,

not emotional, closeness. In their relentless pursuit of satisfying their elusive needs, they may turn to a daughter.

Learning how to meet needs is an essential part of
preventing incestuous behavior, but it is only half the story.
The other half is learning how to handle stress. Stress
threatens or interferes with needs, so one big aspect of
getting needs met is dealing effectively with stress.

STRESS, ITS CAUSES AND CONSEQUENCES

In Part III, on "Why Incest Occurs," we saw that stress
from excessive change puts families under constant pressure and contributes to parents losing control of their behavior. Excessive change (see list of change events on
Pages 114–115) is not the only source of stress for people.
Stress also comes from "nonevents," the failure of people
to gain what they seek or believe they should have, and
from the situations and circumstances in which they find
themselves. Effective stress management or relief ad-
dresses all three of these sources of stress.

What is stress? Stress is any demand, force, or pressure
that requires a person to make an adjustment. It may be
physical stress such as rain that drives a person indoors,
cold that requires him to bundle up, noise that interrupts
his sleep. It may be emotional stress such as separation
from loved ones or death. It may be behavioral stress that
comes from what a person does such as overeating and
smoking. Stress per se is not bad. A certain amount of
stress is necessary to live. We have atmospheric pressure
on us each moment we live. Without it, we would die. We
need other kinds of stress to stimulate our growth, to challenge us, and keep us from getting bored.

What is harmful is too much stress, excessive stress. It
produces inside us a feeling of distress. When stress is only
moderate, we feel tension and enough discomfort to take

action on whatever is causing the stress. When stress is excessive, we become distressed and flounder or lash out.

The consequences of excessive stress may be physical, emotional, or social. Some people have a heart attack, acquire some form of cancer, get ulcers or colitis, have headaches or arthritis. Others get depressed, suffer chronic anxiety, hostility, guilt, or shame. Still others deal with the excessive stress by acting out in such ways as committing incest or physical child abuse, becoming alcoholic and assaultive, or battering wives. A few people express excessive stress in all three areas: the physical, emotional and social.

The sources of stress are external and internal, meaning that stress comes from both outside us and inside us. When both sources are at work then we have excessive stress. As we have seen, the external comes in the form of undergoing multiple changes. The external may also be in the form of chronic stress from a bad marriage, inability to parent or manage children, or a deadend job. More crucial than the external sources of stress is the internal, how the person is his or her own source of stress. When this occurs, we call it self-stressing. Self-stressing is caused by how a person views and responds to the events and changes in his life, situations, and circumstances.

Specifically, self-stressing is caused by (1) "awfulizing" —viewing events, situations, or circumstances as catastrophic, horrible, terrible, unbearable; (2) "shoulding"— demanding (usually silently in the form of self-talk and thoughts) that others should do or be different, that oneself should do or be different, or that the world should be different (fair, just, easy); or (3) overgeneralizing—condemning oneself or others on the basis of a single performance or one set of behaviors or traits ("I'm a failure" or "I'm worthless because I got fired" or "I didn't get promoted" or "I let my family down").

All people carry on an internal dialog with themselves. Most people think in this way, by self-talk. Thoughts are molecular events in the brain that have chemical consequences for the body. When people say demanding and stressful things to themselves, when they are awfulizing, shoulding, or overgeneralizing, they are just as much putting their mind and body under pressure as they would if they were facing a truly threatening external source of stress, such as having a gun pointed at them.

By viewing events as catastrophic or demanding that the world or people be different or by condemning themselves, they are turning on all the chemical juices that the body has for "fight" or "flight." Blood pressure goes up, cholesterol rises, stress hormones (adrenalin and noradrenalin) are released, muscles contract, arteries tighten, blood sugar rises, corticosteroids increase, brain enzymes are altered, and a host of other chemicals course through the body (cortisol, testosterone, throxine, insulin). It is no wonder that people feel distressed when they have their body bathed in chemicals and they are stewing in their own juices. Bad and distressful feelings are chemically based, and the chemicals come as a result of excessive stress, principally self-stressing.

As we noted, different people will express their distress in different ways. In learning how to manage excessive stress, people learn not only to prevent abusive behavior but also physical illness and emotional disorder.

Techniques of Managing Stress

So what can be done about excessive stress and self-stressing? What are the techniques for dealing with it, both for preventing excessive stress and handling it if it does occur? We have a 10-step program we teach people.

STEP 1.   Get rid of the "language of stress." Stop awfulizing, shoulding, overgeneralizing—"aso-ing," for short.

The language of stress consists of demands and commands given to the body by thought and self-talk. Since excessive stress is caused by internal stress added to external, the starting point for managing stress and preventing distress is to change the internal dialogue the person is carrying on. This means editing out (1) all awfuls, terribles, horribles, "I can't stand it"; (2) all shoulds, oughts, musts, and (3) all use of never and always, as in "I never do anything right" or "I always fail, lose, get the short end," etc.

STEP 2.   Adopt a new self-care vocabulary. Tone down the internal dialogue so that it is less stressful and more accurate. When people awfulize, they are insisting that something is completely bad. As Psychologist Albert Ellis points out, nothing is completely bad unless it is being slowly tortured to death. What people really mean is that something is very sad or that it is very irritating, frustrating, deplorable, inconvenient, disappointing, unfortunate. When they say something is horrible or they can't stand it, they really mean they don't like what happened. This is not only more accurate to say to oneself, it is less stressful as internal dialogue.

STEP 3.   Do daily exercise; give release to the "fight" and "flight" chemicals stirred up in the body by running, swimming, or cycling, at least 20 minutes each day, or playing racketball or squash, which are a good catharsis for anger and hostility. We recommend aerobic exercise, running, swimming, cycling, or brisk walking because it not only allows release of fight and flight chemicals but also conditions the heart and interrupts self-stressing. It is impossible to keep awfulizing and shoulding while running.

A number of psychologists and psychiatrists, in addition to ourselves, are runners and recommend running as part of therapy for clients. Some therapists actually have their clients run with them during the treatment hour. We attend professional meetings where there are running workshops as part of the program, and it is becoming clear that aerobic exercise is going to be adopted by more and more therapists to treat psychological and emotional problems. We have found it to be particularly beneficial for someone who is depressed.

STEP 4.   Learn relaxation exercises. Another way to relieve the distress that people feel when they are under excessive stress is to relax the body and mind. Again, the effect is to interrupt the awfulizing-demanding cycle and to engage in a pleasant distraction.

The physiological benefits are that the body loses its tenseness, aches and pains are relieved, and the mind clears. Gaining a state of relaxation requires training and practice just as adopting a self-care vocabulary does. Any number of relaxation exercises are available. The following is a brief one that we use and teach to parents.

> Get in a comfortable position. If you can lie down, fine. If not, sit in a position that is comfortable. For most people this means both feet are flat on the floor, legs and ankles uncrossed, arms uncrossed and hands resting on each thigh. Don't hold anything or have anything in your lap.
>
> Now close your eyes. Take a deep breath and hold it. Let it out very slowly. Now take another deep breath and hold it. Let it out very slowly. Do that a third time.
>
> Now we invite you to breathe this way three more times, but also engage the mind as well as the body in relaxing. To do this, simply say to yourself each time, "I am relaxed." As you inhale slowly, say the words, "I . . . am. . . ." Then, after holding your breath and as you let it out slowly, say the word, "re—lax—ed." Okay. Take a deep breath and say to yourself, "I . . . am. . . ." Now, as you exhale, say: "re—lax —ed."
>
> Do that two more times on your own.

It is impossible for the body to stay uptight and tense when this kind of breathing is practiced. It is impossible for the mind to stay stressed when thoughts are diverted to something positive or pleasant and the "aso-ing" (awfulizing, shoulding, overgeneralizing) cycle is interrupted.

Other relaxation exercises divert the mind in other ways. Some people prefer to say the word, calm, to themselves as they exhale. Some picture the word CALM in big letters. Dr. Herbert Benson of Harvard Medical School has a method that calls for the person to keep silently repeating the word "one" as the person exhales. In transcendental meditation and yoga, mantras are used, sounds that a person repeats or hums out loud.

The breathing exercise can be used anywhere. It can be done with the eyes open, and we recommend it for people to use in traffic, at work, and at home. A longer relaxation exercise that we also use, and have made a regular part of each therapy session with parents, starts with the deep breathing and then goes into imaging. Each person is asked to picture going to the beach on a nice, warm, pleasant day. A few white fluffy clouds float overhead; the blue sky stretches to an unbroken horizon; the water is clear and blue and the waves come rolling in on the shore. All is quiet except for the occasional sounds of sea gulls. The air is fresh and there is a slight salty spray blowing in. The sand is white and clean and warm, and the person is asked to lie down on it.

We then invite each person to go over each part of his body, from the top of his head to the tip of his toes, and let the feeling of relaxation wash away all his tension, all his aches and pains. After relaxing each part, we then invite the person to experience even deeper relaxation by picturing himself at the top of 10 steps. The person is asked to go down the steps one at a time, using our voice as a "handrail," and as he goes down, he experiences deeper and deeper relaxation. At the bottom, we invite the person just to enjoy the feeling of deep relaxation for a few moments. Then we guide the person back up each step one at a time as he becomes progressively alert but remains relaxed.

This is an exercise that people learn to do on their own. It does require practice, just as the short breathing exercise also does. Our experience is that when people practice the exercise, which only takes about 15 minutes, at least once a week, they experience less stress.

Some people prefer other images besides the beach. They may like the woods or mountains or a quiet valley. Any place that a person can picture that represents relaxation will work. Preferably, it is a place that the person has experienced and enjoyed. The mind can flash to that place instantaneously, and if a person will follow through with a relaxation exercise around the image, the effects of stress will melt away.

STEP 5.   Know nutrition. Be diet conscious. Eat right. As we have noted, people add to their stess by stressing their bodies, by eating too much and the wrong food. Junk food falls into this category; many snacks and soft drinks do also. Refined white sugar is one of the most common additives and may stress the body. Evidence implicating it in disease and physical disorder continues to mount. Yet people in the United States consume an average of 126 pounds of sugar a year.

STEP 6.   Develop a social support system; don't depend on strokes from just one other person or any single source but have multiple sources. A person with a social support system is one who feels loved, cared for, valued, and needed.

There is ample research now demonstrating that social support protects people from the consequences of stress coming from hospitalization, surgery, loss of job, bereavement, retirement, and old age.

Having social ties—friends, family, involvement with other people—buffers the effects of undergoing multiple changes in a relatively short period of time. Social support reduces the chances of suicide and depression.

Undoubtedly, good relationships with a number of people provide a buffer against stress. One reason this is true is that when people are experiencing excessive stress and they have someone they can share their problems with, they tend to stop awfulizing and begin saying more positive things to themselves, such as:

> Well, here is someone who went through the same thing and knows what it is like. He survived, so I guess I can, too.

> It's good to know that I've got someone who will back me up and give me some assistance in this crisis. It's not so bad after all.

STEP 7.   Learn to manage change. As we saw in Part III on "Why Incest Occurs," excessive change can wear a person down to the point that he loses control of his physical health, emotional health, or his behavior. All change, good or bad, is stressful and requires adjustment. Techniques for managing change include the following.

A.   Make a weekly check of any changes going on. Take the "Schedule of Recent Experience" (see Chapter 7) and keep count of the change units being accumulated.

B.   Recognize that when more than 150 change units are accumulated in a year, chances of getting physically sick, having an emotional problem or losing control of one's behavior start increasing. Fifty percent of the people who score 200 to 300 units will fall into one of these three problem categories. For those scoring 300 or more, 80 percent will have trouble.

C.   When it becomes clear that the change-unit total for the year is likely to exceed 150, start postponing or rejecting changes and make as few new adjustments as possible. Do not follow one major change with another. A divorce (73 points) or serious illness (53) should not be followed by something as major as a job change (36) or move to a new city (a minimum of 20). Often, people bring unnecessary stress and change into their lives because they do not say "no" enough.

One of the parents we worked with was a woman with six children at home and all the stress anyone needs. A friend had to go into a hospital for a checkup and asked her to take care of her three children, two of whom the woman knew were very difficult to manage. She took the children in, and felt very angry and used when neither her friend nor her friend's husband called to see how things were going nor offered to buy groceries for the children. Meanwhile, the children would not behave and the woman's stress level kept going higher and higher. All of this could have been avoided simply by saying "no."

D.   Be aware that even small changes add to a person's stress. Make only changes that are necessary or will be definitely beneficial once adjustment is completed.

E.   Build "stability zones." The more change people subject themselves to, the more important it is that they have certain areas of their lives that are stable, such as in social support systems. Stable areas require no new adjustments. They are predictable and comfortable. They help offset the effects of excessive change.

Stability zones may be built around holding on to the same old jacket for years, keeping a car past its prime, refusing to take up every new fad. More importantly, stability zones are made up of keeping in touch with old friends, having sustained relationships with parents, maintaining a good marriage. Some people seem to thrive on change and can never get enough of it. A closer look at their lives, though, reveals some carefully-developed stability zones. Alvin Toffler, in *Future Shock,* tells of a man who

> has changed jobs at a mind-staggering rate, has moved his family 13 times in 18 years, travels extensively, rents cars, uses throw-away products, prides himself on leading the neighborhood in trying out new gadgets, and generally lives in a restless whirl of transience, newness and diversity. Once more, however, a second look reveals significant stability zones in his life: a good, tightly woven relationship with his wife of 19 years; continuing ties with his parents; old college friends interspersed with the new acquaintances.

F.   Cling to useful habits; a habit is a routine that is done automatically, requiring no new thought or adjustment. It is another form of a stability zone. Habits help neutralize change.

G.   Observe rituals. Rituals usually involve other people, which is good, and may take on the character of events. But the events are predictable and require no new behavior. They are something that can be counted on and looked forward to. It is important for societies, just as for individuals, to observe rituals. They are part of the glue that holds us together. Many families have rituals: the celebration of birthdays, anniversaries, doing things together at certain times of the year on certain occasions.

STEP 0.   Learn to think and make decisions only when it is necessary. Thoughts and decisions are energy. They require effort. Too much information coming in, too much to remember, too many decisions to make are forms of stress.

A certain amount of cognitive and decisional stress is necessary and good. But too much leads to overload and malfunction. One technique for dealing with this type of stress is to write things down instead of trying to remember them. Dr. Hans Selye, president of the International Institute of Stress in Montreal, observes:

> trying to remember too many things is certainly one of the major sources of psychologic stress. I make a conscious effort to forget immediately all that is unimportant and to jot down data of possible value. . . .

A technique for dealing with decisional stress is to ask someone else to do the deciding when the point of overload has been reached. This takes us back to learning to ask for what we need. If we come in from a day of being overloaded with decisions, we can explain our plight and ask our spouse to take over, to decide what to have for dinner or where to go or what to do.

It is also important for a family to designate quiet havens for its members, a private place in the house where a person can go to get away from further stress or stimulation. This should not be a hole for a person to crawl into for indefinite periods but simply a room or corner where all overload is avoided for the time being, where all noise, decisions, new information, even conversation can be escaped temporarily.

STEP 9.   Cultivate a sense of humor and ways to have fun; self-stressing is rooted in taking things too seriously. People who practice self-stressing overexaggerate the significance of problems and take life too seriously.

People who can laugh at themselves and find humor in life stay clear of a major source of stress. Humor helps a person see events, situations, circumstances, and crises more realistically and keep from defining them as life-and-death issues, which can only lead to distress.

We give "homework assignments" to parents to have fun. Some try to tell us that they do not know what to do that is fun. Everyone has had fun at some time in life doing something. We get people to think back to what they used to enjoy, then ask them to start doing it again. It is particularly important for people who have got themselves depressed.

STEP 10.   Plan and preadjust to keep from getting caught unprepared and off guard. New situations are stressful and, as noted in Step 8, they require ad hoc, unprogrammed decisions that can take a lot out of a person. When a new situation or change is coming up, find people who have had the same or similar experience and get their advice and counsel. This is called anticipatory guidance. Expectant mothers do it all the time. They ask experienced mothers what pregnancy and parenthood are all about and they read books. They prepare themselves for what is coming. They pre-adjust. Any anticipated event can be similarly planned for, whether it is moving to a new city, changing to another job, retiring, or getting a divorce.

We use this technique in group therapy for parents. Someone in the group has information or experience that is useful to someone else who is thinking about making a change or experiencing a certain event. It is part of managing change (see Step 7) in advance.

SUMMARY

Any prevention of incestuous behavior, as well as other problem behavior in the family, must start with parents learning to meet their needs and learning how to handle stress, which interferes with the fulfillment of needs.

As we have noted, when people get under excessive stress, they often lose control and do things they normally would never do. Learning how to keep the amount of stress in one's life to a manageable level, then, is an important step toward prevention. This is not to say that learning to manage stress, by itself, is the answer to incest any more than it is the solution to physical abuse of children or any of the other problems that people under pressure inflict on others and themselves. It is simply one factor to be aware of—and to do something about.

Other factors, such as meeting one's needs in healthy ways, must also be addressed. Some of these factors, as we have suggested, may require professional help—counseling or psychotherapy—as a preventive measure.

Chapter 14

WHAT THE PARENT NEEDS TO DO
FOR THE CHILD

We have seen that the first thing that parents can do to assure healthy relations with their children is to take care of their own needs so they will not turn to their kids to do it for them. We have also seen the importance of parents becoming informed about parent-child sexuality and the difference between physical affection and physical intimacies that become sexual.

What else do parents need to do? A look at the kinds of children (see Chapter 6) who are most vulnerable to becoming involved in incestuous relationships indicates that parents should give particular attention to:

1. Meeting the child's needs for nurturing. This means providing support, protection, and affection. A child who receives nurturing has no need to seek or substitute sexual activity in attempt to get affection and support.

2. Letting the child be a child. When children are allowed to act their age, and complete the developmental tasks of that age, they are not called on to take over func-

tions of a parent. Daughters do not make a habit of preparing meals for fathers, mixing them drinks, doing their laundry, tidying their rooms, disciplining the other kids, sleeping with fathers, becoming their sexual partners. Sons do not become the man of the house, making the decisions and doing everything a husband does, including sleeping with mother.

3. Encouraging the child to grow and separate. Just as children have needs to be nurtured, to be dependent and care-free, they also have needs to develop and separate from their parents. They cannot do this if they become enmeshed in incest. They cannot do this if the parent is threatened by the child's growing up and gives "don't leave me" messages.

The most central issue of any family is meeting people's needs both to belong and to separate, to be a part of others and to be apart from. The family that provides the conditions for both dependence and independence, belonging and separateness, has taken a big step toward preventing problems among its members, incest included.

4. Setting limits for the child. Children are not ready to be grown-up and to separate overnight, although they may insist otherwise. They may be responding to changes in their body or to peer models, they may begin acting sexual or seductive, but they expect to have limits set. They do not expect parents to accept them as mature and experienced or to respond to their sexual overtures.

5. Providing adequate stimulation. This means giving children age-appropriate games, activities, or responsibilities that are challenging and help keep them from becoming bored and unoccupied. Parents who are concerned about their child's excessive masturbation or preoccupation with sex often find that the child's life is barren in other respects.

6. Helping build the child's self-esteem. Children with low self-images do not have anything to lose by re-

sponding to sexual opportunities, taking drugs, drinking or doing anything else that takes their minds off their own insecurity, anxiety, and lack of confidence. Self-esteem can be built by a parent's offering plenty of love and affection (so the child gets a feeling of being lovable), giving no criticism of the child as a person, and providing ample opportunities for the child to acquire new skills and a sense of mastery.

7. Keeping good relations with one's spouse. This is something the parent needs to do not only for himself or herself but also for the child. When there is continued strife between spouses, the child invariably is invited to take sides or to get aligned with one parent against the other. Enmeshment with one parent and alienation from the other spell trouble for the child and can set the stage for problems such as incest. It is under such conditions that a child tends to try to "rescue" the enmeshed parent from his or her unhappiness by taking the alienated parent's place. By keeping good relations with one another, parents stay aligned with each other and avoid a blurring of generational boundaries.

Staying aligned with one another does not mean that mother and father should never disagree in front of the child. "United front" parents can create as many problems in a family as those who are always fighting. Parents who go to great lengths to avoid any disagreement with one another may start "scapegoating" the child and seeing the child as the problem, rather than their own relationship. Mother and father may insist that the daughter seduced the father, completely ignoring the fact that their own lack of love and affection for each other was a primary contributor to the problem.

8. Keeping emotionally close to the child but sexually distant. This is a corollary to previous points on providing generous affection and warmth but not using the child to meet the parent's needs, sexual or otherwise.

9.   Teaching the child a set of moral or ethical values. The best teaching comes from providing the child with a model in terms of what is right and wrong, good or bad, for parents and children to do. Religious teachings may be useful but only if they are practiced and not just preached. As we have seen, religious people may become involved in incest, despite their high principles. Principles and values often go by the board when emotional needs are not met. Principles and values also have little meaning to children unless it is explained why certain behavior is good or bad and unless they can see parents practice moral behavior in everyday life.

10.   Recognizing the rights of the child. Children for so long were regarded as property for parents to treat as they saw fit that the rights of a child are still not considered in many families. The most basic right the child has is the right to a healthy development, free of exploitation or misuse.

Chapter 15

WHAT CAN BE DONE IN TREATMENT

Prevention is what can be done about incest before it occurs. Treatment focuses on steps to be taken once an incestuous relationship occurs. The first step in treatment is knowing what to do and how to handle the problem when it is first detected. How should the discovery of incest be responded to by relatives, neighbors, police, doctors, protective service workers, parents? As we discussed in Part IV, some of the harmful consequences of incest result from inappropriate reactions to the problem, the child, and the family upon discovery. We will look now at what can be done to handle the crisis of discovery so that the child and family are helped, rather than broken, by the experience.

RESPONSE TO THE CHILD

As we have seen, disbelief is a common response to a child who reports incest. For reasons we mentioned in Part IV, a mother may simply refuse to believe that her daughter is telling the truth. Professionals, too, are all too ready to believe the child is making up the whole story. This stance of incredulity means the child is put in the position of proving that the incest took place. It also means that often the problem continues to exist because no intervention is made.

The question could be asked, "Don't some children lie in order to get back at a parent?" Yes, some do, but a child's claiming that a parent had sex with her warrants attention whether it actually happened or not. As Walters has noted:

> Very, very few children accuse a parent of being sexually involved with them. When that does occur, whether the accusation is founded or unfounded, by its very rarity we may suspect a severe disruption in the relationship between a daughter and her father or a son and his mother. It really does not matter whether the abuse occurred or not; treatment is still indicated.

What should be said to a child who has been involved in incest? It is probably easier to list what should *not* be said. "Awfulizing" will only stress the child further. True, it is sad and unfortunate that the child has been abused but telling her she is "ruined for life" or that her father "should be shot" is certainly not helpful.

Adults are likely to react as if the incestuous situation is an "emergency," with the child needing immediate attention. Since the incest has probably been going on for months or even years the "emergency" usually refers to a need to reduce the anxiety of the adults and calm their alarmist behavior before it creates more problems for the child.

The less hysteria and drama that are displayed in response to the discovery, the easier it will be for the child to open up and give more information. It is all too easy to get caught up in seeing the child as a victim and wanting to prosecute, if not persecute, the father. But this stance helps no one. The whole family is a "victim," and steps must be taken to strengthen and support the family, not traumatize it further.

The responses that are more likely to be truly helpful to the child are first, if the child says her father sexually abused her, then she is to be believed and not cross-examined. If she is lying, there is plenty of time to learn that later. At the moment she opens up to tell someone, she is asking for and needs support. Then with an attitude of trust and belief, more information—who, where, when, how—can be asked for. The second thing that the child who has been involved in incest needs to be told is that this sort of thing does happen sometimes, that it is not supposed to happen, and that it will stop. The third thing the child needs to hear is reassurance that she or he was not responsible for the incest happening, that it was her parents' job to see that it did not happen, and that they did not offer the protection they should have.

The emphasis needs to be on the fact that the child is not to be blamed, even if she participated with some willingness. At the same time, not much will be gained by playing up to the child the fact that her parents were irresponsible. The point is to help the child to stop further self-blame and guilt.

We previously discussed how the judicial process can be harmful to the child. What response can be made to mitigate the stress from legal involvement? The courts can be a valuable aid in getting reluctant family members to participate in treatment and in serving to protect the child from further harm. At the same time, the judicial process can unwittingly destroy a family that is already seriously strained, as incestuous families are. We think the most helpful involvement of the court is as a monitor and protector, not as a persecutor. Using the civil rather than criminal courts is one way this can be accomplished.

However, if criminal charges are filed, investigators and authorities can help by being aware of and responding to the child's feelings of fear and embarrassment. Arranging for a child to testify in the judge's chambers instead of in open court is one way the stress for the child can be lessened.

In Israel, a social work orientation is used instead of traditional police investigation in cases of sexual abuse of a child. "Youth examiners" are charged with the double responsibility of creating an aura of reassurance and eliciting the facts of the offense. After assessing how the child has been affected by the abuse, the youth examiner determines whether or not the offender will be prosecuted and whether or not the child will be permitted to testify. A system like this would require legislative changes to implement in this country, but it serves as a model for how the judicial procedure can become a treatment process and how the needs of the sexually abused child can be given priority. Regardless of who is involved, police, physicians, or protective service workers, priority should be given to protecting the child from further emotional, as well as physical, abuse.

RESPONSE TO THE PARENTS

As we have indicated, people react to incest by either denying it could happen or expressing outrage and horror at the offending parent. A certain amount of anger is natural when one hears about an adult who sexually exploits any child, particularly his own child. However, continuing outrage probably has its roots in other feelings, such as wanting to deny that parents can have sexual feelings toward their own offspring.

People prefer to believe we have only nurturing and platonic feelings toward children and that children are sexless creatures. As we discussed in Chapter 12, children are not sexless, and parents do have sexual feelings about their children.

One way to deny these sexual feelings in ourselves is to regard the incestuous parents as completely different from ourselves and be enraged by what they have done. Thus many people, professionals included, look upon these parents as sick, crazy, or maniacs. A few are, as we discussed in Part II, but they make up a very small percentage of incestuous parents. A person who persists in clinging to an intense sense of outrage cannot be an effective helper. She or he will only compound the abusing parent's anxiety, guilt, hostility, distrust, and low self-image. The person who continues to feel outrage wants to punish the parent, not help him.

As therapists, we must be certain when we begin work with an incestuous family that we are not holding on to any outrage or letting the feeling cover our own repressed sexual feelings. We must be equally careful to avoid the other extreme of rationalizing the behavior of the incestuous parent, e.g., "He couldn't help it. He had all these pressures on him. What do you expect since he had poor parenting himself and his wife was so rejecting?" Rationalizations serve the same function as outrage in defending a person against unacceptable feelings toward his or her own children.

But whatever the reason for such a position, rationalization is no more helpful than outright rejection of incestuous parents. Those who reject are inclined to punish; those who rationalize, to dismiss. Although it is important to be aware of the stresses in the lives of incestuous families and how pressure may be a precursor to the incest, these stresses do not justify their behavior. It is possible to understand how incest occurs without condoning or dismissing it.

What should be said to the parents when incest is detected by someone outside the family? Again, it is almost easier to list what should not be said. What should *not* be said is that the parents are horrible, vile, sick people who ought to be horse-whipped or worse!

On the other hand, the incest should not be dismissed as insignificant. The parents need to be told that their daughter is believed to be telling the truth, and even if she is not, the family has a serious problem that cannot be ignored. They should be told to get help and to be guided in finding that help. At this point, the parents need support and guidance in finding professional assistance.

A therapist to the family (counselor or social worker) needs to continue this support and at the same time to confront the problems. The points the therapist should convey are first, if there are legal charges, the parents need to be told that, and what the consequences of those charges might be. Second, the parents should be told in a straight-forward manner that the incestuous behavior is not accept-able behavior and must stop. As we discussed in Part II, some fathers rationalize that sex with their daughters is not wrong, and this belief has to be confronted head-on. Third, the therapist needs to tell the parents that the role-reversal behaviors in the family are harmful to their children and must be changed. Certainly just telling the parents these things will not bring about instant change, but conveying these ideas lays the groundwork for change to take place.

WHAT IS DONE IN THERAPY

Most of the incestuous families we see are referred to us by child welfare agencies, others are referred by probation officers. In about half the families, one or more of the children have been removed from the home by order of the court. The parents are told that their chances of getting the children back are likely to be greatly enhanced if they undergo therapy. Thus most families are angry, resentful, distrusting, and frightened when we first see them.

For the first session the parents and all their children are asked to come for a family therapy session. In that session, we find out from the family members what happened, what they think are problems to be solved in the family, and what has happened to them since the incest was discovered. The family session gives us an opportunity to see how the family relates and to begin to teach them how to relate in more positive ways.

If the parents have not yet verbally acknowledged to the child that they, not she, were responsible for the incest taking place, we ask them to do that in the family session. We also ask them to tell her that they regret her being exploited. In other words, the parents apologize to the child.

If it seems useful, we arrange another family session at a later date. Then we ask the parents to enter our therapy group, which meets once a week for an hour and a half. We do not see the children again until much later, after the parents have made changes in treatment, and the family is functioning well. Some therapists prefer to continue seeing the whole family. Our belief is that the parents are the ones who need to do most of the changing and their being in treatment without the children emphasizes that point; others take a similar stand. Dr. James Simmons, a psychiatrist at the Indiana University School of Medicine, only treats the sexually abused child if he or she is showing recent changes in behavior, attitudes, thinking, or outward appearance. His position is that extensive psychiatric investigation of the child can sometimes harm more than help, and that it is important "to keep in mind the dictum 'primum non nocere,' first do no harm."

We believe families can change without every member being involved in the treatment sessions. Our approach is to enable the parents to set up a new system for the family members to use in relating and then to help the children adjust to and fit into that system.

The first night a new couple comes to group, they are given a checklist that presents several problems any family might have, but the list is designed around problems most common to abusive families. We ask them to check any problems that apply to them and to rank order the problems. We have found the checklist to be an easy way for people to say they have problems without having to verbalize them right away. The parents new to the group fill out the checklist while they listen to other group members work on their problems and concerns.

Using the list as a starting point, we write down the problems the parents want to work on. The problems are listed on a Goal Attainment Scale (GAS), which is a technique used both as a therapeutic tool and a means for evaluating results. GAS involves identifying the main areas of concern in an incestuous family and setting goals in each area to be attained in therapy (see Goal Attainment Follow-Up Guide, on Page 247, of Gene, a client, as an example). We set goals for three-month intervals and re-evaluate them at the end of that period.

The typical problems we work on with each parent include symbiosis, marital relationship, stress reduction, sexual climate, isolation, and alcoholism. Parents make "contracts" with us under each problem area—agreements as to what they will do toward solving that problem in the next three months. Since the contracts are stated in terms of behavior it is possible to measure change. Either the parents have done what they said they would do by the end of the period or they have not. With both parents in group, there is more pressure to be honest in self-reporting. As people begin to make changes for the better, their whole demeanor and appearance improve, so change can often be verified by observation.

FIGURE 15–1 Goal Attainment Follow-Up Guide for Gene

Level at Intake:
Level at Follow-up: *

Level at Intake:
Goal Attainment Score
(Level at Follow-up):

GOAL ATTAINMENT FOLLOW-UP GUIDE
Goals for 3 Months for Gene

SCALE ATTAINMENT LEVELS	SCALE 1: Symbiosis (weight$_1$ = 25)	SCALE 2: Marital Relationship (weight$_2$ = 20)	SCALE 3: Stress Reduction (weight$_3$ = 20)	SCALE 4: Sexual Climate (weight$_4$ = 10)	SCALE 5: Isolation (weight$_5$ = 15)	SCALE 6: Alcoholism (weight$_6$ = 15)
most unfavorable outcome thought likely (−2)	Not ask wife for any nurturing (such as back rub, ask her to phone, do him a favor)	Not have sex with wife	Not do relaxation exercises	Use obscenity in front of children or wife every day	Not go out or visit friends at all	Drink daily
less than expected success (−1)						
expected level of success (0)	Ask wife for nurturing twice a week	Have sex with wife once a week	Practice relaxation exercises once a week	Use obscenity in front of children or wife once a week	Go out with friends or have them over once every two weeks	Drink once a month
more than expected success (+1)						
most favorable outcome thought likely (+2)	Ask wife for nurturing once a day	Have sex with wife twice a week	Practice relaxation exercises once a day	Not use obscenities in front of children or wife	Go out with friends or have them over once a week	Be totally abstinent

What do we do about each problem? Symbiosis is typically the most important area we treat. In Part III, we discussed symbiosis in terms of role-reversal, the parent turning to the child to meet needs of the parent instead of the child. Symbiosis begins as a life-sustaining relationship between mother and child in the earliest state of development. An example of a normal, healthy symbiosis is illustrated by a mother who awakens at her infant's first whimper and gets up to feed, change, or in some other way attend to his or her needs. In this type of symbiosis, the experience is one of meeting mutually shared needs: the infant's need to be nurtured and the mother's need to nurture.

In an incestuous family, the symbiosis takes the form of the parent forcing the child to meet the parent's needs for nurturing by engaging in sexual behavior with him or her. The symbiosis becomes exploitive, not mutually satisfying, because the child's needs are ignored. True, the child may receive some attention in the process, but the relationship is still exploitive. In father-daughter incest, the mother, too, forces the child into taking care of her. She does this by being sick or unavailable, so that the child becomes the "mother" to the family.

In group therapy with incestuous families, we begin breaking up the symbiosis by teaching parents about their feelings and how to meet their needs in a nonexploitive way. We may begin by asking a father to request from his wife a back rub or compliment each day or in some other way to be directly responsible for getting nurtured. As the father becomes more successful at getting strokes and nurturing from his wife, he begins to give up his fantasies of an all-loving mother. He comes to have a more realistic picture of his stroke needs and how to meet them without exploiting his daughter or anyone else. At the same time the father is learning about nurturing, we are teaching the mother to be straight about her need for strokes and attention and to ask for them directly instead of getting a migraine so that her daughter has to take over her responsibilities in the home.

As is clear from what we have said previously, the relationship between the husband and wife is severely strained. We think the chances of the incest recurring remain present if the marriage is not strengthened and made more satisfying to both partners. So the second problem area we focus on is the marital relationship. One problem in the marital relationship lies simply in how the mates talk to each other. Most husbands and wives in incestuous families exchange either negative strokes or no strokes at all. In other words, if they do say something to one another it is only for the purpose of complaining or expressing anger. So we teach the parents how to change their stroking patterns.

Sometimes the parents have not spoken kindly to each other for so many years they have almost forgotten how. One man in our group even sounded angry when he was telling his wife he loved her! We start by asking the parents to exchange positive strokes in the room. This gives us and the rest of the group a chance to hear what voice tone and facial gesture are used, and to share those observations with the parent. Of course, teaching how to relate positively comes only after the parents have said they want to improve their relationship. We also teach the use of "I messages" and "active listening," which are techniques for stating a complaint without blaming and giving a response without defending or judging

Another serious problem in the marital relationship is sex between husband and wife, or more accurately, lack of sex. As we have said, one of the reasons the father turns to his daughter for sex is that the mother has retreated from him sexually, as well as in other ways. In group we ask the couple to discuss openly their sexual difficulties and to make contracts with each other around sex that will make the experience satisfying to both. The contracts often involve compromises, and the group is helpful in aiding the couple to work out the compromises. Too, just talking about sex in group lets the parents feel freer to discuss their likes and dislikes with each other.

When the parents find greater satisfaction, emotionally and sexually, with each other, they are less likely to turn to a child to get their needs met. As a result, generational boundaries are strengthened.

Getting parents involved in a group is a first step toward breaking up the isolation of incestuous families. They make friends with people who have similar problems, who will listen to them, and who do not condemn them. Because distrust underlies the isolation, we encourage the parents to begin trusting by reaching out. For this reason, we give them both our office and home telephone numbers and ask them to call. In addition to being in group and calling us when they need help outside group, parents make contracts to meet new friends and to socialize more with other couples.

Stress, as we have said, is a major factor contributing to incest. For this reason, we also emphasize stress reduction in our work with incestuous families. We begin by teaching them much of the material presented in Chapter 13. Once they understand how stress happens and what effects it can have, we teach the techniques for managing stress. One technique we use in group is a relaxation exercise that all the group members participate in. The final 15 to 20 minutes of each group session consist of listening to a tape we made of one of our relaxation exercises and practicing relaxing. Parts of the exercise the group members can practice on their own at home, and they contract to do so.

Parents also agree to limit the number of change events they will initiate in the three-month period. At first, the parents act as if all the events in their lives are outside their control, when, in fact, they could have prevented many of the changes had they planned ahead. For example, one couple moved four times in six months, when they could have moved only once by carefully thinking out their needs in terms of space, money, and transportation. In group, each parent fills out a Schedule of Recent Experience (see Chapter 7) and keeps track of change units as they accumulate.

The sexual climate in the home where incest occurs often needs modifying before the home will be safe. Sexual climate includes sexual attitudes of both parents. For example, one father who had been sexually involved with his daughter described how he let her get in bed with him and sleep there all night because she was frightened by the country sounds she was unfamiliar with since she had lived only in the city. The daughter was 14. Changing the sexual climate in the home meant telling the father that there were alternative ways to comfort his daughter that do not blur generational boundaries. He was told that his taking her to bed was inappropriate, whether anything happened or not. The father contracted to learn new nonsexual ways to relate to his daughter. Changing the sexual climate also involves telling the parent directly that incest is wrong, why it is, and getting a contract that it will stop.

Alcoholism is not a problem in all incestuous families, but it has played a part in many families we have worked with. We find the back-up of Alcoholics Anonymous (AA) most helpful in aiding alcoholic parents to stop drinking. Some can do it without the aid of a support group like AA, but most need the structure and reinforcement AA provides. Even if the parent does not elect to go to AA, we work out a contract with him to stop drinking and to do in group whatever he has to do to be able to keep that contract. One thing he often has to do is find alternative ways of structuring his time other than hanging out where drinking is going on or keeping to himself with a bottle.

These six problem areas are not the only ones we focus on in group, nor are they present in every family we have worked with. They are *typical* problems in incestuous families, though, and need to be addressed when they are present.

GENE: A GROUP MEMBER

Gene, a father we described in Chapter 4, and his wife, Lillian, were members of our group. Gene's GAS Follow-up Guide (see p. 247) illustrates the typical problems and contracts around each problem. When Gene first came to group, he had just been sentenced to 10 years on probation for sexually molesting his three stepdaughters. He was alcoholic and out of work. Fighting between Gene and Lillian was almost continuous, with his regularly shouting obscenities at her and at the children. They rarely visited friends and did not go out socially, even just the two of them. Sex between Gene and Lillian was almost nonexistent, as were other forms of positive stroking.

The first problem Gene decided to tackle even before he came to group was his alcoholism. A week before starting therapy with us, he vowed never to drink again and joined Alcoholics Anonymous. He began attending their meetings regularly. Lillian was supportive of his decision, and went to the meetings with him. Gene has stuck by his decision. When he stopped coming to group he had been abstinent just over one year.

The martial relationship was the next problem area for attention. It was typical of their relationship that when Lillian was saying something that was of concern to her, Gene would either laugh or interrupt her and start in on a long-winded harangue. We confronted his behavior and suggested for a contract that Gene learn to really listen to what Lillian was saying and to respond in a nonblaming way. He agreed, and by the time they left group, Gene not only was not berating Lillian and discounting her feelings, but he was showing her open affection and giving her positive verbal strokes. Understandably, Lillian was responding in kind. As they began to relate more positively, they found they were interested in having sex with each other again.

Gene was feeling much stress from having been laid off his job. The stress was both financial and emotional. He was constantly telling himself that he was no good, worthless, and had not amounted to anything. We confronted his self-stressing talk by exposing him to our Stress Seminar. He found the information very useful and began applying it to himself. One way Gene learned he was not "all bad" or a "worthless person" was to make a list of every possible way in which he could compare himself to other men his age and to do an evaluation using two or three men he knew to use for comparison. Gene did a very thorough job and was amazed to see that in many categories he scored higher than his friends. He got the point that he had positive as well as negative qualities and he began to feel much more self-confident. Just after making the comparison, Gene found work, and his self-confidence rose even more. He was still on the same job when he stopped group.

To further aid Gene in reducing his stress, he contracted to practice on his own the relaxation exercises learned in group. He did this at least once a day and noticed a big improvement in his ability to feel relaxed and calm.

On the problem of symbiosis, Gene learned to ask directly for nurturing from Lillian. Gene presented a "macho" front—tough, mean, and stubborn. In fact, his nickname in group was "the Armadillo." This tough guy image stood in the way of his asking for or accepting nurturing. He believed that to do so would be "soft" and, therefore, unmanly. To break down his macho image, we asked Gene to make a contract that at least once a day, he would ask Lillian to do something for him, even if it was something as simple as asking her to call him when she got to work so he would know she had arrived safely. Since they were fighting much less and Lillian was feeling more stroked, she was quite willing to nurture Gene when he asked for it.

Gene and Lillian began to break up their isolation by coming to group and scheduling a time to have dinner together either before or after group. They also joined a church and began going fairly regularly. Even when they did not go, they made arrangements for their children to go to the Sunday school. Lillian began to go out to lunch with some of her co-workers without Gene feeling threatened, and Gene started taking some job-related courses one evening a week and meeting new people there. He also met many new friends at his AA meetings.

In terms of changing the sexual climate, Lillian asked Gene to stop using obscenities around the children and around her. He agreed and has kept his agreement. Perhaps most importantly, he vowed never to sexually abuse his daughters again and has not. There are no indications he will have any trouble keeping this commitment.

When Gene and Lillian left group after participating regularly for a year, they were happy, their marriage was better than it had ever been, there had been no recurrence of the incest, and they had both made changes that would make any recurrence unlikely. The protective services agency had returned full custody of their daughters to them, and the probation officer was going to recommend that the probation be discontinued.

OTHER APPROACHES TO TREATING THE FAMILY

Some other approaches to helping incestuous families change involve methods and programs we have not incorporated into our treatment. At the Child Sexual Abuse Treatment Program (CSATP) in California, Henry Giarretto's experience has been that the family members must be counseled separately before family therapy is useful. For this reason, his team first counsels individually with the child, mother, and father. Next they see the mother and daughter together, then the husband and wife. Family therapy follows the marital counseling, and last comes group counseling.

In 1972, some of the parents in treatment in the CSATP formed a self-help group called Parents United. The members meet weekly. After a brief meeting with the group as a whole at the beginning of the session, the members form into various smaller groups. The smaller groups are made up of couples, men, women, and mixed singles and couples. The daughters, too, have formed a self-help group which they call Daughters United. Their group is composed of teenage girls and meets on the same evenings as the Parents United groups. Whatever the approach to treating incestuous families, we think it is most important that they do receive professional help and, preferably, from specialists in the area. Although the incest may not recur once it is disclosed the family is still very troubled.

For instance, months after Harry Lewis (Chapters 4 and 7) had stopped molesting his daughter, Annie, she reported to her teacher and a school nurse that Harry was again having intercourse with her and that she had missed school in order to have a pregnancy test. We had a family therapy session in which Annie admitted making up the whole story. She had done so for two reasons: first, she was going to get a C in a class where she had previously made all As, and she feared her parents' reaction, and, secondly, she was angry that her mother had had little time to spend with her since the new baby had been born. Obviously, there were major communication problems in the family, even though the incest was no longer of concern.

Another reason why treatment is necessary is there are many problems in families in which a child is sexually abused that parallel those in families where physical abuse takes place. In both types of families, the parents are turning to the child to get their needs met. In the physically abusive family, the parent tries to beat the child into meeting his or her needs. In the incestuous family, the parent uses sex and seduction. Parents in both types of families come from similar backgrounds, deprived in terms of nurturing and closeness. If treatment is not offered, incest may occur with another child in the family or physical abuse may begin.

One teenager we treated reported to the child protective workers that her father had been sexually molesting her for years, in fact since she was three. She was removed from the home for a few months. Her father saw a psychiatrist briefly and then dropped out of treatment. The daughter was returned home for one week for a trial visit. During that week her father did not molest her sexually, but he beat her so badly that a child welfare worker commented she "looked like she'd been in the ring with Muhammad Ali." Clearly, for such a family, serious problems still exist, even if the incestuous behavior ceases.

THE CHILD GROWN UP

Even though there is still a heavy taboo around the subject of incest and many victims of incest will not admit to having been involved in it as a child, people are starting to deal with the problem more frankly and are asking for help. What can be done for the person who experienced incest as a child? Fortunately, there is much that can be done to mitigate the long-term consequences we discussed in Part IV.

The first step is being willing to reach out for help. Many people stop themselves from going to a professional for treatment because of their feelings of guilt and shame. As we said, many children believe they are uniquely different, that they are the only ones who have ever had sex with a parent. Those feelings persist into adulthood, and the person thinks a therapist would react with shock or disbelief. While this is possible, it is unlikely if an experienced therapist is chosen. In our experience, virtually all therapists who have been in practice a few years have seen clients who had incest in their backgrounds. An experienced therapist is not likely to be shocked and will certainly not be critical or blaming. If a therapist does react negatively to the disclosure of the incest or responds with disbelief or indifference, another professional should be sought. Local mental health or psychological associations can be helpful in guiding someone to a therapist who has experience in dealing with specific kinds of problems.

Our approach to working with adults who experienced incest as a child focuses on changing the person's self-image, sharing information on how incest happens, and helping the person to work through old feelings of depression, guilt, shame, and anger. If the woman or man is married, problems in the marriage will be dealt with, including any that have to do with sexual dysfunction.

We usually see our clients for a few sessions individually and then ask them to go into group therapy. We find the group experience helps the person to build trust, to learn to be nurtured, and close in a nonsexual way, and to learn how to relate without trying to be responsible for everyone around. Another benefit of group is that the person learns her secret is not so horrible after all and can be shared without her being abandoned, ostracized or blamed.

DIANNE IN TREATMENT

Dianne (see Chapters 4 and 7) was considering suicide when she first came to see us. Her younger sister had committed suicide two months before, and Dianne herself had

had a close brush with death when a man broke into her apartment, beat her up, and raped her three weeks earlier. Dianne viewed herself as totally worthless and saw no point in living.

The first step in treatment was to deal with her depression. We asked her to make a contract to stay alive just one week at a time for the present. She agreed. We also arranged that she start eating better, exercising, and keeping friends around her. While restructuring her living habits, we helped her work through feelings of rage and sadness, which were first directed at the rapist and then at her father. In the first session, Dianne had revealed her incestuous involvement with her father. Many clients do not open up until they have more time to develop a sense of trust in the therapist.

As Dianne began to eat better, exercise more, and get more strokes from people, she started to feel less overwhelmed by all that had happened. After a few weeks, she joined one of our therapy groups. In the group, she met people who would hold her, listen to her, not judge her, and not exploit her. She also learned that she did not have to be responsible for other people's feelings and that she did not have to meet other people's needs if she did not want to.

In group, Dianne learned to sort out the "games" she was playing with her husband-to-be and to see what role she had in initiating them or keeping them going. She stopped relying on him for all her strokes and learned to be more assertive in asking for what she needed. She also realized how the man she had picked to marry was in many ways like her father—bright, impulsive, immature, and irresponsible. Fortunately, he was willing to come into therapy too and made many changes in terms of growing up and becoming more responsible.

Dianne now is a successful public relations specialist, working with a prestigious firm, and getting promotions rapidly. She has many friends and a rich social life. She and her husband are still working out their relationship so that both of them can feel satisfied and rewarded. Although some of the old feelings and behaviors still resurface for Dianne, she is basically happy, healthy, and enjoying life. She understands her past and how it affects her today, but she is not letting the past stop her from getting where she wants to go and being the kind of person she wishes to be.

We hope Dianne's story will be an encouragement to the many people who grew up, or are growing up, in incestuous families. While it is true that Dianne had to overcome many handicaps to be where she is today, her success serves as testimony to the fact that change is possible and the consequences of incest need not be crippling.

Chapter 16

WHAT CAN BE DONE ON THE
PUBLIC LEVEL

A taboo in any society is meant to regulate the behavior of people so that the social system works and stays in balance. In the words of anthopologist Margaret Mead, taboos are "the deeply and intensely felt prohibitions against 'unthinkable' behavior." The problem with the taboo against incest is that it has not kept sex in the family from occurring as much as it has kept people from reporting the problem, becoming informed about incest, and taking steps to treat and prevent incest.

Until incest stops being considered an "unthinkable" subject, in terms of public discussion and recognition, and is brought out of the closet and backroom into the light of day, little action can be expected.

The first order of business, then, is a public information campaign. States across the nation have greatly increased public consciousness and reporting of physical child abuse through such campaigns. Sexual abuse, which may be even more prevalent, now needs to be emphasized. One young woman, who had been involved in incest with her father, remarked: "A lot of people don't even know what the word means and it is going on all the time."

The subject needs to be demystified and desexualized. By this we mean that the public needs to be told that it is not a rare, "unthinkable" occurrence that is found only among members of primitive tribes in far-off lands, and that it is not essentially a sexual problem but one of troubled families that do not know how to meet their emotional needs.

Federal, state, and local welfare agencies, as well as departments of human resources, should take the lead in conducting a public information campaign, just as they have done with physical child abuse. Schools also have a special responsibility.

For years, children have been warned to stay out of cars with strangers and to beware of men offering candy. Said one young woman who was sexually abused by her father:

> The pamphlets say beware of this man who is going to offer you candy and get you in his car. You're not taught what to beware of or that he might do something sexual with you. The last thing you are taught is that it might be a family member, an uncle or father. There is this bogey man who is going to get you. But you don't know what he is going to get.

A study in New York City of "child sex vicitimization" found that only 2 percent of the cases occurred on school grounds and another 2 percent in automobiles, yet all the warnings to children continue to focus exclusively on the stranger.

In 1974 the U.S. Department of Health, Education, and Welfare funded a pilot project aimed at informing high school students, teachers, and administrators about physical child abuse. In Houston, "Lift a Finger" was so successful, the project was extended to other areas. Students developed their own curriculum about the causes, treatment, and prevention of abuse. Teachers learned how to detect early signs of abuse and how to report it. Principals and administrators learned about the problem and started cooperating on doing something about it. Similar efforts are needed on incest. Children will not have faith in their parents undermined by knowing what constitutes healthy and unhealthy parenting. They need information and training in order to be good parents themselves some day.

Children must also know where they can get help if they need to seek it on their own. If a child's parents do not intervene in his or her behalf, then the child must take action. So many children with problems at home, such as incest, feel helpless because they know that their parents are not going to do anything to get help yet help is needed and they do not know where to turn. A crisis center or a children's shelter is one possibility. Some cities, such as Knoxville, Tenn., have hotlines for children in distress to use. But there must be posters, billboards, pamphlets, and public service announcements for children to know such facilities exist, and what kind of problems they help with.

As we saw in Chapter 11, all Peggy needed was to see one poster to know she was not alone with her problem and something could be done. Another young woman said, ". . . if there had been a big billboard when I was 8 years old," she would have known what to do.

One of the prerequisites to getting such help for children and to launching campaigns in their behalf is recognition of the rights of children. The law still emphasizes the rights of parents.

> The child is not guaranteed—nor does he have an absolute right to—parental care that will provide him with adequate food, clothing, and shelter. The child does not have a right to medical and health care that will insure his future. . . .

Also, the child's right to a safe home and a healthy development is not established. Another basic right that has not been emphasized and taught to children is the right of the child to his or her own body. Almost a decade ago, the Joint Commission on Mental Health of Children stated that children have the right to be wanted, to live in a healthy environment, to have their basic needs satisfied, and to receive loving care. Yet, such rights are still not recognized.

So laws need to be changed and public attitudes modified. To guarantee the right of a child to a healthy development, we need health visitors who would go to the homes of children and assist parents with problems. In *The Abusing Family,* we pointed out that the United Kingdom has had such a program since the early 1900s. The purpose of the health visitor is not to spy or to report bad parents but to assist parents in meeting the emotional and physical needs of their children, particularly in the early years.

As Dr. Henry Kempe, a pioneer in child abuse work who studied the health visitors program abroad, has pointed out:

> All ... [health visitors] are able nurses who go to every house, rich, poor, middle class, knock on the door and say, "How are you, Mrs. Jones?" They are always courteous to the mother. Eventually they have some tea in the kitchen and eventually they see the child and they then do what amounts to an advocacy job for the child.

A wide range of problems, not just incest, could be headed off with this kind of personal intervention. Much of the solution to incest, as well as to a number of emotional problems, delinquency, and drug abuse, lies in strengthening parents and families.

MEASURES TO STRENGTHEN PARENTS AND FAMILIES

As we saw in earlier parts of the book, incestuous parents tend to be isolated or stressed individuals who use sex with their children in an attempt to meet needs for nurturing, closeness, and stimulation. Several steps can be taken through legislative and public action to shore up families and strengthen parents so that serious problems are less likely to occur:

1. *Full employment.* Unemployed fathers constitute a high-risk group, vulnerable to any number of problems of which incest is one. A national policy that recognizes employment as a right and guarantees employment to every able individual is essential.

2. *Restore neighborhoods.* Troubled families, incestuous families, are often cut off from neighbors and live in areas where there is little sense of community. They need strokes from social contacts. One starting point for restoring a sense of neighborliness would be to make fuller use of neighborhood schools, keeping them open at night, on weekends and during the summer to offer programs and bring parents and children together from the area.

3. *Courses for parents.* As we noted in our previous book, parenting is a skill and requires training. We do not expect a brain surgeon or even a clerk-typist to do his or her job without training, yet one of the most important jobs that nearly all adults face is being a parent, but no training is offered. Many people learn from the models their own parents provided, but many learn the wrong things or have the wrong models. So it is essential that public schools offer parenting courses for both kids and adults. It should be mandatory for all children starting in at least junior high school and should include experience in nurseries and day care centers. For adults, such courses would help relieve the stress many parents are under, stress that contributes to the problems they have in their lives.

Another course that would be particularly useful to parents who are potentially abusive would be one on the nature of human needs and how to meet those needs. As we have emphasized, it is the failure to meet the needs that leads parents to abuse children.

4. *Family service centers.*   Although most cities have a wide range of services to offer people in need, they are usually scattered, uncoordinated, and often inaccessible. Neighborhood centers are needed that pull together all the services that a troubled family may need: counseling, housing, employment, vocational, and welfare. Again, the neighborhood school or its campus may well be the most attractive and feasible site for such centers.

5. *Mobilization of employers.*   The private sector is in a strategic position to influence the mental and emotional health of a large number of people. Incentives should be provided to encourage companies and organizations to restructure jobs so that workers will have a greater sense of accomplishment, recognition, and meaning. Incentives also should be given for offering services to employees that help them reduce the stress in their lives. These include:

A. *Situational groupings.*   This is the name given to a group of people who are brought together as they confront an impending situation, change, or problem. The situation may be a move to another city, retirement, termination, promotion, or divorce. Those facing the situation are given guidance and information by people who have already undergone the same experience and are functioning effectively. Such guidance can be enormously helpful as a stress-management technique for employees facing changes.

B. *Exercise breaks.*   Some companies already are giving workers 15- to 30-minute breaks to engage in calisthenics or other forms of exercise. Larger companies are also furnishing jogging tracks or paths, exercise machines, weight rooms, and swimming pools. Even some smaller organizations are encouraging employees to lose weight or stop smoking by offering bonuses and cash incentives.

C. *Stress-management seminars.*   Many of the techniques we proposed in Chapter 13 lend themselves to be
taught at company-sponsored seminars for employees and
management. Both the worker and company benefit. The
worker is better able to cope with the stress in his or her
life, and the company has less absenteeism, accidents, alcoholism, poor morale and low productivity.

Any program or service, whether initiated by an em-
ployer or a community, that helps parents and families
reduce the stress in their lives and better meet their needs
will be a preventive measure in incest.

THE ROLE OF PROFESSIONALS IN PREVENTION

Just as the public and private sectors must be mobilized, so
must the professionals. Just as a public information campaign is needed to raise people's awareness of incest and
to promote prevention, so must there be education of the
professionals—physicians, teachers, lawyers, judges, psychologists, and all those in the helping professions.

Their tendency to deny that incest is going on and is
a widespread problem is just as strong as other people's.
When confronted with its existence, their response is often
just like everyone else's: to turn away blindly or to seek
severe retribution. As Dr. Diane Browning and Ms. Bonny
Boatman of the University of Oregon Health Sciences Center have pointed out:

> Physicians need to overcome their own denial and become
> aware of the prevalence of incest. They must be alert to the
> possibility of incest in high-risk families and may need to
> overcome their own discomfort and initiate frank, sensitive
> discussion of the matter with family members. In doing so,
> they give families a chance to unburden themselves and seek
> appropriate action.

To be effective in helping a child or family, a professional must have worked through his own feelings about
incest so he or she is still not finding it too "unthinkable"
to deal with. The tendency often is, both by professionals
and nonprofessionals alike, to talk about something else.
One young woman who sought help encountered this kind
of situation:

> I had a lot of pain to deal with. The minute I'd try to deal
> with the incest, people would hush me up . . . nobody would
> let me deal with that.

Physicians, teachers and others who are in daily interaction with families and children are in a strategic position to spot signs of trouble and to help head incest off
before it occurs or to detect it in the early stages. But to do
this, they must know what the cues are and to receive training in what incest is all about and what can be done. They
must know to look for role-reversal and symbiosis in a
family, to understand the meaning of a child's becoming
withdrawn or depressed or having sleeping or eating disturbances (see cues list in Chapter 10).

In the study by Browning and Boatman, they found it
"distressing" that only two of 14 cases of incest were referred by physicians "in spite of the fact that many of these
families had been in recent contact" with doctors.

Besides being trained in how to identify high-risk families and children and to detect cues of ongoing incest,
members of the helping professions must also know how to
get appropriate services for those in need. They must know
what community resources exist and what specialists, if any,
there are in treating and helping incestuous families.

The professionals also need to know the reporting
laws governing incest. In a number of states, incest is covered under child abuse—as it should be—and must be reported to the local or state child welfare or protective

services agency. In states where incest and sexual abuse are still not a reportable problem, that is, no law says that anyone with knowledge of a case must report it, professionals must take the lead in getting legislatures to make it a reportable condition.

Every community also needs a coordinated team to deal with incest, a team equipped to investigate every report, make a joint decision on what is wrong and what should be done, take whatever court action is necessary to protect the child and get the family into treatment, and to see that the child and family get treated. On the team should be psychologists, psychiatrists, social workers, attorneys, child advocates, and representatives of the court.

Legal action should be taken in civil court under child abuse statutes. As suggested, every effort should be made to minimize the effects that the investigation and court action have on the child. Every effort should be made to keep the family together.

We agree that many incestuous families will not go to treatment or remain in therapy unless they are made to. They should be given to understand that unless they undergo and complete therapy, criminal charges will be brought against the offending parent or that court action will be taken to remove the child—or the offending parent —from the home.

In some cases, it is necessary to remove the child anyway. This is particularly true in cases where the father, for instance, is psychopathic (see Chapter 4) and may have committed both physical and sexual abuse of the child. Criminal charges may also be necessary. We do not know if the treatment we have outlined (see Chapter 15) is effective for psychopaths or some psychotics.

In the majority of cases, however, the parent is not a psychopath or psychotic and physical abuse is not involved. In these cases, the best interest of both the child and the family are served if the child stays in the home and treatment is provided. In these cases, it is necessary to have sufficient staff so that caseworkers can make frequent visits to the home to assure that no further abuse is occurring while the family undergoes treatment. None has occurred in families undergoing therapy with us.

By keeping families together and taking a therapeutic rather than a punitive approach to incest, reporting of the problem is encouraged. As long as family members think that if they report the problem, the father will be jailed, the child will be taken away, and there will be a "scandal," then all are likely to remain silent.

Shaping Public Policy

We have emphasized that both on the public and professional level, there is a pressing need for more awareness of incest and knowledge of what to do about it. We agree with Brant and Tisza that "a social climate that allows for freer communication about sexuality, and the recent focus on the sexually-assaulted female" are likely to contribute to constructive action.

However, it should be noted that in some quarters, there is the idea that more open acknowledgement of sexuality should encompass a license to behave without sexual restraints. The René Guyon Society, headquartered in California, lobbies for legislative action to permit adult-child sex, as well as other kinds of sexual behavior that heretofore have been considered illegal. On incest, the Guyon Society believes there must be "sex before 8 or else it is too late," contending that if a child is not allowed sex he or she will develop any number of later problems. No valid evidence is presented for such a position and none is offered to refute the many studies, such as our own and those we have cited, showing the many negative consequences of incest.

At the other end of the spectrum are people who are pressing for harsher and more punitive treatment of all sexual abuse cases. Some of these argue that the rise in child pornography and child prostitution is due to "pampering" of offenders. We believe that those in the pornography or prostitution business should not be confused with troubled families in which incest occurs. Sending a parent to prison does nothing to rehabilitate a family.

We believe it is important that public sentiment be mobilized against both extremes as they touch on the problem of incest so that constructive laws and policy will emerge. We do not believe that the law should be used to prosecute sexual activity between consenting adults, regardless of whether they are related or not, but that it should be concerned with children who are abused.

SUMMARY

Incest is a form of child abuse that needs to be demystified and desexualized. The taboo around it has served to keep people from recognizing how widespread it is, from reporting it or taking action to prevent or treat it. It is time to recognize that incest is not some unthinkable sin or sexual aberration, but a problem growing out of parents not knowing how to meet their needs for closeness, nurturing, and stimulation or how to deal with stress, which interferes with fulfillment of needs.

Prevention lies in parents learning how to meet their needs and to manage stress, as well as becoming informed about how to deal with their own sexuality and the sexuality of their child. Parents under stress or those who are lonely and isolated may let physical affection for the child spill over into physical contact that becomes sexual.

On the public level, a child's right to a healthy development must be recognized. Steps need to be taken to strengthen and support families through full employment, restoring a sense of community to neighborhoods, providing courses in parenting and stress management to parents and children alike, and mobilizing employers to help workers lead more satisfying and less stressful lives.

Finally, the law must be used to make incest a reportable problem and to get help and treatment for incestuous families. It should not be used to take the child away, send a parent to prison and break the family up.

All this requires that both the public and professionals alike became aware of the widespread extent of incest and make the necessary commitment to prevention and treatment.

NOTES

Introduction

PAGE

14   On the home being more dangerous to a child than the streets, Vincent De Francis of the American Humane Association found in a study of sexual abuse in New York that in only 25 percent of the cases was a stranger involved. See De Francis' *Protecting the Child Victim of Sex Crimes Committed by Adults,* p. 70.

15   Masters, p. 65, is among those who discusses how common incestuous thoughts are.

15   Both Weinberg and Weiner have reported on worldwide incidences of known incest, which are now recognized as gross underestimates.

16   Houston figures are from Harris County Child Welfare Unit and the Texas statistics come from the Texas Department of Human Resources.

16   See Henry Giarretto's chapter in Helfer and Kempe's *Child Abuse and Neglect: The Family and the Community,* for the Santa Clara figures.

16   See Weber, p. 65, for national estimates on sexual abuse.

16   William H. Young, Jr., M.D., assistant clinical professor of psy-
        chiatry at George Washington University School of Medicine and
        University of Virginia School of Medicine, gave the estimate of 4
        to 5 percent in the U.S. population. He spoke at the American
        Society for Adolescent Psychiatry in Toronto April 30, 1977.

16   Psychologist John Woodbury conducted a national survey on in-
        cest and concluded that 5 to 15 percent of the population is
        involved. His estimate is in *The Silent Sin: A Case History of Incest,*
        p. vi.

16   See Weeks, p. 848, for more on perpetrators of incest.

16–   See Walters, p. 116, for the survey among university freshman
17   and sophomores. Figures from the San Francisco Sexual Trauma
        Center were given by CBS Morning News October 24, 1977.

17   An idea of how much bigger the problem of sexual abuse is than
        physical abuse of children can be gained from De Francis' study,
        p. 37, in which it was estimated that in one year, the number of
        cases of "child sex victimization" in New York City alone was half
        the total of physical abuse cases for the entire nation.

17   The report of the huge increase in incest, from one in a million
        to one in 20, is on p. vi in Woodbury and Schwartz.

18   For more on the permissive sexual climate, see Socarides, pp.
        385–92.

18   Giarretto's quote is from his chapter in Helfer and Kempe.

18   Toffler presents a vivid account of the effects of change in *Future
        Shock* and discusses the precarious position of the family.

PART I   WHAT INCEST IS

Chapter 1   More Than a Matter of Sex

26   See Goldsten and Katz, p. 386, for the New York law on incest and
        a discussion of its development.

26   Leslie A. White gives a comprehensive account of the original
        purposes served by the incest taboo, particularly in terms of es-

tablishing expanding alliances and defenses for a society's survival, in his paper on "The Definition and Prohibition of Incest."

26–   See Lindzey's 1967 paper for one of the most extensive reviews
27   of studies suggesting that inbreeding results in such problems as mental deficiency, deaf-mutism, physical malformations like dwarfism and albinism. It is true that such conditions may be produced if a family has "hidden" defective genes and incest occurs between father and daughter, mother and son or brother and sister. However, as sociologist George P. Murdock noted in *Social Structure,* if the "hidden" genes are positive rather than negative, inbreeding can result in "superior" offspring. Cleopatra, noted for both her brains and beauty, was the product of generation after generation of incest among the Pharaohs of Egypt. Some authorities have noted that when defective offspring do occur from incestuous unions, the partners were of subintelligence or in some way overtly defective themselves. As White said, "if the offspring of a union of brother and sister are inferior it is because the parents were of inferior stock, not because they were brother and sister." Nevertheless, the part that inbreeding may play in producing defective offspring continues to be investigated. See Chapter 11 in this book for more on this.

27   The State of Texas Penal Code, Section 25.02, contains the comment on "protection of family solidarity" as being the rationale for incest taboos.

27   For definitions of incest as sexual activity between family members or any intimate physical contact or act that is accompanied by sexual excitement, see Giarretto's "Humanistic Treatment of Father-Daughter Incest," Henderson's paper on "Incest," and the National Center on Child Abuse and Neglect's resource paper on "Intra-Family Sexual Abuse of Children."

28   For Parson's view on the psychological and social functions of the incest taboo, see his book, *Essays in Sociological Theory.* Jung discusses the incest taboo in *Psychology of the Unconscious.*

28   Freud's theory on the beginning of human culture and the origin of the incest taboo is in *Totem and Taboo.* How ambition and accomplishment in the outside world are tied to the surrendering of sexual impulses inside the family is discussed by Wahl in his paper on "The Psychodynamics of Consummated Maternal Incest."

29   Fromm sees mother and home standing for "the natural ties" that must be surrendered for a child to grow up and reach out to the

world. Adults and children alike long for security and "rooted-ness" but roots, Fromm says, must be established beyond mother and one's original home for human growth and development to occur. See *The Sane Society,* pp. 44–45.

30   On pseudoincest, see Masters and Johnson's article on "Incest: The Ultimate Sexual Taboo," p. 57.

31   In discussing "sexual misuse" as opposed to "sexual abuse," Brant and Tisza, p. 811, note that "children are not always the passive victims of adults." Sexual abuse is a term that "tends to make one view cases in terms of adult 'abusers' and child victims." Sexual misuse is preferable because "it is less pejorative and does not compel one to think only in terms of victims and abusers." In sexual misuse, as Brant and Tisza see it, the whole family has problems and all members suffer to some extent. Schechter and Roberge, p. 129, use the term "sexual exploitation" and see incest as exploitation or child molestation taking place in the home. They view incest as the "more insidious, collusive, secretive, and chronically pervasive" form of molestation.

32   Walters, p. 116, tells of a father installing a one-way mirror in the bathroom so he could observe his daughters taking showers. "Was he sexually abusive?" is Walters' question. He also tells of being asked by a university professor to see the professor's 11-year-old daughter because of a "problem" the girl was having. When pressed for details, the father complained that "she no longer likes to take baths with me."

33   On the problem with penal codes covering incest, De Francis' report on sex crimes shows that nearly half the cases in New York were dismissed because of the requirement for corroboration of the child's testimony. Brant and Tisza, p. 89, argue that "the criminal process is long and complicated and often creates stresses for children and their families beyond those resulting from the actual misuse." The process is traumatic for the child, who gets caught in the middle. For more on this, see Chapter 11.

Chapter 2   Incest in History and Religion

35   See Mueller's article in the *Christian Century* for a complete list of the remotely-related kin prohibited to marry under "A Table of Kindred and Affinity."

36 One theory on why people marry outside the family is that there is a "natural" or "instinctive" aversion to sex with family members. If this were true, there would be no need for an incest taboo or for laws against intrafamily marriage. Although the theory still appeals to those who want to believe that incest does not occur, that it is "a violation of nature," the evidence refutes the theory.

36 On the adaptive value of the incest taboo, Frances and Frances, p. 235, note that there have been three complementary, nonbiological theories on the origin of the taboo: the psychoanalytic theory emphasizes the taboo's value in controlling conflict and competition in the family; the anthropological theory stresses the benefits gained by the nuclear family's forging links with surrounding families or tribes, and the sociological theory views the taboo as controlling eroticism in the family as a means to socialize the child for a functional role in the family and society. We have combined these theories in our discussion of the purposes served by the incest taboo.

36–37 The quote by Leslie White on the importance of establishing ties between families for social evolution to occur is from his paper on "The Definition and Prohibition of Incest." The quote by Parsons is from *Essays in Sociological Theory*, p. 134.

37 See Mead's *Temperament and Sex*, p. 84, for the Arapesh position on incest.

37 Masters, p. 28, touches on the Church's fear of wealth being concentrated in a few families. Exemptions from the incest taboo have also been observed among the Northeast Bantus of East Africa, who may marry their mothers, and among the Kalangs in Java who actually encourage mother-son marriages. According to Maisch, the Dyaks in the hinterland of Borneo have no concept of incest.

37–38 Concerning the practice of incest in ancient Egypt, see Maisch, p. 22, for the estimate that two-thirds of the city of Arsinoe was made up of incestuous marriages, largely brother-sister. Bullough said that the Persians encouraged marriage between parents and children as well as between brother and sister. Among the Romans, the story is told that Nero had incestuous relations with his mother whenever he rode with her in a litter. He would emerge with stains on his clothing (Bullough, p. 140). Nero's mother, Julia Agrippina, was the niece of Emperor Claudius, who forced the Roman Senate to legalize unions between uncles and nieces so he could marry Agrippina. It was 300 years later before the law against such marriages was restored.

38   Bullough, p. 259, tells of the belief among members of the Hindu Sakta sect in India that incest is a higher grade of sexual intercourse and that the highest grade is relations with a goddess. Schroeder, in "Incest in Mormonism," gave an extensive review of instances of incestuous relations among Mormon families prior to the Utah legislation of 1892.

39   The extremes to which incest laws were extended, such as forbidding marriages closer than sixth or seventh degrees of kinships, can be traced in part to the spread of power of the Roman Catholic Church and its "abhorrence" of sexuality. Maisch, p. 26, notes that the Church regarded sex as "sinful and promiscuous" and ultimately persuaded secular lawmakers even to prohibit marriage between two baptismal witnesses of the same child. Under Innocent III (1198–1216), the Church relaxed such prohibitions and adopted a rule allowing cousins beyond the third degree of kinship to marry.

39   Raglan, pp. 99–100, discusses incest as a crime and sin according to English law and the Church of England. Maisch, pp. 27–31, discusses incest in the Catholic Church.

40   See Lord Raglan, p. 3, for more on superstitions about catastrophes that occur as a result of incest, including the belief among French peasants that crops fail and epidemics occur when first cousins marry.

41   Reference to the sons of Adam marrying their sisters is in Jubilees 4. The story of Lot and his daughters is in Genesis 19:31–35. Genesis 20:13 tells of Abraham and his half-sister, Sarah. A discussion of incest in scripture can be found in both Masters' *Patterns of Incest,* pp. 9–14, and Schechter and Roberge, pp. 128–129. Masters observes that we can all be considered "children of incest" since Eve was made from Adam's rib.

Chapter 3   A New Look at Incest

42   Among the arguments against incest laws is the one that consenting adults, such as a grown brother and sister, nephew and aunt,

should be free to pursue sexual relationships together since no child's welfare is in jeopardy and society is in no way threatened. We take the position that criminal laws on incest further the myth and mystery that have historically kept the subject secret and that a child's welfare can better be protected by a number of other laws on the books and by public education, which can help strip the secretiveness away from the subject.

43   The quote on infringement of the child's rights is in the preface by Tisza in Weinberg, p. x.

44   See DeMause, pp. 86–87, for some of the history of sexual abuse that children have suffered at the hands of parents and other adults. Maisch, p. 37, notes that superstitions account for the practice of parents masturbating their children. It is believed that masturbation encourages the growth of genitals in boys, assures sexuality in girls, and helps keep a child quiet in general.

46   Cory and Masters, pp. 12–19, explore the treatment that writers have given the incest theme since John Ford's play *'Tis Pity She's a Whore*. Maisch, pp. 12–21, also traces the "incest motif," noting that "almost all the most important writers in world literature have dealt with the incest theme. . . ." Practically all have focused on conflict, condemnation, guilt, and punishment generated by incest, except in the case of brother-sister relationships, which have been portrayed as socially unacceptable but "moving and lovable."

47   Brown's "The Case of Richard Loftus" in *Bedeviled* presents a chilling account of the guilt and anger that characterized a mother-son sexual union.

48   In discussing incest as "the riskiest of family secrets," Schechter and Roberge, p. 129, speculate as to the role "the Bible's ferocious proscriptions in Leviticus" may have played in shaping people's view of the subject and their reaction to it in terms of humor, denial, or retribution.

49   See the preface in Weinberg's book by Tisza for more on the increasing concern that both the public and professionals have today with sexual behavior. Weinberg, p. xxi, tells of the increased openness toward incest extending to letter-writing to

newspaper columnists. He says that of the thousands of letters received by Ann Landers, 6 percent pertain to incest.

49   See *Playboy,* p. 43, for more comments on incest from "The Playboy's Advisor."

50   In addition to the definition of a virgin in the Ozarks, Masters, p. 47, also says there is an Indian saying that "for a girl to still be a virgin at 10 years old, she must have neither brothers nor cousins nor father." Weeks was quoted in *Pediatric News,* p. 3.

50   For more on "rustic environment" incest, see "Sexual Abuse of Children: A Clinical Spectrum" by Summit and Kryso. Another saying, regarding sisters as subjects of incest, is the proverb of the Central African Asandes: "The search for a woman begins with the sister."

51   See Berry's paper on "Incest: Some Clinical Variations on a Classical Theme," p. 152.

51   A more recent serious novel which includes mother-son incest is *Flesh and Blood,* by Pete Hamill.

53   Unconscious incest is a term that authorities use in various ways. To Maisch it means unwittingly committing incest, as Oedipus did with his mother. Psychoanalysts interpret what Oedipus did as the expression of unconscious incestuous impulses even though, at the time he married his mother, he was not aware they were related. Maisch uses the term "subconscious incest wish" to describe the motivation involved in behavior where the attraction between family members is felt and acted on short of consummating the act.

55   The quote by Stendhal (real name Henri Beyle) is from Rank's 1912 work in which he examined incest themes in literature and the lives of writers.

PART II   WHO COMMITS INCEST

Chapter 4   From Teachers to Tyrants

60   Giarretto, in "Humanistic Treatment of Father-Daughter Incest," pp. 148–149, noted that the $13,413 income and other socioeconomic features of incestuous families in his study contra-

dict the picture often presented of such families as being poor, black and subnormal in intelligence.

61   Average age of the fathers in our survey was 39. In Maisch's study, the average age was 40.7, and in Weinberg's 1955 survey it was 43.5. More recent studies have found the average age to be in the late thirties, when many men are starting to become disenchanted with their jobs and marriages.

65   The incestuous father who says, "it is a sin to go with other women," is discussed by Cormier et al., p. 211, of McGill University. They point out that the daughter is "thus placed in the special role; she is not a woman outside the family with whom it is a sin to commit adultery, but someone who belongs to him, a permissible alternative to the wife."

66–   See Weinberg, pp. 94–102, for a discussion of the "endogamic"
67   type and the case of Ho.

68–   The descriptions of how Barbara's father played the "love game"
69   with her are from pages 34 and 48–50 in Woodbury and Schwartz' *The Silent Sin.*

70   See Sarles, p. 639; Lustig et al., p. 36, and Schechter and Roberge, p. 135, for fathers who provided "sex education" for their daughters.

71   The full story of Citizen William K. is given by Karpman, in Masters, pp. 159–178.

74   Oliver, p. 39, describes the father who considered incest acceptable but sex by his daughters with boyfriends as improper.

76   See Rosenfeld et al., p. 336, for the case of Mr. D. and Mary.

78   See Maisch, pp. 126–127, for a discussion of tyrants and aggressiveness as a characteristic of one type of incestuous father.

79   The jealous, controlling father described by Maisch, p. 140, was normal in his behavior at work and outside the family.

80   Maisch, p. 139, lists "drinker" (24 percent) as among a number of disruptive factors in incest. He found 5 percent of the wives to be drinkers, which is consistent with our findings.

Chapter 5   Psychopaths and Sex Cultures

83   In McCord and McCord, pp. 1–22 and pp. 70–97, the psychopath is described as being asocial, driven by uncontrolled de-

sires, highly impulsive, aggressive, feels little guilt, and has a warped capacity for love. These personality features stem from a childhood of emotional deprivation and rejection, coupled, in some instances, with brain damage.

86   The number of "hypersexed" men involved in incest is no greater than 14 percent, according to Maisch, p. 128. "Even the idea of the 'hypersexual' or 'instinctive' committer of incest is hardly tenable for any length of time," he says.

86   Caprio and Brenner, pp. 241–244, said that the man who raped his daughter had hallucinations of longstanding. He said "he did what he did because of his love" for his daughters. He also had incestuous relations with a younger daughter.

87   Weinberg, p. 97, in presenting the case of Mr. J., notes the promiscuous psychopath's turning to a family sex partner is "precipitated by the absence, refusal, or declining attraction of his wife and by the inaccessibility of other women. He may be too infirm or 'too old' to attract other women."

89   Carolyn Swift, Ph.D., of the Wyandot Mental Center in Kansas City, Kan., gave testimony in January 1978 before a subcommittee of the U. S. House of Representatives that boys "are being victimized at rates equal to or surpassing girls," but that probably 50 to 80 percent of the incidents go unreported.

90   Drs. J. W. Mohr, R. E. Turner, and M. B. Jerry, p. 19, note that the pedophilic act often "represents an arrested development in which the offender has never grown psychosexually beyond the immature prepubertal stage, or a regression or return to this stage due to certain stresses in adult life, or a modification of the sexual drive in old age."

90   Drs. E. Revitch and R. G. Weiss, p. 75, point out that pedophilia is "more common in those individuals who are emotionally immature, physically underdeveloped or have physical and mental defects. Pedophilia is also likely to occur in individuals who are in states of regression such as loss of potency, alcoholic inebriation, and early senility."

Chapter 6   *Mothers, Daughters and Siblings in Incest*

93–   The descriptions of Barbara are from *The Silent Sin,* pp. 181, 35
94   and 56.

96   The young woman who tried to hold her family together and help her father talked on her incestuous experiences in Gary Mitchell's documentary film *Incest: The Victim Nobody Believes.*

96   Julia's case is presented in Weitzel, Powell, and Penick, pp. 127–130.

98   The daughter of the beautiful woman described by Yorukoglu and Kemph, p. 122, looked upon her father "more as a sick child than as a father."

99   See Browning and Boatman, p. 72, for more on depressed mothers.

99–   Mrs. L., described by Lustig et al., pp. 35–36, had long attached
100   herself to others for nurturance: to a sister, teachers, girl friends, finally her daughter Ann. Her husband felt no guilt from the incest with Ann, justifying it on the basis of "sex education" for the daughter.

100   See Kaufman, Peck, and Taguiuri, pp. 271–274, for the case of Mrs. Smith and June.

101   The quotation by Barbara's mother is from Woodbury and Schwartz, p. 208.

102–   Schechter and Roberge, p. 134, tell of the mother whose son
103   began sleeping with her at 10.

103   See Walters, pp. 127–128, for three instances of mothers sexually abusing their sons in the absence of a husband in the home.

103–   Weinberg, p. 92, reports that a mother may be promiscuous but
104   still oppose sex with her son, as in the case of N.

106   In regard to brother-sister incest, Weinberg, p. 169, says that when the sister cooperates, she "no longer has the carefree social intimacy, the frank but friendly disregard which siblings have for each other." She vies with other girls for her brother's attention.

Part III   Why Incest Occurs

Chapter 7   When Sex Stops Between Father and Mother

112   The first chapter of our book *The Abusing Family,* pp. 25–36, describes research we did in investigating excessive change and

PAGE

"Life Crisis As a Precursor of Child Abuse." Dr. T. H. Holmes, professor of psychiatry at the University of Washington School of Medicine in Seattle, and Dr. R. H. Rahe, who formerly worked with Holmes and is now at the Naval Health Research Center in San Diego, have demonstrated that 80 percent of people whose life change scores are 300 or higher will fall sick. For those with scores under 300 but more than 150, 51 percent will get sick. For those scoring less than 150, 37 percent will get sick in the next two years.

113   The original work on the Social Readjustment Rating Scale was reported by Holmes and Rahe in the *Journal of Psychosomatic Research* in 1967.

113   The passage about Somerset Maugham's father is from Maugham's autobiography, *The Summing Up*, p. 15 and p. 18.

118   June Smith's case comes from p. 273 in Kaufman, Peck and Tagiuri.

119   Maisch's case is from p. 177 of *Incest.* The figure on fathers staying at home alone with the daughter is from p. 175.

120   The incident involving the mother who put her daughter in bed with the father is in Kaufman et al., p. 276.

121   The account of Hortense and Dickie Loftus is from Wenzell Brown's "Murder Rooted in Incest" in Masters' *Patterns of Incest,* pp. 301–327.

121–   The quotes from the Loftus case are on p. 308 in Masters.
122

Chapter 8   Taboos in Twilight

PAGE

125   See Toffler, p. 103, for the wife who made 11 moves and pp. 49–181 for a graphic account of transience in American society.

127   Newsweek's "Anything Goes" special report appeared in the November 13, 1967, issue, pp. 74–78. Its cover story on "Sex and TV" was in the February 20, 1978, issue, pp. 54–61.

129   See "The Liberation of Sexual Fantasy" by Daniel Goleman and Sherida Bush in *Psychology Today,* October 1977, pp. 48–53, for organizations dedicated to deviations in sexual styles and expression.

129   Wallace told of the incest publications in an interview.

130   Lesse is quoted· from "Factors Influencing Sexual Behavior in Our Future Society," p. 373. Socarides is quoted from "Beyond Sexual Freedom: Clinical Fallout," pp. 387–388.

130   Ryder was quoted in the *Los Angeles Times*, February 16, 1975, Part 1.

131   See Weinberg, pp. 65–66, for ways that fathers are sexually familiar with their daughters before incest occurs. "One father burned a hole in the door of the bathroom with a poker so he could watch his daughter bathe."

132   Weinberg's case of V. is on p. 92 in *Incest Behavior.*

135   See Weinberg, p. 66, for case of H.

136   Regarding anger toward one's spouse as the basic reasons for incest, Walters, p. 121, argues: "If your husband/wife were to become sexually involved with another person, would you prefer that person be another adult or your child? The answer, universally, is another adult. We must then ask why one selects one's child. An adult has or can create all kinds of opportunities for sexual involvement with another adult, for adult partners are available in every community. The basic reason for being involved with one's child is anger toward one's spouse." As we noted, the adults who get involved in incest have limited capacities for developing relationships outside the family, and that is a basic problem.

136–   Maisch, p. 176, discusses "temptation" factors. The quote about
137   parent and child sleeping in the same bed is on p. 175 and the case of the 43-year-old man is on p. 177.

137   For figures on the number of persons per room in Weinberg's study and previous studies, see Weinberg, p. 58.

Chapter 9   Fantasies of An All-Loving Mother

143–   Cormier, Kennedy, and Sangowicz's case of F. is in "Psychody-
144   namics of Father Daughter Incest," pp. 209–210.

144   See Weiss, Rogers, Darwin, and Dutton, "A Study of Girl Sex Victims," p. 9, for the case of Mr. R.

144   The feeling that Barbara's father, Henry, retained for his first wife, Tina, are discussed in Woodbury and Schwartz, p. 146 and p. 200.

PART IV CUES AND CONSEQUENCES

Chapter 10   Cues That Incest Is Going On

PAGE

156   The case of Cindy was reported by Finch, pp. 181, 185.

158   For more information on the cues of incest and the Maryland study on venereal diseases in children, see Brant and Tisza, pp. 83–85.

158   The quote from Brant and Tisza is on p. 84.

159   The case of Tim was reported by Mary Murphy in an unpublished paper. Ms. Murphy is a psychologist working in the Developmental Pediatrics Clinic of Texas Children's Hospital in Houston.

159– See Bender and Blau, pp. 501–502, for the case of Mary V.
160

160   Finch, pp. 170–187, discusses in depth how overstimulation affects a child emotionally.

161   The quote by Barbara describing her father's immaturity is from Woodbury and Schwartz, p. 82.

162   The relationship between Barbara and her mother is described in Woodbury and Schwartz, pp. 206–208.

162   Weinberg gives a more complete description of mother-daughter competition on pp. 157–171.

163   The brother-sister incest case is from Weinberg, pp. 168–169.

Chapter 11   Consequences of Incest

PAGE

167   The American Humane Association, under the direction of Dr. Vincent De Francis, studied 250 families in which a child had been sexually abused. In 66 percent of the families, there was some major impact as a result of the abuse. See pp. 144–145 in De Francis.

170   For a discussion of guilt as it relates to the break-up of the incestuous relationship, see Rosenfeld et al., p. 334.

173   Weinberg's statistics about pregnancy in the daughters are on p. 51.

174   Brant and Tisza, on pp. 85–86, give a detailed description of how the incestuous relationship was detected in one family.

174   The quote from Maisch is on p. 208.

175   How the child's needs are forgotten in the legal process is discussed by De Francis, pp. 1–3. The quote regarding parental dissatisfaction with the judicial process is from the same source, p. 194.

175   See Finch, p. 185, for Cindy's case.

178   Summit and Kryso's discussion of the labeling process is on p. 244.

178   The quote of the woman who was afraid to report the incest is from the film, *Incest: The Victim Nobody Believes.*

178–   Maisch gives an analysis of the effects of incest in the families he
179   studied on pp. 207–216.

180   The quotes about the mother's responses are from Weinberg, pp. 195–196.

182   Dr. Noel Lustig, a psychiatrist at the University of California at Los Angeles, discusses the contribution role reversal makes to the daughter's depression. His comments are in the paper by Finch, p. 185.

183–   Unless identified otherwise, all the quotations on these pages are
188   from women interviewed in the film, *Incest: The Victim Nobody Believes.*

186   The other effects of incest experienced by the daughter of William K. are discussed by Karpman in Masters' *Patterns of Incest,* pp. 172–176.

188   See Giarretto, pp. 145–146, for more information on drug abuse and prostitution as a consequence of incest.

188   Weiner discusses the findings of the Chicago Vice Commission, pp. 615–616.

190   The statistics about the number of wives reuniting with their husbands are in Kennedy and Cormier, p. 194.

190   The interview by Dr. Pittman is in the article by Machotka et al., p. 107.

194   The quote is from Masters and Johnson, p. 58.

195   See Finch, p. 15, for more on the effeminate 12-year-old boy.

PART V   WHAT CAN BE DONE ABOUT INCEST

Chapter 12   Parent-Child Sexuality

209   The descriptions of Deborah and Ruth and their attempts to monopolize their fathers are on pages 84 and 281 of *Three Babies.*

209   The takeover of mother by Pat is from Dorothy Baruch's *New Ways in Sex Education,* as quoted in Dodson, p. 188.

210–
211   The problem of the overstimulated 5-year-old who takes showers with his mother is from Summit and Kryso, p. 241. They describe the sex counselor's experiment on p. 242.

212   The quotes are from Summit and Kryson, pp. 243–244.

215   See Dodson, p. 187, for the case of the 9-year-old boy who was turned on by his mother's going around in bra and panties.

216   Summit and Kryso, p. 240, discuss "loving sensuality" and "abusive sexuality."

Chapter 13   What Parents Should Do About Their Own Needs

PAGE

220   See "The Varieties of Intimacy," condensed from *No-Fault Marriage* in *Reader's Digest,* pp. 115–118, for more on Marian and Ray and for ways to develop closeness between spouses.

221   See Alberti and Emmons' book *Your Perfect Right* as an example of how to learn to be assertive, and Zimbardo's book on *Shyness: What It Is, What To Do About It.*

222–
233   Blair Justice is currently writing a book on self-stressing, its causes, consequences, and treatment.

223   For more on self-talk and awfulizing, see just about any of Albert Ellis' long list of books and papers. His best known is *A New Guide to Rational Living,* with Robert A. Harper.

227   In his book *The Relaxation Response,* Benson reviews a number of techniques, including transcendental meditation, yoga, and progressive relaxation, that he says produce the physiologic changes he has identified with the relaxation response.

228–
229   Sidney Cobb, M.D., presented a review of "Social Support As a Moderator of Life Stress" in *Psychosomatic Medicine,* pp. 300–314.

230–
231   See Toffler, pp. 377–382, for more on how people can offset the effects of rapid change with "stability zones."

232   The Selye quote is from *Stress of Life,* p. 269.

Chapter 14   What the Parent Needs to Do for the Child

238   For a good overview of the question of children's rights, see Brian Fraser's "The Child and His Parents: A Delicate Balance of Rights." A representative of one of the most liberal positions on children's rights is Richard Farson, who argues that a child has the right to sexual freedom. Included in this freedom is the right for children to have sex with each other and with adults, including parents, if they choose. In his book *Birthrights,* on pp. 129–154, Farson cites skimpy evidence that incest has no negative consequences and says that children should have the option to refuse if they do not want sex. He does not explain how a child turns down a persuasive, persistent or aggressive father, or keeps from being manipulated or duped into consent.

Chapter 15   What Can Be Done in Treatment

240   The quote about children rarely accusing their parents of being sexually involved with them is from Walters, p. 121.

240   Simmons, in his comments in Finch's paper, explains his position on the "emergency" referrals and why he and his associates work first with the parents or concerned adults, see p. 187.

242   For more information on the Israeli system of handling sexual abuse of children, see De Francis, pp. 8–11.

245   For more information on Simmons' treatment approach to sexual abuse of children, see Finch, p. 187.

248   For more on the nature of symbiosis and how we treat problems involving it, see our paper, "Shifting Symbiosis."

249   See Gordon's *Parent Effectiveness Training* for more on "I messages" and "active listening."

254–   Giarretto describes the treatment approach of the Child Sexual
255   Abuse Treatment Program in detail in his article, "Humanistic Treatment of Father-Daughter Incest," pp. 149–150.

256   Walters, p. 62, takes the position that "Sexual abuse is quite different from physical abuse and more difficult to treat." While

there are some differences between physically and sexually abusive families, there are even more similarities. In our experience, treatment is not more difficult in cases of sexual abuse. The background of parents who commit incest is similar to that of parents who physically abuse.

Chapter 16 What Can Be Done on the Public Level

PAGE

260   See Mead's "A Proposal," p. 31, for more on the nature of taboos.

261   The young woman who lamented the lack of accurate information given children on sexual abuse appeared in the documentary film *Incest: The Victim Nobody Believes.* She is one of among many who are convinced that for children to protect themselves or know how to get help, they must have accurate information on sexual abuse and who commits it.

261   See De Francis, pp. 40–41, for more on how infrequently strangers are involved.

262   Child and Family Services of Knoxville operates a sex-abuse hotline.

262   The quote on the rights not guaranteed a child is from Fraser, p. 327.

263   Numerous proclamations have been issued on the rights of children, including a declaration from the Joint Commission on Mental Health of Children and one from the General Assembly of the United Nations, but the law favors parents. We agree with Kempe and Fraser when they say that children do not belong to their parents, but to themselves in the care of their parents.

263   Kempe's quote on health visitors is from "A Practical Approach to the Protection of the Abused Child." See *The Abusing Family,* pp. 231–234, for more on health visitors, and pp. 235–240, for courses on parenting and the nature of human needs.

264   The use of schools to develop a sense of community and to help restore neighborhoods fits in with recommendations that The President's Commission on Mental Health made in 1978 in its report on the need for greater community support.

265   For more on situational groupings, see Dr. Herbert Gerjuoy in Toffler, pp. 383–385.

266 The quotes by Browning and Boatman are from "Incest: Children at Risk," p. 72 and p. 69.

267 See *Incest: The Victim Nobody Believes* for the young woman discussing how she would be hushed up when she tried to tell what had happened to her.

269 In addition to a social climate that allows for freer communication about sexuality, Brant and Tisza, p. 80, also believe that sexual abuse is receiving more attention now because of laws making it a reportable condition and professionals becoming more aware of child abuse generally.

269 René Guyon wrote a book called *The Ethics of Sexual Acts* in 1934 in which he found little reason to restrict any kind of sexual behavior.

269 The Guyon Society seeks to revise penal codes to permit, heterosexually, "penis-vagina copulation" among children and adults with children, and to allow masturbation of children. Homosexually, the society is for anal copulation among children and adults with children, as well as oral copulation.

BIBLIOGRAPHY

Adams, M. S., & Neel, J. V. Children of incest. *Pediatrics,* 1957, *40,* 55–62.

Alberti, R. E., & Emmons, M. L. *Your perfect right.* San Luis Obispo, Ca.: Impact, 1974.

Baruch, D. *New ways in sex education.* New York: McGraw-Hill, 1959.

Bender, L., & Blau, A. The reaction of children to sexual relations with adults. *American Journal of Orthopsychiatry,* 1937, *7,* 500–518.

Benson, H., with Klipper, M. Z. *The relaxation response.* New York: Avon, 1976.

Berry, G. W. Incest: Some clinical variations on a classical theme. *Journal of the American Academy of Psychoanalysis,* 1975, *3,* 151–161.

Blumberg, M. L. Child sexual abuse. *New York State Journal of Medicine,* 1978, *78,* 612–616.

Brant, R. S. T., & Tisza, V. B. The sexually misused child. *American Journal of Orthopsychiatry,* 1977, *47,* 80–90.

Brown, W. *Bedeviled: The true story of the interplay of the aggressor and the victim in sexual attacks.* Derby, Conn.: Monarch Books, 1961.

Browning, D. H., & Boatman, B. Incest: Children at risk. *American Journal of Psychiatry,* 1977, *134,* 69–72.

Bullough, V. L. *Sexual variance in society and history.* New York: Wiley, 1976.

Caprio, F. S., & Brenner, D. R. *Sexual behavior: Psycho-legal aspects.* New York: Citadel Press, 1961.

Bullough, V. L. *Sexual variance in society and history.* New York: Wiley, 1976.

Caprio, F. S., & Brenner, D. R. *Sexual behavior: Psycho-legal aspects.* New York: Citadel Press, 1961.

Carter, C. O. Risk to offspring of incest. *The Lancet,* February 25, 1967, 436.

Church, J. (Ed.) *Three babies: Biographies of cognitive development.* New York: Random House, 1966.

Church, J. *Understanding your child from birth to three.* New York: Random House, 1973.

Cobb, S. Social support as a moderator of life stress. *Psychosomatic Medicine,* 1976, *38,* 300–314.

Cormier, B. M., Kennedy, M., & Sangowicz, J. Psychodynamics of father daughter incest. *Canadian Psychiatric Association Journal,* 1962, *7,* 203–217.

Cory, D. W., & Masters, R. E. L. *Violation of taboo.* New York: Julian Press, 1963.

De Francis, V. *Protecting the child victim of sex crimes committed by adults.* Denver, Colo.: American Humane Association, Children's Division, 1969.

DeMause, L. Our forebears made childhood a nightmare. *Psychology Today,* 1975, *8,* 85–88.

Dodson, F. *How to parent.* New York: New American Library, 1971.

Ellis, A., & Harper, R. A. *A new guide to rational living.* Englewood Cliffs, N. J.: Prentice-Hall, 1975.

Farson, R. *Birthrights.* New York: Macmillan, 1974.

Finch, S. M. Adult seduction of the child: Effects on the child. *Human Sexuality,* 1973, *7,* 170–187.

Frances, V., & Frances, A. The incest taboo and family structure. *Family Process,* 1976, *15,* 235–243.

Fraser, B. G. The child and his parents: A delicate balance of rights. In R. E. Helfer, & C. H. Kempe (Eds.), *Child abuse and neglect: The family and the community.* Cambridge, Mass.: Ballinger, 1976.

Freud, S. *Totem and taboo.* New York: The New Republic Edition, 1931.

Fromm, E. *The sane society.* Greenwich, Conn.: Fawcett, 1955.

Giarretto, H. Humanistic treatment of father-daughter incest. In R. E. Helfer, & C. H. Kempe (Eds.), *Child abuse and neglect: The family and the community.* Cambridge, Mass.: Ballinger, 1976.

Goldsten, J., & Katz, J. *The family and the law.* New York: The Free Press, 1965.

Goleman, D., & Bush, S. The liberation of sexual fantasy. *Psychology Today,* 1977, *11,* 48–53, 104–107.

Gordon, T. *Parent effectiveness training.* New York: Wyden, 1970.

Guyon, R. *The ethics of sexual acts.* New York: Knopf, 1934.

Henderson, D. J. Incest: A synthesis of data. *Canadian Psychiatric Association Journal,* 1972, *17,* 299–313.

Holmes, T. H., & Rahe, R. H. The social readjustment rating scale. *Journal of Psychosomatic Research,* 1967, *11,* 213–218.

Incest: The Victim Nobody Believes, a film produced by Gary Mitchell Film Co., Sausalito, Ca., 1976.

Jung, C. *Psychology of the unconscious.* New York: Moffat, Yard, 1916.

Justice, B., & Justice, R. *The abusing family.* New York: Human Sciences Press, 1976.

Justice, B., & Duncan, D. Life crisis as a precursor to child abuse. *Public Health Reports,* 1976, *91,* 110–115.

Justice, R., & Justice, B. Shifting symbiosis in abusive families. *Transactional Analysis Journal,* 1976, *6,* 423–427.

Karpman, B. Citizen William K. In R. E. L. Masters (Ed.), *Patterns of incest.* New York: Julian Press, 1963.

Kaufman, I., Peck, A. L., & Tagiuri, C. K. Family constellation and overt incestuous relations between father and daughter. *American Journal of Orthopsychiatry,* 1954, *24,* 266–279.

Kempe, C. H. A practical approach to the protection of the abused child. *Pediatrics,* 1973, *51,* 791–809.

Kennedy, M., & Cormier, B. M. Father daughter incest: Treatment of a family. In W. C. Reckless, & C. L. Newman (Eds.), *Interdisciplinary problems in criminology: Papers of the American Society of Criminology.* Columbus, Ohio: Ohio State University, 1965.

Krafsur, R. P. (Ed.). *American Film Institute catalog of motion pictures feature films 1961–70.* New York: Bowker, 1976.

Landis, J. T. Experiences of 500 children with adult sexual deviation. *The Psychiatric Quarterly,* 1956, *30,* 91–109.

Langsley, D. G., Schwartz, M. N., & Fairbain, R. H. Father-son incest. *Comprehensive Psychiatry,* 1968, *9,* 218–226.

Lasswell, M., & Lobsenz, N. *No-fault marriage.* New York: Doubleday, 1976.

Lesse, S. Factors influencing sexual behavior in our future society. *American Journal of Psychotherapy,* 1976, *30,* 366–385.

Lewis, M., & Sarrel, P. M. Some psychological aspects of seduction, incest, and rape in childhood. *Journal of Child Psychiatry,* 1969, *8,* 606–619.

Lindzey, G. Some remarks concerning incest, the incest taboo, and psychoanalytic theory. *American Psychologist,* 1967, *22,* 1051–1059.

Los Angeles Times, A new honesty in mending marriages, February 16, 1975, part I.

Lukianowicz, N. Incest. *British Journal of Psychiatry,* 1972, *120,* 301–313.

Lustig, N., Dresser, J. W., Spellman, S. W., & Murray, T. B. Incest: A family group survival pattern. *Archives of General Psychiatry,* 1966, *41,* 31–40.

Machotka, P., Pittman, F. S., & Flomenhaft, K. Incest as a family affair. *Family Process,* 1967, *6,* 98–116.

Maisch, H. *Incest.* London: Andre Deutsch, 1973.

Masters, R. E. L. *Patterns of incest.* New York: Julian Press, 1963.

Masters, W. H., & Johnson, V. E. Incest: The ultimate taboo. *Redbook,* April 1976, pp. 54–58.

Maugham, W. S. *The summing up.* New York: Doubleday, Doran, 1938.

McCord, W., & McCord, J. *The psychopath.* Princeton, N.J.: D. Van Nostrand, 1964.

Mead, M. *Sex and temperament.* New York: William Morrow, 1935.

Mead, M. A proposal: We need taboos on sex at work. *Redbook,* April 1978, p. 31.

Mitchell, G. Study guide for *Incest: The victim nobody believes,* Sausalito, Calif., 1976.

Mohr, J. W., Turner, R. E., & Jerry, M. B. *Pedophilia and exhibitionism.* Toronto: University of Toronto Press, 1964.

Mueller, W. R. I'm a congregationalist, you know. *The Christian Century,* 1976, *93,* 476–477.

Munden, K. W. (Ed.). *American Film Institute catalog of motion pictures feature films 1921–30.* New York: Bowker, 1971.

Murdock, G. P. *Social structure.* New York: Macmillan, 1949.

Murphy, M. Sexual abuse of children. Unpublished paper, University of Texas School of Public Health, 1976.

National Center on Child Abuse and Neglect. *Intra-family sexual abuse of children* (unit 6). Washington, D.C., 1976.

Newsweek, Taboos in twilight, November 13, 1967, pp. 74–48.

Oliver, B. J. *Sexual deviation in American society.* New Haven, Conn.: College and University Press, 1967.

Parsons, T. *Essays in sociological theory.* Glencoe, Ill.: Free Press, 1949.

Pediatric News, Sex abuse of child more common than is realized, March 1975, p. 3.

Playboy, The Playboy advisor, October 1965, p. 43.

Raglan, F. R. R. S. *Jocasta's crime: A anthropological study.* New York: Dutton, 1933.

Rank, O. *Das inzest-motiv in dichtung und sage.* Leipzig-Vienna: F. Deuticke, 1912.

Raybin, J. B. Homosexual incest: Report of a case of homosexual incest involving three generations of a family. *Journal of Nervous and Mental Disease*, 1969, *148*, 105–109.

Reader's Digest, The varieties of intimacy, November 1977, pp. 115–118.

Report to the President from President's commission on mental health (vol. 1). Washington, D.C.: U.S. Government Printing Office, 1978.

Revitch, E., & Weiss, R. G. The pedophilia offender. *Diseases of the Nervous System*, 1962, *23*, 73–78.

Rosenfeld, A. A., Nadelson, C. C., Krieger, M., & Backman, J. H. Incest and sexual abuse of children. *Journal of Child Psychiatry*, 1977, *16*, 327–339.

Sarles, R. M. Incest. *Pediatric Clinics of North America*, 1975, *22*, 633–642.

Schechter, M. D., & Roberge, L. Sexual exploitation. In R. E. Helfer, & C. H. Kempe (Eds.), *Child abuse and neglect: The family and the community*. Cambridge, Mass.: Ballinger, 1976.

Schroeder, T. Incest in mormonism. *American Journal of Urology and Sexology*, 1915, *11*, 409–416.

Seemanova, E. A study of children in incestuous matings. *Human Heredity*, 1971, *21*, 108–128.

Selye, H. *Stress of life*. New York: McGraw-Hill, 1956.

Socarides, C. W. Beyond sexual freedom: Clinical fallout. *American Journal of Psychotherapy*, 1976, *30*, 385–397.

Swift, C. Sexual assault of children and adolescents. Testimony prepared for presentation to the Domestic and International Scientific Planning, Analysis, and Cooperation Subcommittee of the Committee on Science and Technology of the U.S. House of Representatives, January 11, 1978, New York City.

Summit, R., & Kryso, J. Sexual abuse of children: A clinical spectrum. *American Journal of Orthopsychiatry*, 1978, *48*, 237–251.

The Holy Bible. Chicago: Catholic Press, 1967.

The State of Texas Penal Code, Chapter 25, revised 1974, 608–610.

Tisza, V. B. Preface in S. K. Weinberg, *Incest behavior* (rev. ed.). Secaucus, N.J.: Citadel Press, 1976.

Toffler, A. *Future shock*. New York: Bantam Books, 1971.

Wahl, C. W. The psychodynamics of consummated maternal incest. *Archives of General Psychiatry*, 1960, *3*, 188–193.

Walters, D. R. *Physical and sexual abuse of children*. Bloomington, Ind.: Indiana University Press, 1975.

Waters, H. F., Kasindorf, M., & Carter, B. Sex and TV. *Newsweek*, February 20, 1978, pp. 54–61.

Weber, E. Sexual abuse begins at home. *Ms*, April 1977, pp. 63–67.

Weeks, R. B. The sexually exploited child. *Southern Medical Journal,* 1976, *69,* 848–850.

Weinberg, S. K. *Incest behavior* (rev. ed.). Secaucus, N.J.: Citadel Press, 1976.

Weiner, I. B. Father-daughter incest: A clinical report. *Psychiatric Quarterly,* 1962, *36,* 607–632.

Weiss, J., Rogers, E., Darwin, M. R., & Dutton, C. E. A study of girl sex victims. *Psychiatric Quarterly,* 1955, *29,* 1–26.

Weitzel, W. D., Powell, B. J., & Penick, E. C. Clinical management of father-daughter incest. *American Journal of Diseases of Children,* 1978, *132,* 127–130.

White, L. A. The definition and prohibition of incest. *American Anthropologist,* 1948, *50,* 416–436.

Woodbury, J., & Schwartz, E. *The silent sin: A case history of incest.* New York: Signet Books, 1971.

Zimbardo, P. *Shyness: What it is, what to do about it.* Reading, Mass.: Addison-Wesley, 1977.

ABOUT THE AUTHORS

Blair Justice has written extensively about the problems of children and families, both in the scientific literature and for magazines and newspapers. He was a medical writer and science editor at several large dailies before becoming a psychologist. He received degrees from the University of Texas at Austin, Columbia University, and Rice University. Dr. Justice is a professor of psychology at the University of Texas School of Public Health in Houston and is a senior psychologist and group therapist at the Texas Research Institute of Mental Sciences.

Rita Justice is a psychologist in private practice and codirector of the Southwestern Institute for Group and Family Therapy in Houston. She received both her bachelor and doctoral degrees in psychology from the University of Texas at Austin and completed a postdoctoral fellowship at Baylor College of Medicine in the Department of Pediatrics. Dr. Justice has done extensive training and teaching in transactional analysis and is currently a Clinical member with a teaching contract in the International Transactional Analysis Association.

Blair and Rita Justice are the authors of *The Abusing Family* and have a 14-year-old daughter, Liz, living with them in Houston. They have served as consultants to a number of child welfare departments and protective service agencies and have lectured widely in this country and abroad on the subject of physical and sexual abuse.

INDEX

VISTA

HQ
71
J84

Justice, Blair.

The broken taboo

c.2

HQ
71
J84

Justice, Blair
The broken taboo

c.2   013725   Vista card2

DATE	ISSUED TO	
AUG 0 6 1993	*signature* 0958678	

013725